‖‖ ‖ ‖‖‖‖‖ ‖ ‖‖ ‖‖‖‖‖‖‖‖‖‖‖‖‖‖ ‖‖ ‖‖
W9-BSP-520

Praise for *All Is Well*

*"**All Is Well** is simply excellent. Dr. Mona Lisa Schulz has blended her expertise in health with the healing wisdom of Louise Hay, one of the leading icons of the human consciousness community. This book is a tribute to the intuitive genius of Louise, whose work as a role model for positive thinking pioneered healing first for people with AIDS and then for countless others."*

—**Caroline Myss,**
New York Times best-selling author of
Archetypes: A Beginner's Guide to Your Inner-net

*"In today's world of too much information and too little wisdom, there is very little that gets to the heart of any matter—especially regarding health. But **All Is Well** does just that by combining medical science and intuition. As a former RN, I insist on the latest medically proven scientific evidence when looking after my own health. But I also honor my story, my personal experiences, and my unique sense of intuition; I use these to inform my ability to find inner peace, health, and balance in everyday life. This book takes this same approach, and so when I started to read, I began to feel better immediately. If you read only one book about health this year, this is the one for you!"*

—**Naomi Judd,**
author of *Naomi's Breakthrough Guide*

*"**All Is Well** is a must-read manual for the coming times when we will need to be our own spiritual physicians. The best health insurance is to learn how to stay healthy, and Louise Hay and Dr. Mona Lisa Schulz are wonderful teachers."*

—**Doreen Virtue,**
author of *The Healing Miracles of Archangel Raphael*

"We know the mind affects the body's physiology. We know there are emotional roots that underlie disease and that few diseases are purely biological. We know the benefits of affirmations like the ones Louise Hay has been teaching for decades. Yet never before have the scientific medical data, psychology, and spirituality—as well as the brilliant perspectives of Louise Hay and Dr. Mona Lisa Schulz—interlaced with each other so effortlessly. Whether you're facing an illness, working with patients, or simply seeking to live an optimally healthy life, read this wonderful book and let it inspire you. . . . The answers that follow may be your best medicine yet."

—**Lissa Rankin, M.D.,**
author of *Mind Over Medicine* and blogger at LissaRankin.com

ALSO BY LOUISE HAY

Overcoming Fears

The Power Is Within You
(audio book)

The Power of Your Spoken Word

Receiving Prosperity

Self-Esteem Affirmations
(subliminal)

Self-Healing

Stress-Free (subliminal)

Totality of Possibilities

*What I Believe and Deep
Relaxation*

You Can Heal Your Life
(audio book)

*You Can Heal Your Life
Study Course*

Your Thoughts Create Your Life

DVDs

Dissolving Barriers

Receiving Prosperity

*You Can Heal Your Life
Study Course*

*You Can Heal Your Life,
THE MOVIE* (also available
in an expanded edition)

CARD DECKS

Healthy Body Cards

I Can Do It® Cards

*I Can Do It® Cards . . .
for Creativity, Forgiveness,
Health, Job Success, Wealth,
Romance*

Power Thought Cards

Power Thoughts for Teens

Power Thought Sticky Cards

Wisdom Cards

CALENDAR

I Can Do It® Calendar
(for each individual year)

and

**THE LOUISE L. HAY BOOK
COLLECTION**
(comprising the gift versions
of *Meditations to Heal Your
Life, You Can Heal Your Life,*
and *You Can Heal Your Life
Companion Book*)

All of the above are available at your local bookstore, or may be ordered by visiting:

Hay House USA: **www.hayhouse.com®**
Hay House Australia: **www.hayhouse.com.au**
Hay House UK: **www.hayhouse.co.uk**
Hay House South Africa: **www.hayhouse.co.za**
Hay House India: **www.hayhouse.co.in**

ALSO BY MONA LISA SCHULZ, M.D., PH.D.

*Awakening Intuition: Using Your Mind-Body
Network for Insight and Healing*

*The Intuitive Advisor: A Medical Doctor Teaches
You How to Solve Your Most Pressing Health Problems*＊

The New Feminine Brain: Developing Your Intuitive Genius

＊Available from Hay House

Please visit:

Hay House USA: **www.hayhouse.com**®
Hay House Australia: **www.hayhouse.com.au**
Hay House UK: **www.hayhouse.co.uk**
Hay House South Africa: **www.hayhouse.co.za**
Hay House India: **www.hayhouse.co.in**

SASKATOON PUBLIC LIBRARY **RM**
36001401402267
All is well : heal your body with

ALL *is* WELL

HEAL YOUR BODY *with* MEDICINE, AFFIRMATIONS, *and* INTUITION

LOUISE HAY
and
MONA LISA SCHULZ
M.D., P H.D.

HAY HOUSE, INC.
Carlsbad, California • New York City
London • Sydney • Johannesburg
Vancouver • Hong Kong • New Delhi

Copyright © 2013 by Louise Hay and Mona Lisa Schulz

Published and distributed in the United States by: Hay House, Inc.: www.hayhouse.com® • *Published and distributed in Australia by:* Hay House Australia Pty. Ltd.: www.hayhouse.com.au • *Published and distributed in the United Kingdom by:* Hay House UK, Ltd.: www.hayhouse.co.uk • *Published and distributed in the Republic of South Africa by:* Hay House SA (Pty), Ltd.: www.hayhouse.co.za • *Distributed in Canada by:* Raincoast Books: www.raincoast.com • *Published in India by:* Hay House Publishers India: www.hayhouse.co.in

Cover design: Amy Rose Grigoriou • *Interior design*: Riann Bender

All rights reserved. No part of this book may be reproduced by any mechanical, photographic, or electronic process, or in the form of a phonographic recording; nor may it be stored in a retrieval system, transmitted, or otherwise be copied for public or private use—other than for "fair use" as brief quotations embodied in articles and reviews—without prior written permission of the publisher.

The authors of this book do not dispense medical advice or prescribe the use of any technique as a form of treatment for physical, emotional, or medical problems without the advice of a physician, either directly or indirectly. The intent of the authors is only to offer information of a general nature to help you in your quest for emotional and spiritual well-being. In the event you use any of the information in this book for yourself, the authors and the publisher assume no responsibility for your actions.

Note: The case studies found in this book are composites drawn from years of clinical work. These are true to the spirit of the teaching and the treatment provided, although not to the experience of any one particular person.

Library of Congress Cataloging-in-Publication Data

Hay, Louise L.
  All is well : heal your body with medicine, affirmations, and intuition / Louise L. Hay and Mona Lisa Schulz, M.D., Ph.D. -- 1st edition.
      pages cm
  Includes bibliographical references.
  ISBN 978-1-4019-3501-6 (hardcover : alk. paper) 1. Mental healing. 2. Mind and body therapies. 3. Spiritual healing. I. Schulz, Mona Lisa. II. Title.

RZ400.H342 2013

615.8'528--dc23

2012038724

Tradepaper ISBN: 978-1-4019-3502-3
Hardcover ISBN: 978-1-4019-3501-6
Digital ISBN: 978-1-4019-3505-4

17 16 15 14   7 6 5 4
1st edition, March 2013
4th edition, May 2014

Printed in the United States of America

Whenever there is a problem, repeat over and over:

All is well.
Everything is working out for my highest good.
Out of this situation only good will come.
I am safe.

It will work miracles in your life.

JOY & BLESSINGS,
LOUISE HAY

Contents

A Welcome from Louise

It thrills my heart to present this book to you, dearest reader, whether you're new to my work or a longtime follower.

All Is Well looks at my teachings from a fresh and exciting angle. My co-author, Mona Lisa Schulz, whom I love and adore, has been promising me for ages that she would pull together scientific evidence to support what I have been teaching for years. While I personally do not need proof to know that these methods work—I rely on what I call my "Inner Ding" to evaluate things—I know there are many people who will only consider a new idea if there is science behind it. So here we present the science to you. With this added information, I know that a whole new segment of people will become aware of the power they have to heal their bodies.

So let this book be your guide. In the following pages, Mona Lisa will show clearly, step by step, how you can move from illness to wellness—outlining the connections between emotional wellness and health and the prescriptions we give for healing. This book combines medical health, holistic health, nutritional health, and emotional health in one nice, tidy package that can be followed by anyone, anytime, anywhere.

Chapter 1

INTEGRATING HEALING METHODS

Healing the mind and body with affirmations, medicine, and intuition is territory that has been increasingly explored over the last 30 years. And though there are many brilliant and gifted individuals who have helped lead the way, few would argue with the fact that the first pioneer in this field was Louise Hay. In fact, this movement began en masse in the 1980s, when we all bought her "little blue book," *Heal Your Body: The Mental Causes for Physical Illness and the Metaphysical Way to Overcome Them*, and discovered the thought patterns that led to the health problems we all had.

Who knew what a turn my life would take because of this little blue book, but it truly has changed everything. It helped me sculpt my own medical practice, and its theory has guided me along the path to better health for my patients and myself. As you can imagine, I was thrilled—actually beyond thrilled—when Hay House proposed that I write a book with Louise that brought together the healing power of intuition, affirmations, and medicine: both traditional Western medicine and alternative therapies. It's the ultimate healing system! To work with this material . . . and with Louise! How could I say no?

I had dragged *Heal Your Body* along with me to medical school and later as I spent long years researching the brain in pursuit of my Ph.D. I used it when I cried through the ups and downs of my medical and scientific training. And the times I didn't cry and came down with sinusitis and postnasal drip. I would look up in the book the associated thought pattern: postnasal drip, also known as "inner crying." When I got nervous about taking out one student loan after another to pay tuition, I started to get sciatica, lower-back problems. Once again I turned to the little blue book. Sciatica was associated with "fear of money and of the future."

Time after time, the book made sense, but I could never figure out where Louise got her affirmation system. What motivated her, nearly 35 years ago, to start her "clinical observation study" on the association between human thoughts and health? How could someone with no scientific background or medical training observe client after client, see a consistent correlation between certain thought patterns and their associated health problems, and then write a book that so accurately addresses our health concerns? Her prescriptions worked but I didn't know why or how. It simply drove me crazy.

So, as necessity—or aggravation—is the mother of invention, I decided to delve into the science behind her affirmation system, mapping out the emotional aspects of illness in the brain and body. And the correlations I found helped me create a treatment system that has guided me through more than 25 years of intuitive consultations and an equal number of years as a physician and scientist. But it wasn't until Louise and I started down the path of writing this book that I realized how powerful combining the healing methods I use with Louise's affirmations could be.

The Importance of Intuition

Back in 1991, I had finished two years of medical school training plus three years of my Ph.D., and I needed to go back to the hospital floor to finish my studies. Armed with a white coat, stethoscope, and lots of little books, I entered the floors of what at that time was Boston City Hospital.

On the first day, my resident came to me, gave me the name and age of my first patient, and said simply, "Work her up." That was it. I was terrified. How was I supposed to figure out what was wrong with her when I had no information other than her name and age?

In the elevator on the way down to the emergency room, I fidgeted nervously. I knew only the rudiments about how to work up a patient, let alone how to operate the stethoscope around my neck. Momentarily trapped in the elevator, I stood with clipboard in hand. And there, in an instant, I saw in my mind's eye an image of the patient I was about to evaluate. She was moderately obese, in lime-green stretch pants, clutching the right upper part of her abdomen, screaming, "Doctor, doctor! It's my gallbladder!"

Wow! I thought. *In the event that the patient I am about to meet does have a gallbladder problem, how would I evaluate that medical problem?* As the elevator slowly crept between floors, I flipped through the pages of the numerous manuals stuffed in my pockets and quickly researched how I would work up a patient with a gallbladder problem. On my clipboard, I sketched out the classic workup one does for a gallbladder problem: check an ultrasound of the liver, check liver enzymes, observe the whites of the patient's eyes.

The doors opened. I ran down to the emergency room and threw open the curtain, and there, to my surprise, was a woman lying on the gurney in, yes, lime-green stretch pants, screaming, "Doctor, doctor! It's my gallbladder!"

It had to be a coincidence, right?

The second day, once again, the resident barked out the name and age of my patient, telling me to go down to the emergency room. Again an image of the patient popped into my mind, this time with a bladder infection. So, I ran the drill again: how would I treat a patient with a bladder infection. Lo and behold, it was a bladder infection. On the third day, I repeated the process again, and again my impressions were accurate. After three days, I realized that there was something unique about my brain, that my mind's eye could see ahead of time what my trained medical eye would eventually see on the floors of the hospital.

I could see just how useful intuition was in helping me assess my patients, but I soon realized that intuition played an even larger role than I initially thought.

The Body's Intuition

The human body is an amazing machine, and as a machine it requires regular maintenance and care to run as efficiently as possible. There are a variety of reasons your body can break down and get sick: genetics, the environment, diet, and so on. But as Louise found in her career—and published in *Heal Your Body*—every illness is affected by emotional factors in your life. And decades after Louise presented her conclusions, the scientific community has put forth studies that support them.

Research has shown that fear, anger, sadness, love, and joy have specific effects on the body. We know that anger makes muscles clamp down and blood vessels constrict, leading to hypertension and resistance to blood flow. Cardiac medicine tells us that joy and love tend to have the opposite effect. If you look at Louise's little blue book, a heart attack and other heart problems are "squeezing all the joy" out of the heart, a "hardening of the heart," and a "lack of joy." And her affirmation to reverse these problems? "I bring joy back to the center of my heart," and "I joyously release the past. I am in peace."

Specific thought patterns affect our bodies in predictable ways, releasing certain chemicals in response to each emotion. When fear is your dominant mood over a long period of time, the constant release of stress hormones, specifically cortisol, triggers a domino effect of chemicals that lead to heart disease, weight gain, and depression. As with fear, other emotions and thoughts follow a typical pattern as they are projected onto the body in the form of illness. In my work, I have also found that while emotions travel everywhere in the body, they affect organs differently

4

depending on what is happening in your life. This is where intuition comes in.

Often if we are not aware of an emotional situation in our life or the life of a loved one, this information comes to us through intuition. We have five earthbound senses that can evoke our feelings: seeing, hearing, body sensation, smell, and taste. And we have five parallel "intuitive senses"—clairvoyance (seeing), clairaudience (hearing), clairsentience (body sensation), clairalience (smelling), and clairgustance (tasting)—through which we can gain additional information. For example, you may anxiously receive an intuitive image, a clairvoyant flash that a friend is in danger. Or you may feel dread when you hear the phone ring in your head five minutes before it actually does, relaying bad news about a loved one's death. You may get that famous "bad taste in your mouth" or feel like you "smell something suspicious" right before someone asks you to agree to a bad business deal. Or you may experience a bad feeling in your body, whether it's that "gut feeling" or that "heartache" warning you about a problem you will be facing in your relationship.

In addition to the commonly understood intuition that guides us in these matters where we have insufficient information—like the intuition that has helped me throughout my medical career—our bodies also have innate intuition. Our bodies can tell when something is out of balance in our lives, even if this knowledge is unclear in our conscious minds.

If we are to fully heal, we must bring our attention to the messages our bodies relay through intuition. But we also need logic and facts to fully understand which imbalances in our lifestyle are affecting our health. Just like needing both tires inflated on a bicycle, you need to balance emotions and intuition with logic and fact. Both extreme logic without intuition and intuition without logic breed disaster. We must use both of these tools to create health. Throughout this book we will discuss how to do this, focusing on four approaches:

1. Becoming conscious of our emotions and those of other people in our life, making note of the warnings that come with fear, anger, and sadness

2. Figuring out what thoughts accompany these feelings that keep swirling around our heads

3. Identifying symptoms of distress and locating them in our bodies

4. Decoding the intuitive/emotional thought-pattern information underlying the symptoms and understanding that every illness is also in part due to diet, environment, genetics, and injury

The Intuitive Emergency Dashboard

So how do we tap into our body's intuition to read and interpret the messages it is trying to send us?

Think of your body as a car dashboard; it has a series of emergency warning lights—regions that light up symptomatically when something in your life needs attention. Who hasn't experienced that irritating gas light? Always going on at an inopportune time, this dashboard warning light aggravates you when you drive your car until it's so low on fuel that it's almost running on fumes. Similarly, if an area of your life is empty—or running on excess—a part of your body will hint, murmur, even scream out in distress.

You have seven warning lights, each consisting of a group of organs. The health of the organs in each group is associated with specific types of thought patterns and behaviors. For example, the organs associated with feeling safe and secure in the world are the bones, blood, immune system, and skin. If you do not feel safe and secure, you are more likely to experience illness in one of these organs than if you do. We refer to this group of organs as an *emotional center* because their health is connected to the same emotional issues.

Each chapter in this book is dedicated to the health of the organs of one emotional center. For example, Chapter 4 looks at the organs of the first emotional center—the bones, blood, organs of the immune system, and skin—and helps you interpret what illness in each of those organs means. It looks at the balance in your life surrounding the core emotion associated with the organs. So, in essence, if your sense of safety and security has been thrown out of balance, you will likely become ill in your first emotional center organs.

Just as we need a balanced diet to be healthy, we also need to make sure we have healthy sources of love and happiness. By working to invest our energy among various areas of life—family, money, work, relationships, communication, education, and spirituality—we can create physical and emotional health.

How to Use This Book

When Louise and I began our discussions about how to create the most useful book for you, we decided to structure it so you could look up the part of your body that is experiencing illness and work from there—just like in *You Can Heal Your Life*. However, you must remember that people are not simply individual organs bound together, so the illness in one part of your body will generally affect the health of another part. And emotions about feeling safe and secure in your family (first emotional center) also play into emotions about self-esteem (third emotional center). To fully heal, you must look at your life as a whole while giving extra attention to the organ or illness that's causing you the most trouble. Feel free to flip directly to the part of the book discussing your personal problem area, but remember that you may also find important information about other imbalances in your life by reading through the entire book. Having a complete picture of your strengths and weaknesses can help you create a long-term plan for a healthy life in all your emotional centers.

As you work your way through the book, I'll help you tap into your body's intuition surrounding the organs in each emotional center so you can understand the messages your body is sending. But remember, only you can decide what your body is really telling you. This book is a general guide that matches what is commonly seen and what the science mostly supports.

After you have determined what your body is telling you, Louise and I will walk you through healing techniques that address the numerous reasons why we get sick. While we won't give specific medical advice in this book because good medical advice is unique to each individual, we will provide case studies that give you an idea of some of the basic types of medical interventions to consider. More important, we will lay out affirmations that you can repeat to yourself multiple times throughout your day and behavioral suggestions that you can immediately incorporate into your own life. These tools will help you change your thoughts and habits to create health.

There is one thing to note about the case studies. These sections highlight the extremes of people with problems in a single emotional center. However, it's important to remember that most people don't have just one problem—they can have many, whether it's infertility, arthritis, and fatigue or some other combination of issues. In our case studies we focus only on the predominant issue that is associated with each emotional center. To cover all the imbalances and problems in each person's life would lead to an encyclopedic tome that wouldn't be nearly as accessible to the vast majority of people as we have crafted this book to be. So don't be surprised if you recognize yourself in *many* of the descriptions we lay out.

While you're reading, your intuition may scream out, or perhaps it will simply make a quiet squeak. The important thing is to listen to what comes up and work with it.

I've learned a couple very important guiding principles throughout my career: The first is that every single one of us, no matter our uniqueness, no matter what our personality quirks or our past emotional or physical trials, all of us can improve our health. The second is that we need to be open to every healing modality available to create health and happiness. Whether it's vitamins and nutritional supplements, herbs and medicines, surgery, meditation, affirmations, or psychotherapy, everything can be helpful if you use it under the guidance of a skilled, healing professional you trust. *All Is Well* will help you find the combination of methods that is right for you.

Chapter 2

YOUR *ALL IS WELL*
SELF-ASSESSMENT QUIZ

Louise and I have each worked with thousands of people, and one of the most important parts of this work is our initial intake—let's just call it a getting-to-know-you process. This process allows us to assess where you stand now with your health and your emotions and gives us hints about the best way to help you.

The quiz in this chapter will guide you in doing the same thing for yourself. And by the time you finish it, you should have a better idea of where to start on your path to healing.

There are seven sections, each with questions covering both physical health problems and lifestyle habits. Answer yes or no to each of the questions. At the end of the quiz, there is a scoring guide to help you evaluate your current emotional and physical health. Then have a close friend take the quiz as though that person were you and compare the scores. It's helpful to get outside perspectives because sometimes we cannot see our own lives clearly.

Quiz

Section 1

Body Health Questions:

1. Do you have arthritis?
2. Do you have spinal problems, disk disease, or scoliosis?
3. Do you have osteoporosis?
4. Are you prone to accidents, muscle spasms, or chronic pain?
5. Do you have anemia, bleeding disorders, or a tendency toward viruses or fatigue?
6. Do you have psoriasis, eczema, acne, or other skin disorders?

Lifestyle Questions:

1. Do you tend to give more than you receive?
2. Do you have trouble feeling loved by an independent person?
3. When you see someone in pain, do you feel that you have to rescue them?
4. Are you not good with group politics, or do you lack social savvy?
5. Were you bullied growing up?
6. Are you bullied in your current life?
7. Does your health tend to suffer during changes in seasons?
8. Does change make you nervous?

9. Is the boundary between your moods and someone else's too easily penetrated?

10. Were or are you the black sheep of the family?

11. Are you the person everyone automatically goes to when they have a problem?

12. Do you tend to burn bridges in relationships after arguments?

SECTION 2

Body Health Questions:

1. Do you have health concerns associated with your female reproductive organs—your uterus or ovaries, for example?

2. Do you have vaginitis or other vagina problems?

3. Do you have problems with your male reproductive organs: prostate, testicles, or others?

4. Do you experience impotence or problems with sexual desire?

Lifestyle Questions:

1. If you lend money to a loved one, do you have a hard time charging interest?

2. Do you usually go into debt during the holidays?

3. Do you thrive on competition, or do people tend to say you are just a little too competitive?

4. Have you ever broken up a relationship over a career choice?

5. Do you have a lifelong pattern of being overeducated and underemployed?

SECTION 3

Body Health Questions:

1. Do you have digestion problems, such as a peptic ulcer?
2. Do you have problems with addiction?
3. Are you overweight?
4. Do you have anorexia or bulimia?

Lifestyle Questions:

1. Do you think it's vain to have a facial?
2. Do you tend to attract people who have trouble with addiction?
3. Do you know exactly how much fat there is in your love handle and hip region?
4. Do you have compulsive habits—shopping or eating, for example—that you use to calm your nerves?
5. Is your personal style—your fashion, mannerisms, and even your way of speaking—behind the times?

SECTION 4

Body Health Questions:

1. Do you have problems with your arteries or blood vessels?
2. Do you have arteriosclerosis?

3. Do you have hypertension?

4. Do you have high cholesterol?

5. Have you had a heart attack?

6. Do you have asthma?

7. Do you have any breast disorders?

Lifestyle Questions:

1. Do people often tell you how you are feeling?

2. Have you been told that you are too sensitive?

3. Are your moods sensitive to weather and season changes?

4. Have you cried at work?

5. Do you cry easily?

6. Is it hard for you to get angry at a loved one?

7. Do you have a short fuse?

8. Do you stay home or away from people because you feel overwhelmed by emotion?

SECTION 5

Body Health Questions:

1. Do you have jaw problems?

2. Do you have thyroid problems?

3. Do you have neck problems?

4. Do you often get a sore throat?

5. Do you have other throat problems?

Lifestyle Questions:

1. Did you have trouble following directions when you were young?
2. Do you have trouble following directions now?
3. Is it hard for you to concentrate on cell phones or a speakerphone call?
4. Do you tend to have long arguments or misunderstandings with friends or loved ones over e-mail?
5. Do you say yes simply to end an argument?
6. Do you have dyslexia or problems with stuttering, learning languages, or public speaking?
7. Do you communicate better with animals than people?
8. Do people often turn to you to fight their battles for them?

Section 6

Body Health Questions:

1. Do you have problems with insomnia?
2. Do you get migraine headaches?
3. Are you worried about getting or looking older?
4. Do you have Alzheimer's disease?
5. Have you had cataracts?
6. Do you experience dizziness?

Lifestyle Questions:

1. Do you have trouble keeping within the word limits on essay tests?
2. Do you have problems with multiple-choice tests?
3. Is your mind always in the clouds?
4. Do you drag your feet when it comes to learning new technology?
5. Have you ever experienced serious trauma or abuse?
6. Can you feel "spirit" when you're in nature?

SECTION 7

Body Health Questions:

1. Are you experiencing a chronic illness?
2. Have you been diagnosed with an incurable disease?
3. Do you have cancer?
4. Is your health so bad that you are on the verge of death?

Lifestyle Questions:

1. Do you have a driven, indomitable spirit?
2. Are you always working—never taking a sick day?
3. Are you lost as to what your true life's purpose is?
4. Do you tend to have one life or health crisis after another?
5. Do most of your friends and family seem to be moving away or leaving you in other ways?

Scoring

To score the quiz, simply count the number of yeses in each section.

SECTION 1

We Are Family—The First Emotional Center: Bones, Joints, Blood, Immune System, and Skin

If you answered yes to:

- **0 to 6 questions:** You are truly at home in the world, and your healthy bones, joints, blood, and immune system reflect this. Your health challenges are likely to be in other areas.

- **7 to 11 questions:** You have occasional family problems, and that twinge of joint pain, the frustration of skin problems, or the discomfort of immune system issues will let you know. So make sure to tune in and try to get these things under control before they grow into something much worse.

- **12 to 18 questions:** Brace yourself! It's time to reevaluate how to get family or other group support. You need to focus on the health of the first emotional center right away by working to create a more secure life. Go to Chapter 4 to learn what changes you can make to help rid you of your bone, joint, blood, immune, and skin problems.

SECTION 2

It Takes Two—The Second Emotional Center: Bladder, Reproductive Organs, Lower Back, and Hips

If you answered yes to:

- **0 to 2 questions:** You are truly a powerhouse in your capacity to financially and romantically negotiate your way through life. With your ability to balance love and money, your health challenges are more likely to come from other body regions.

- **3 to 5 questions:** You have average ups and downs with love and finances. However, that occasional hormonal mood swing or lower-back pain may indicate that you need to look for an unstable relationship or financial issue somewhere. Just remember to keep vigilant in your efforts.

- **6 to 9 questions:** Your life has been a struggle over how to handle both financial independence and intimate relationships. Your health challenges with lower-back and hip pain or hormonal, reproductive, or bladder problems are likely to help give you intuitive warnings that you need to find a better way to balance money and love. Go to Chapter 5 right away to gain insight on how to create this balance.

SECTION 3

A New Attitude—The Third Emotional Center: Digestive System, Weight, Adrenal Glands, Pancreas, and Addiction

If you answered yes to:

- **0 to 2 questions:** You have an innate sense that you are lovable and can focus on your own needs, yet you have enough discipline and responsibility to handle a job and meet your responsibilities to others. Take a bow. This is rare. With your capacity to balance your own identity, your challenges are more likely to come from other body regions.

- **3 to 5 questions:** Your occasional struggles with work and your self-esteem are likely to materialize in only occasional problems of indigestion, constipation, bowel irregularity, or weight concerns. So keep an eye out for any growing imbalances in these areas.

- **6 to 9 questions:** You know you have self-esteem issues. Your lifelong struggle to feel empowered by a career and to simultaneously love yourself is likely to have resulted in illness of your digestive tract and kidneys or in issues with weight or addiction. Chapter 6 can help you learn important ways to change your thoughts and behavior to lead to health in this emotional center.

Section 4

Sweet Emotion—The Fourth Emotional Center: Heart, Lungs, and Breasts

If you answered yes to:

- **0 to 4 questions:** You are one of those rare individuals who can take care of a child, an aging parent, or anyone for that matter and still manage to keep your wits about you. You were born with a strong mental and emotional constitution. Good for you.

- **5 to 10 questions:** Your heart, respiratory, or breast problems might signal sadness, anxiety, or frustration with a child or partner, but you won't be sidetracked for long. You have resilience, and somehow you know how to bounce back!

- **11 to 15 questions:** Watch out! Your lifelong struggle managing your emotions in your relationships can make life seem like a soap opera or bad reality show. Sometimes you may want to run away and live in a monastery just to get away from it all. But your health is within reach. Check out Chapter 7 to see what you can do to heal yourself.

SECTION 5

Something to Talk About—The Fifth Emotional Center: Mouth, Neck, and Thyroid

If you answered yes to:

- **0 to 4 questions:** Congratulations on your impressive communication skills. You know how to express your own needs and listen to the point of view of those around you. You know yourself and how to be strong and empathetic at the same time. Good for you.

- **5 to 8 questions:** You have only the occasional disagreement with friends, children, parents, co-workers, or your partner. And even though you lock horns, your conflict doesn't last long and neither do the health problems that tend to develop in your neck, thyroid, jaw, or mouth. When a communication style isn't working, you will temporarily get neck or jaw tightness or dental problems that will quickly help you reevaluate a better way to communicate.

- **9 to 13 questions:** You probably don't need to hear this from us, but you have had a lifelong struggle to feel heard and understood by others. You've also had problems listening to those around you. It's important that you learn to communicate while being aware of all sides of a situation—peacefully having a voice and simultaneously hearing. Chapter 8 will set you on the right path.

Section 6

Suddenly I See—The Sixth Emotional Center: Brain, Eyes, and Ears

If you answered yes to:

- **0 to 3 questions:** How do you do it? You are one of those rare individuals who was born with a stable mind-set and doesn't tend to struggle with the unknown. Call it faith. Or call it traveling through life on autopilot. It doesn't matter. You've learned not to struggle, and you gracefully adapt to the changes in life. Your health problems are probably not to be found in the brain, eyes, and ears.

- **4 to 8 questions:** You have only the occasional problem struggling with pessimism and narrow-mindedness about the future. However, an inner voice eventually tells you that your mind is not your friend. And the headache, dry eyes, or bout of dizziness that occurs when you are in a pessimistic funk will soon get your attention and force you to look at your world with a healthier perspective.

- **9 to 12 questions:** Take a deep breath. The cause of your problems is your lifelong struggle to clearly see and hear the world as it really is. You need to widen your scope of perception, making your mind-set more adaptive and flexible. By being open to how life flows, and releasing your expectations about how you think life should be, you can create better health in your brain, eyes, and ears. Learn more about this in Chapter 9.

SECTION **7**

Changes—The Seventh Emotional Center: Chronic and Degenerative Disorders and Life-Threatening Illnesses

If you answered yes to:

- **0 to 2 questions:** You are at a stable point in life. You've watched other people suffer health disasters but you've remained healthy. Congratulations, and keep it up.

- **3 to 5 questions:** You have only the occasional medical issue. Your faith may have been tested on those few times when you got the painful medical results back from the doctor. Since you've had these experiences before, keep an eye out for anything your body may be trying to tell you before it gets to the point of dealing with these dramatic situations again.

- **6 to 9 questions:** Don't worry; you have company. You've known for a while that you need help. You meditate, pray, and have an array of medical support people to help guide you through the crises. However, you are worn down. To have a better life, you need to examine how to change and grow in partnership

with Divine spirit. Join us for the adventure in
Chapter 10.

Now that you've evaluated your current situation, let us take
the next steps to create health together.

Chapter 3

A PERSPECTIVE
ON USING MEDICINE

Some readers who are drawn to this book may be tempted to opt out of the healing options modern medicine provides. This could be because they see using these as proof that other options won't work, or perhaps because of some level of distrust of the modern system. But in my experience—both with my own health and through my patients—I've found that medicine is an essential part of the equation.

Around the world over a period of some years, health care has undergone seismic shifts. For centuries or perhaps millennia, when it came to healing, people focused on engaging skilled practitioners who used techniques such as dream interpretation and intuition. Because they didn't have the technology we use today, they relied on these mystical skills to lead them toward a cause and a cure. For example, in ancient Greece, instead of employing a radiologist to get an MRI or CT scan, ancient physicians would go into an altered, dreamlike state and intuitively accessed information about their patients' illnesses. Healing involved looking at the whole person and attempting to restore balance to restore health.

In recent years, science has changed this whole-person, balance-focused perspective on health. Diagnostic tests, drugs, specialists, and many technical advances have made the world a healthier place. Average life expectancy has gone up. The incidence of maternal death during childbirth has plummeted. We have medications that can eradicate horrible diseases. Think of the havoc wreaked on Europe during the mid-14th century. The bubonic plague—the Black Death—killed somewhere between 30 and 60 percent of the entire population. Can you imagine? And the bubonic plague is still around, but its impact has been minimized by treatment with antibiotics. Modern medicine really has accomplished amazing feats.

As a physician and healer, I cannot stress enough the importance medicine plays in healing. If you are ill, you should contact a medical practitioner. These professionals have the knowledge and skill to use technology to your advantage. They can prescribe unique practices and medicines based on the combination of symptoms and ailments you present.

But it is also important to remember that medicine has its limits. That's why we're writing this book.

As the field of healing has shifted, many people have moved away from any interaction with the mystical. The miraculous cures that technology has brought about seem to offer more modern and tidy solutions. But remember that technology makes mistakes, too. Blood tests and pregnancy tests frequently come back with faulty results. Medications have side effects. Things go wrong.

So what's my point? That technology without limits is folly. And intuition alone is equally foolish. We must use a combination of techniques—and employ a combination of experts—to achieve true health. In fact, my life is a perfect demonstration of how medicine, intuition, and affirmations can heal your life.

Back in 1972 when I was 12, my family had a lot of financial stress, and we had many conversations about money. Within a period of three months my spine curved into a severe case of scoliosis, which necessitated surgery. Because of my spine's altered structure, I developed an enlarged heart and decreased lung capacity as well. The surgery was dramatic and lifesaving—complete with rods and screws.

I remember walking down Longwood Avenue in Boston before the surgery, looking up at the tall medical buildings and saying to anyone who would listen, "Someday, I'm going to come back here, and I'm going to study medicine and science." That surgery changed my future. The doctors saved my life by using medicine; as a result, I became a physician and a scientist so I, too, could save people's lives.

But life has a way of not working out exactly the way we expect it to. As a pre-med student, I developed narcolepsy that made my consciousness—my intellect—go on the blink. I couldn't stay awake in my classes. It looked like my dreams of being a doctor and a scientist were going down the drain. They simply weren't going to materialize because I couldn't keep my grades up if I couldn't keep my eyes open.

So again I turned to medicine. And again the doctors helped; they found a drug that would keep me awake. But I soon had to stop taking it because of a life-threatening side effect. Sadly, my dependable world of medicine had nothing else to help me.

This development launched a series of voyages into other healing methods. I tried one after another: alternative, complementary, integrative—you name it. I tried Chinese herbs, acupuncture, and even a macrobiotic healing diet for three years. All these methods helped me somewhat, but none completely worked in my quest to stay awake.

A wonderful thing that came out of this exploration was that I learned, through seeking help from a medical intuitive, about my brain's facility for intuition. Out of desperation, I also went to a shaman, who told me that when I learned how to access my intuition, my health problems would get better.

But all these advisors could only take me so far. There was one element of my health that was not being addressed—my emotions! I had begun to see a pattern developing. I found that if I was angry about something for a very long time, or if I was around irritating, angry people, my narcolepsy would act up and I would end up falling asleep—against my will—within 24 to 48 hours. Believe me, I timed it; it was always 24 to 48 hours. And I figured out that if I was nervous about something, or around anxious, high-strung people, I would eventually start feeling sleepy. Lights out! The same thing was true for people who were sad or depressed.

One day I walked into a bookstore and found Louise's little blue book. While I had seen that certain thought patterns were associated with illness, I didn't know how to use this knowledge to get healthy—other than to avoid certain people or situations, which just isn't practical in the long run. But Louise's book offered me the tools I needed to neutralize the negative thought patterns that I knew were contributing to my health problems: affirmations!

It was certainly worth a try. Conventional, alternative, and complementary medicines were all helping some, but not completely, and avoiding someone else's emotions or my own was getting exhausting. So I got out a notebook, and with some choice pens started writing specific affirmations that seemed to be associated with my health problems:

I choose to see life as eternal and joyous. I love myself just the way I am. I love myself just the way I am.

I, Mona Lisa, rely on Divine wisdom and guidance to protect me at all times. I am safe.

I, Mona Lisa, rely on Divine wisdom and guidance to protect me at all times. I am safe.

These are classic Louise Hay–isms. I repeated them over and over again, and slowly but surely my sleep spells decreased. I got into medical school and graduated with an M.D. and a Ph.D. I never would have been able to do this without affirmations.

I've had my share of ups and downs with my health over the years. (Haven't we all?) Each time I had a down, I'd turn to conventional and integrative medicine. I'd also take out Louise Hay's book, and I'd use medical intuition to find the imbalances in my life. This combination always did the trick.

This is how I stay well. Medicine, intuition, and affirmations. It's also how I help other people.

Recently, the spine problem that started when I was 12 began to escalate. I started to list forward like the Leaning Tower of

Pisa—I stood at a 70-degree angle, always facing toward the ground. The surgeons I saw in Phoenix, Arizona, said it was straight back syndrome, a complication of the extensive scoliosis surgery I had had nearly 40 years before. I couldn't walk very far or lift my arms. Intuition told me to reevaluate the structure and support in my life, and I did. I looked at my purpose with the help of spiritual advisors and friends. I also worked with a Chinese acupuncturist and *qigong* master, but all these remedies only took me so far.

I still wanted to be able to walk. The surgeon said that an operation was necessary or I'd be in a wheelchair. So on February 13, 2012, I went to the operating room—and almost died when an abnormal vein blew during surgery. Medicine again saved my life. The surgeon stopped the bleeding, resuscitated me, and fixed my spine, making me three inches taller. And he gave me back my life.

I would love to tell you that medicine alone—so neat, so tidy, so rational—was the saving grace. I was in the ICU for more than two weeks and in the hospital for four weeks: let us say recovery was tricky. But now I'm better than ever. So what was it that brought me back? Of course, in the hospital, I used medicine. And I used intuition to figure out how to strengthen my body and create balance in my life. I relied heavily on affirmations to change my thoughts. And believe me, they needed changing! This is how you heal the whole person. How you create lasting health. Medicine alone wouldn't do it, and neither would intuition or affirmations. Only a balanced approach holds the full promise of healing.

Chapter 4

WE ARE FAMILY

The First Emotional Center: Bones, Joints, Blood, Immune System, and Skin

The health of the first emotional center depends on your feeling safe in the world. If you don't have the support of family and friends that you need to thrive, you will see this insecurity manifest in your blood, immune system, bones, joints, and skin. The key to enjoying health in this center is balancing your own needs with those of the meaningful social groups in your life. Family and friends, work, and an organization to which you are devoted all take up time and energy. But they are also meant to give back, in the form of friendship, safety, and security; they should provide a sense of belonging. These are all reasons human beings seek out other people and groups. However, the needs of the group should never be allowed to overshadow your own needs—particularly your health.

When you are not getting what you need from relationships or activities on which you spend considerable time, your body and mind will start to tell you. At first the signs may be as simple as fatigue, skin rashes, or joint pain. Mild problems in the first emotional center can serve as an early-warning system, letting you know when you have gone off track. Ignoring your body's warnings could lead to a world of hurt: chronic fatigue syndrome, fibromyalgia, osteoarthritis, rheumatoid arthritis, Epstein-Barr virus, hepatitis (A, B, or C), mononucleosis, Lyme disease, allergies, rashes, psoriasis, joint pain, and autoimmune disorders like lupus all stem from an imbalance in the first emotional center.

The part of your body in which the sickness manifests depends on what's causing the feeling of insecurity. For example, if you feel so overwhelmed by family responsibilities that you put your own needs on the back burner, the insecurity you feel will create illness in your bones. Feeling hopeless and helpless will show up in your blood. Feeling completely alone and outcast from your family will bring illness to your immune system. And being unable to set boundaries with those around you will show up in skin ailments. We'll get into more specifics as we move through each organ system. For now, just remember: it is important to listen to your body's warnings and take action. By focusing on *why* you are not feeling safe and secure, you can change thought and behavior patterns that may be adding to your sickness.

First Emotional Center Affirmations and Science

So what's the importance of affirmations? If you fundamentally don't believe that you are capable or worthy of receiving support, foundation, and security, medicine alone won't be able to cure what ails you. You must address the underlying beliefs that led you down the road of health problems in the first place. If you are experiencing illness in your blood, immune system, bones, joints, or skin, you are probably also having negative thoughts, such as:

- I can't independently support myself.
- I have nobody to help support me.

- I feel depressed, joyless, hopeless, and helpless.
- I am unloved and alone.

This is where affirmations come in; they help you change these core beliefs. If you use affirmations to address the negative thought patterns and beliefs—the doubts and fears—*and* apply available medical science, you will start to see huge changes in your health and in your emotional life.

If you look at the affirmations that address illness in organs of the first emotional center, you'll see that they have to do with building support, foundation, security, structure, family, movement, and flexibility. The health of your bones in general reflects the structure of your life and how you draw on and use the support others offer you. If you feel loved and supported, your spine will feel structurally strong and flexible. Conversely, if you feel a lack of support and security in your life, you may suffer from osteoporosis and bone fractures.

A lack of security doesn't necessarily come only from relationships around you. It can also come from a weak relationship with yourself. Louise's affirmations note that an inability to support yourself independently in the world is associated with a weakened immune system and susceptibility to viruses, which can result in illnesses such as Epstein-Barr and mononucleosis. She refers to this as a "draining of your inner support." If you look at the biological basis of this, you'll see that a suppressed immune system often comes from problems in your bone marrow, which is responsible for producing new blood cells and is a key component of the lymphatic system, which supports the immune system.

What can science tell us about the connection between mind and body health and the affirmation system?

Family—a sense of belonging—is fundamentally important for health in our bodies.[1] Social interaction plays a vital role in everyday regulation of our body systems. If you isolate yourself, you remove the metabolic regulators that are present when you interact with a group, and your rhythms—your life, it seems—goes kind of kaflooey, which affects the health of your first emotional center.[2]

Research has shown that there is a biology of belonging, an actual biological nutrient passing between people who live together—a nutrient that has physical and metabolic consequences.[3] All our body rhythms having to do with sleeping, eating, dreaming, hormones, immunity, cortisol levels, heart rate, and endocrine systems are governed by these metabolic regulators. And when people are together in a communal situation, their biological body rhythms become synchronized and regular. Being together in close and constant fashion the way we are in a family—eating, sleeping, conversing, playing, working, praying—causes us to synchronize our biological watches. In one study, for example, the individual members of B-52 bomber crews were all found to have similar levels of stress hormones while they were working together.[4]

When you lose this nutrient of belonging, feelings of isolation and lack of meaningful relationships give rise to a sense of hopelessness, helplessness, and despair. And these emotions can cause problems with your physical health. Quite literally, your immune system becomes inflamed when you are depressed. Prolonged despair, loss, and bereavement that turn to chronic depression make your immune system pump out inflammatory substances like cortisol, IL1, IL6, and TNF-alpha. These can make your joints ache with pain; make you feel tired, like you have the flu; and increase your risk for a host of bone, joint, blood, and immune system disorders, including osteoporosis.[5]

Another instance of health being affected by losing the feeling of belonging was shown in people who were separated from their parents too early or grew up with mothers who were depressed or unavailable. These folks had a tendency toward depression and immune system dysfunction. Because of this early and painful separation, they were unable to negotiate their sense of loneliness in the world.[6] They often unwittingly found themselves in situations that re-created—emotionally, nutritionally, and biologically—their initial feeling of abandonment. They lived sparse, frugal, and solitary lives that led to a sense of deprivation. The hopelessness they experienced throughout life ultimately rendered them more vulnerable to cancer.[7]

A lack of security can also come after a huge shock: the loss of a beloved family member, an abrupt and painful move, or anything else that leaves you feeling disoriented—like a plant that's been pulled up by its roots, or like being traumatically pulled from your home and sent to a foreign land. And science shows us that during these moments we can also lose our biological "roots"—our hair. When there is chaos between family members, there is an increased risk of hair loss (alopecia), not to mention psoriasis and other skin problems.[8]

So as you can see, having solid external relationships is essential to our health. Science backs this up by showing that "social integration"—wide social networks and social support—creates stronger immune systems. In fact, studies show that more and better relationships mean more and better white blood cells, which help us resist infections and protect us from a wide variety of health perils, including arthritis, depression, and the worsening of symptoms of conditions like tuberculosis. Social interaction also decreases the amount of medication people need and accelerates their recovery from illness.[9]

Other studies show that those who had three or fewer relationships caught more colds and were more susceptible to viruses than those with more relationships. Those who had six or more relationships got the least, and when they did develop colds, they had the mildest symptoms.[10]

This isn't what you'd expect, is it? You'd think that having more friends would expose you to more germs and therefore cause more colds. But germ theory obviously doesn't have the full answer to why we get colds and infections. The reason people with fewer friends are more susceptible may be because they experience stress from being alone and unsupported most of the time. That stress causes the adrenal glands to release norepinephrine and suppress the immune system. In fact, it's been shown that people who have few friends are at greater risk for health problems than smokers or the obese. They also have higher levels of corticosteroids, immunosuppressants that make them more susceptible to chronic fatigue, fibromyalgia, rheumatoid arthritis, lupus, HIV, frequent colds and infections, and osteoporosis.[11]

Depressive thought patterns are also potent. Depression's capacity to increase one's risk of osteoporosis is equal to the risk of having low calcium intake or smoking.[12] So next time you see yet another TV commercial or magazine advertisement for calcium supplements to prevent bone loss, your thoughts should also go to lifestyle changes and affirmations to support your health.

If you are unlovable to other people—you are frightened socially or have grief that causes you to seclude yourself—you must aggressively try to change the thought patterns that keep you entrenched in self-imposed exile, or soon your bones, joints, blood, skin, and immune system will let you know that your solitude is unhealthy. But enough of all this scientific, medical stuff. What do we actually do to heal ourselves?

Bone and Joint Problems

People who tend to have bone and joint problems like arthritis, fractures, osteoporosis, back pain, joint pain, or slipped disks likely feel overwhelmed by the responsibilities of caring for family and friends, always putting the needs of everyone else before their own. They have become so obsessed with caring for others that they don't have the ability to stand up for themselves. If you are one of the millions of people who have bone and joint problems, listen up. It is critical that you identify what it is about your interaction with family and friends that is making you feel unsafe or insecure. You must address these behavioral patterns and beliefs if you are going to fully heal.

For individuals with illness in the first emotional center, there is hope. Using medicine and affirmations to address the intuitive signs your body is giving you, you can create a strong, healthy body. While your doctor can give you specific instructions for how to address your medical concern, no prescription for long-term health is complete without changing the negative thought patterns that have paved the way for illness. A good general affirmation for bone and joint problems is: "I lovingly release the past. They are free and I am free. I am my own authority. I love and approve of myself. Life is good. All is well in my heart now."

While the overall theme of the affirmations addressing health in the first emotional center is about creating a feeling of safety among your family and other social groups, your affirmation varies depending upon the specific body location of your bone or joint problem (see the table on page 183). For example, if your entire back gives you problems, you have general issues with support. However, if you feel pain in only one part of your back, your affirmation becomes more specific. If you suffer from chronic lower-back pain, you probably have financial fears, while upper-back pain relates to feeling very alone, without having enough emotional support.

Louise also looks at the illnesses that can occur *between* bones and joints, and these, too, are addressed with different affirmations. Arthritis is about experiencing criticism in unsupportive families. So for arthritis sufferers in difficult families, the affirmation would be: "I am love. I now choose to love and approve of myself. I see others with love."

And as you are changing your thinking to a healthier mindset, turn your attention outward and look at the balance between your needs and the needs of your family or other social group. Are you letting these people take advantage of you? Are you not standing up for yourself? Do you seem to give more to your friends and family than you receive? Remember, to feel safe and secure you need to learn how to protect and support yourself in addition to adding to the safety and security of these other people. Always remember that you are not the sole resource for everyone—they can look to others for help and advice, too. If you have a problem stepping aside every once in a while, there are groups you can join. Look into Co-Dependents Anonymous (CoDA) or other groups that can help you learn to balance your own needs with the needs of others.

So remember, love your family, but love yourself, too. Worry and care about your friends, but spend some time looking at your own life and make positive changes. Think of yourself in the same way you would a good friend, and don't neglect that relationship.

We all have times when we lose sight of our own needs. The key is to recognize and rectify this behavior before more serious health problems occur.

From the Clinic Files: Immune System Case Study

Starting at age eight, Andrea, now 17, was caretaker to her five younger brothers and sisters. Her parents were unavailable to the children, so Andrea took responsibility for creating a more stable home environment. But her siblings' comfort came at a great personal cost to Andrea. She sacrificed her own needs and even her safety time and time again, and she never had the chance to enjoy a carefree childhood or cultivate an independent identity.

Too young to handle the role of surrogate mom, Andrea developed a series of health problems from an early age—she had a mild curvature of her spine, which was treated with a brace. She tended to get joint and back pain when family stress became unbearable. After her parents died, her spine and joint pain was agonizing and she developed a butterfly rash. This combination sent her to the doctor, who eventually diagnosed her with lupus, or systemic lupus erythematosus (SLE). She had been getting warning signs for years in the form of bone and joint problems but disregarded them because she was handling the turbulent lives of her siblings.

The first thing we did for Andrea was recommend a specific test to verify that she actually had lupus. She went to her internal medicine doctor, who administered a test to find out if the antibody ANA DS (antinuclear antibody double strand) was present. With lupus the body makes these cells that can "attack" almost every organ of the body—whether it's in its mildest form (fever, bone, joint, skin, or thyroid illness) or its more severe cases (lung, kidney, and brain ailments).

The test came back positive, so we knew that lupus was indeed the cause of her pain. If this and other blood tests had repeatedly come back negative, lupus wouldn't be the issue. In addition to the ANA DS test, her physician tested blood cell counts, checking the total number of white and red blood cells and platelets; lupus tends to lower these numbers.

Like most "autoimmune illnesses," lupus goes through ups and downs—there are periods of painful joint, skin, respiratory, fatigue, and other symptoms, and then there are symptom-free intervals of remission. We directed Andrea's treatment toward getting her immune system into remission, which involved getting control of the cells that were making the tissue-attacking antibodies. Our treatment plan was aimed at making them "go to sleep," or calm down.

As a team, including Andrea and other practitioners, we worked to create a treatment strategy to address all of her options, which included everything from potent drugs to supplements to *qigong*—an ancient Chinese practice that uses a combination of breathing, postures, and mental focus for healing. Because the severity of Andrea's lupus wasn't over the top, she could work to heal with or without the use of medication. After discussing the pros and cons with her internal medicine doctor, Andrea started on the steroid prednisone to reduce the inflammation in her autoimmune system. Prednisone is a strong medicine and can have many side effects on bone density, weight, blood pressure, skin, hair, blood sugar, mood, sleep, eyes, and the digestive tract. Although Andrea didn't require such aggressive steps at the point when we were working together, if her symptoms became more severe in the future, she might have to consider taking immunosuppressant drugs such as methotrexate, Azathioprine, or chlorambucil, which have their own list of side effects.

To counter the effects of the drugs she was taking, we suggested Andrea see an acupuncturist and herbalist. We also recommended that she take a calcium-and-magnesium supplement, vitamin D, and a good multivitamin. In addition, she took DHA to repair injured body cells and an herb called Tripterygium wilfordii (TW), using the roots and stems each day to modulate the immune system and ease the symptoms of her lupus. Like any strong medicine, herbs also have side effects. TW can cause reversible changes in hormone levels, amenorrhea, and infertility, so use it only with your medical team's supervision.

We also asked Andrea to cut out a number of things from her diet. Alfalfa sprouts specifically may make lupus symptoms worse. And we suggested that she work with a nutritionist to see if she could identify other foods that seemed to aggravate her symptoms. Luckily, they didn't find anything more.

Finally, we started addressing Andrea's thought patterns and behaviors that could be contributing to her illnesses. We gave her specific affirmations for lupus (I speak up for myself freely and easily. I claim my own power. I love and approve of myself. I am free and safe); bone health (In my world, I am the only authority, for I am the only one who thinks in my mind. I am well structured and balanced); scoliosis (I release all fears. I now trust the process of life. I know that life is for me. I stand straight and tall with love); back pain (I know that Life always supports me. All I need is always taken care of. I am safe); joint pain (I easily flow with change. My life is Divinely guided, and I am always going in the best direction); and rash (I lovingly protect myself with thoughts of joy and peace. The past is forgiven and forgotten. I am free in this moment. I feel safe to be me).

She also followed the advice outlined earlier in this chapter and learned how to balance her personal needs with those of her family. She started going to Co-Dependents Anonymous meetings and took up journaling to explore her emotions. She also practiced expressing her needs to those closest to her. Within months, Andrea was feeling better—emotionally and physically—and we knew she would be better able to tackle the challenges that lay ahead for someone with lupus.

Blood Problems

People who have anemia, bleeding, bruising, or other blood problems tend to feel as though they've hit bottom—that they are completely alone with no support from family and friends. They have become so destabilized that they trust no one, and they live in a world filled with seemingly endless chaos. If this sounds like you, your health depends on your ability to dig yourself out of this pit of hopelessness and create some order and balance in your life.

The area of blood disorders covers a wide spectrum, ranging from anemia to acute leukemia. Some of these disorders are benign, meaning they resolve completely with therapy or do not cause symptoms or are not life threatening. Others, such as sickle-cell anemia, acute leukemia, or certain lymphomas, are more serious in that they cause chronic illness or are life threatening.

Determining the origin of blood problems can be confusing because many of them can be associated with imbalances in either the first or fourth emotional center. Lack of emotional nurturance, a fourth emotional center problem, affects the organs that move the blood, including the heart, arteries, and veins, so the problem is with the organ of the fourth emotional center rather than the blood itself. For disorders of the heart such as high blood pressure and blocked arteries, turn to Chapter 7. The goal in this section is to help change the negative thought patterns and behaviors associated with blood problems of the first emotional center.

The first step in this journey is to identify the messages your body is sending you about the emotions underlying your illness and create health with affirmations. For example, anemia stems from both a lack of joy and a fear of life, plus an underlying belief that you're not good enough. So to address this joylessness and insecurity, use the affirmation "It is safe for me to experience joy in every area of my life. I love life." Bruising is about having trouble managing the little bumps in life and punishing instead of forgiving yourself. Remind yourself that you are worthy of forgiveness and love with the affirmation "I love and cherish myself. I am kind and gentle with me. All is well." Bleeding problems can be seen as joy running out, and anger is often associated with the bleeding. If this sounds like you, try to calm the anger and find the joy in life with the affirmation "I am the joy of Life expressing and receiving in perfect rhythm." Blood clotting involves the shutting down of joy. If you feel blocked emotionally, try repeating "I awaken new life within me. I flow."

In the realm of the blood, health problems are a reflection of not only your feelings but also the chaos around you—whether it's caused by a painful family life, a chaotic relationship, or a demanding boss. Intuitively your body, specifically your blood, is letting you know that you need more support. You must do everything you can to establish secure roots. Even if it's uncomfortable, ask more of the people around you. Leaning on family, friends, and community is a vital part of achieving health in the first emotional center. This is a process. Start small. Ask for help in the little things rather than requesting that someone provide a big service. With the success of each request, you will gain a little more trust in the relationships you have. And if someone fails you time after time, you will be better able to recognize the stable relationships in your life. Your goal is to identify the solid people and then find a balance between providing support for yourself and accepting help from others.

From the Clinic Files: Blood Problems Case Study

As a child, Denise moved a lot because of her father's gambling addiction. The family was uprooted time and time again, fleeing from her father's creditors. There was never enough money for food, and Denise and her brother and sisters went to school hungry almost every day.

When she was in her 20s, Denise's boyfriend hit her; she suffered multiple injuries that she hid from family and friends. One morning Denise woke to find that she could hardly walk. She was so exhausted that she could barely make it to the phone to call for help. Eventually, her doctor diagnosed her with severe anemia.

After talking to Denise we came to see that she had hit her physical and emotional rock bottom. What she craved, but did not have, was family support. And because she had never had it, she did not know how to get that support elsewhere. To Denise the world was a dangerous and lonely place, and she was unable to trust even her closest friends. She was empathetic and understanding with her friends and family. She was the one people came to with *their* problems. However, she was so sensitive to others' needs that she tended to absorb the emotional and physical pain of those around her. Because she had done this for years without an emotional outlet for her own fears, her body began to react to the stress.

Denise was emotionally and physically anemic, so it was important to identify both the energetic and hematologic "leaks" that she was experiencing. A medical intuitive reading helped us pinpoint where she was overly giving of her life energy—in her unhealthy relationship with her boyfriend and with her family. The next step was to figure out where the physical "leak" in her body was. We had to determine what was causing her to lose red blood cells so much that she was becoming anemic. I told Denise to go to her physician and get a test called a complete blood count, or CBC. This test would analyze all of the different components of her blood, and it would help us know why she was anemic.

Many doctors try to cure all cases of anemia by just giving patients iron. However, not looking at the underlying reason why someone is anemic may lead to a more serious problem.

There are three reasons why people become anemic:

1. Loss of red blood cells: This could be a result of trauma (Denise had been hit by her boyfriend, how seriously we don't know), a gastric ulcer, excessively heavy periods, blood in the urine, or internal injuries.

2. Inadequate red blood cell production: This could be caused by iron deficiency (why doctors usually give iron); heredity, including thalassemia; drug use, including alcohol; and chronic illness, like hypothyroidism, low adrenal gland hormone production, chronic hepatitis, and B12 and folate deficiency (called megaloblastic anemia).

3. Red blood cell destruction: This can come from an enlarged spleen, from lupus, as a side effect to medicines like penicillin or sulfonamide, from mononucleosis, or from other viral infections.

Looking only at Denise's age (not yet menopausal), most people would assume that her anemia resulted from heavy periods. If this were true, the iron cure would be great for her. However, by studying her CBC test results, we saw that the number of immature red blood cells (called the reticulocytes) were at a very low level. She was not making enough red blood cells. Iron, blood loss, and heavy periods were *not* the problem. By looking at the size of the red blood cells that she did have—Denise's cells were bigger than usual—her physician figured out that she had a very rare condition called macrocytic anemia, which is caused by low B12 in her diet and low B12 absorption because of long-term stress and antacid use. We verified our suspicions with another blood test to measure her B12 and found that we were correct.

Under the care of a nurse practitioner, Denise got regular B12 shots until her B12 levels normalized. She began taking a pharmaceutical-grade multivitamin B complex and had regular B12 tests to confirm that she was absorbing it.

To remove the barrier to B12 absorption, I had Denise go to a Chinese acupuncturist and herbalist to address her anxiety and heartburn. In addition to relationship counseling about the stressors with her boyfriend, Denise began taking an herbal blend that contained rhizoma, Atractylodis macrocephalae, Radix, Codonopsis pilosulae, and other herbs too numerous to list here.

Denise also started working with the affirmations for general blood health (I am the joy of Life expressing and receiving in perfect rhythm. Joyous new ideas are circulating freely within me); anemia (It is safe for me to experience joy in every area of my life. I love life); and fatigue (I am enthusiastic about life and filled with energy and enthusiasm). Working to shift her mind-set helped her bring joy back into her life by helping her release her fears and begin to realize her self-worth. Within six months her anemia was resolved.

Immune System Disorders

People who have immune system–related problems such as allergies to food and the environment, who catch colds or the flu frequently, and who have more serious autoimmune disorders often feel that they don't fit in anywhere and tend to be loners. These people isolate themselves because, in many instances, they feel that their needs don't match the needs of people around them—so any mingling feels overwhelming. Even on a one-on-one basis, these very sensitive people are unable to relate, so they can't create and maintain relationships that would provide them with a feeling of safety and security. This alienation makes them feel that the world is against them.

If you have allergies and immune system disorders, take heart! There are medical options available. Immune and allergy problems can often be treated effectively with a range of pharmaceuticals and herbal supplements. However, it is an imperfect science. We encourage people to also find ways to lessen the stress that is often at the root of immune system disorders. The first step in doing this is identifying the emotional component of their health problems and incorporating healing affirmations into their regimen. This is vital to achieving and maintaining health. The overall theme for these kinds of disorders is trust, safety, and self-love.

As in all the other areas, your affirmations will differ depending on the thought or behavior and the ailment. For example, people who are allergy prone may tell themselves that they are allergic to everything and everyone or that they have no control over their lives. These kinds of negative thoughts can be replaced with the following affirmation: "The world is a safe and friendly place. I am safe. I am at peace with life."

On the other hand, if you are susceptible to a disorder such as EBV, you may have fears of not being good enough. You may feel your inner support is being drained, or that you are not receiving love and appreciation from those around you. To transform this mind-set, Louise recommends the healing affirmation "I relax and recognize my self-worth. I am good enough. Life is easy and joyful."

People who get the flu frequently tend to respond to mass negativity. They can defuse this negativity with the affirmation "I am beyond group beliefs or the calendar. I am free from all congestion and influence." For those who have mononucleosis, negative thoughts are associated with anger at not receiving love. A healing affirmation is "I love and appreciate and take care of myself. I am enough."

You must also look at your behavior in your day-to-day life. Are you shutting yourself off from other people? Do you feel like nobody understands you? The first thing you need to do is identify what events or people make you feel rejected, criticized, or judged. Though people may seem to do and express things without tact, most of the time they are expressing a legitimate need. Try to remove the emotion from these requests and look at the underlying need. This may help take some of the sting out of what is happening or being said. It will help create tolerance in both your external world and your internal world. The activity of your white bloods cells pushing away and attacking foreign objects is the same as you doing this in your life, so working on emotional tolerance often translates into physical tolerance—creating a stronger immune system.

The other important behavior change is simply to force yourself to be around people. Just as I said before, start small. Once a week, try to take part in one activity where you are not alone. Easing into relationships will help things go more smoothly. You can try out any number of activities—gaming clubs, church groups, and even family get-togethers will help you see that the world isn't your enemy.

Address these two aspects of health—the physical and emotional—and you will begin to see the world through new eyes. Your mood will be more stable and you will feel more content. You will begin to consider the needs of the group as well as your own. Instead of constantly assuming you are being betrayed and attacked, you will react to challenges calmly and with proper emotion. You will come to see value and safety in other people. And finally, you will find balance in your responsibilities to yourself and your family, friends, and co-workers. This balance is the key to health in the first emotional center.

From the Clinic Files: Immune System Disorders Case Study

Larry, now age 32, grew up painfully shy and gawky and spent much of his time on his own. His brothers even found him odd, and he felt like an outcast in his own family. Things did not get, better for him when he was on his own. At work he stayed to himself and quickly became known as unapproachable.

While he had had problems with allergies his whole life, they became increasingly worse over the years, and he developed more complicated immune system disorders. One day Larry came down with a fever; he was exhausted, feverish, and achy all the time. Eventually he was diagnosed with mononucleosis and the Epstein-Barr virus.

Larry had difficulty feeling safe and secure in the world, and his social phobia became symbolized in his body's defense mechanism—the white blood cells of the immune system. While allergies can manifest in many ways—skin rashes, runny nose, itchy eyes, irritable bowels, and so on—these all fall under the category of immune dysfunction because the symptoms come from a reaction of your white blood cells against a foreign body. Basically what happens is that the body senses a foreign object, determines that it is a threat, and sends the white blood cells to destroy it. These cells release irritating substances like histamines, leukotrienes, and prostaglandins in an attempt to attack the allergen. This flood of chemicals causes the inflammation response, which brings with it runny eyes and nose, wheezing and sneezing, itching and twitching, and digestive distress.

With a healthy immune system, the body can tolerate the allergens without mounting such an intense attack, meaning fewer and less intense symptoms.

Since Larry had many of these allergies, he had a few standard medical options:

1. Restriction: The goal in this method is to stay away from allergens that bring about symptoms. All I have to say about that is, good luck. This is a very

temporary solution for most people. They may have improved symptoms for a month or two, but soon the wheezing, sneezing, and itching return. Also, not being in contact with substances on a regular basis weakens the immune system further, thus leading to more intolerance in the body. Continuing on this path leads to life becoming more and more limited and controlled.

2. Medication: There are many medications on the market that counteract the allergic response. Just as with restriction, this method doesn't address the underlying cause of allergies; it simply treats the symptoms. For milder allergies, antihistamines like Benadryl, Clarinex, Atarax, Allegra, and so on offer a good option. These target the histamines being released by the white blood cells. Keep in mind that antihistamines are only recommended for people under the age of 70 because they can lead to problems with memory and urination in older people. In addition to antihistamines, there are medicines, including Singulair and Accolate, that target leukotriene production. Oral, topical, and inhaled steroids are the mainstay for the most severe allergy cases. While the other medications work against inflammation by preventing the production of histamines and leukotrienes, steroids take more drastic action, blocking both the body's release and acceptance of these chemicals. Because of the drastic effects of steroids, you cannot stay on them forever without experiencing severe long-term side effects, including osteoporosis, ulcers, and immune suppression. This is likely why Larry came down with EBV and mono—his immune system had become compromised.

3. Immunotherapy: In this process you are actually injected with minute amounts of what you are

allergic to in an attempt to train your white blood cells to tolerate the allergen. The shots are given in an arm once or twice a week for several months. These treatments are recommended for people with severe allergies, or for those who have symptoms for more than three months per year.

Since Larry had been taking steroids for years, the first thing we did was to gradually taper off his usage. We also had him work with an acupuncturist and Chinese herbalist to strengthen his immune system's ability to fight viruses and at the same time be calm enough to tolerate his environment. One herb among many that was recommended to him is called Wu Cha Seng, and it is said to improve white blood cell function, especially after prolonged chemotherapy treatment. In addition, Larry worked with a nutritionist to make sure he had a good, balanced diet full of dark, leafy vegetables. We also recommended that he take a good pharmaceutical-grade vitamin supplement that contained vitamin C, magnesium, zinc, and B complex. He also started taking astragalus, DHA, turmeric, and ginger because these supplements have been known to ease the symptoms of EBV.

Along with the treatments Larry's medical team helped lay out, he also began to work with affirmations for fever (I am the cool, calm expression of peace and love); mono (I love and appreciate and take care of myself. I am enough); EBV (I relax and recognize my self-worth. I am good enough. Life is easy and joyful); and muscle aches (I experience life as a joyous dance). These helped him change the negative thoughts that kept him locked in illness. He also worked hard to put himself in situations where he was forced to interact with other people. This healing package of medicine, behavioral changes, and affirmations worked together to put Larry's health back on the right track.

Skin Problems

Do you have skin problems such as psoriasis, eczema, hives, or acne? If the answer is yes, you may want to focus on your relationship with the concept of feeling safe and secure in the world. While people with skin problems often have a seemingly put-together life, it is managed with extreme control. These folks are rock solid and dependable . . . as long as nothing changes. Their lives focus on routine, routine, routine because routine is safe and familiar. But real life isn't always safe and predictable, and this is where these people start to encounter problems. The natural ebb and flow of life causes great anxiety, and this in turn manifests as skin problems. Interestingly, the emotions and tendencies associated with skin problems, such as inflexibility in life, are also involved in many joint problems. People who tend toward one of these ailments often have the other as well.

So let's look at our prescription for health that includes first identifying the messages your body is sending you and then using affirmations to promote healthy thought patterns that will lead to clear and glowing skin. A good general affirmation for skin problems that stem from the fear and anxiety surrounding change is "I lovingly protect myself with thoughts of joy and peace. The past is forgiven and forgotten. I am free in this moment."

Skin disorders can take many forms; thus the affirmations that will help you address them vary from one condition to the next. If you have acne, for example, the negative thought patterns are associated with not accepting yourself, so the affirmation is "I love and accept myself where I am right now." Eczema has to do with antagonism and bottled-up emotions coming out. To counteract the effects of these emotions, the healing affirmation is "Harmony and peace, love and joy surround me and indwell me. I am safe and secure." Hives are about small, hidden fears and the tendency to turn small problems into big ones. The healing affirmation for hives is "I bring peace to every corner of my life." Rashes in general have to do with irritation because things have not turned out exactly as planned, and the affirmation for these is directed toward patience: "I love and approve of myself. I am at peace with the process of life." If you have psoriasis, you fear being hurt and may refuse to take responsibility for your own feelings. In this case, the affirmation would be "I am alive to the joys of living. I deserve and accept the very best in life. I love and approve of myself." Try some of the affirmations set out here or refer to the table on page 183 to find an affirmation for your specific ailment.

To address some of the other emotional issues that create skin problems, it is necessary to work on your ability to handle change. As they say, change is the only constant in life. So what can you do? Probably the easiest way to work on this is by shaking up your routine, routine, routine. Though it's seemingly counterintuitive, plan some spontaneity into your life. Every once in a while, set aside a time to just let life take you where it wants. For example, you could leave an hour in your calendar and simply start walking. See what you come in contact with. You'll be introducing a little variety, which can help you see that a world without back-to-back plans isn't necessarily terrible. You could also take a bold action by stepping into a particular role *because* chaos comes with the territory. Put yourself in a situation where it's not possible to control everything—volunteer at a shelter or in a kindergarten classroom. Who knows what could happen there?

You might also want to sit down with your schedule to determine whether there are certain areas of your life where you can focus on letting go of a tiny bit of control. You may not want to give up the power in the boardroom, but perhaps your child's playtime could be freer. The goal with all of these suggestions is to develop flexibility. If you are more flexible, you'll be better able to handle change. The confidence this will inspire in your ability to work with the world—rather than against it—will decrease the amount of anxiety you feel on a day-to-day basis.

From the Clinic Files: Skin Problems Case Study

Carl, age 52, is a family man. He also is a successful businessman who is involved in his community, volunteering for local charities and attending city and family events alike. To the world, including his family and friends, he is grounded and reliable—a pillar of the community.

But inside, Carl is obsessive and rigid in his ways and he hates change. As long as things stay within his control and he feels safe, Carl is able to run a company and be there for his family, friends, and community.

After years of being vigilantly in control, Carl started developing itchy rashes and scaliness on the skin found at the creases in his joints. After a visit to the dermatologist, Carl was told that he had a severe case of psoriasis.

While psoriasis is a skin condition, it often indicates a problem in the immune system, which can be associated with other serious health conditions, including diabetes, heart disease, depression, inflammatory bowel disease, arthritis, skin cancer, and lymphoma. Along with psoriasis, we often see an overproduction of a protein called tumor necrosis factor (TNF) that causes cells to grow too quickly. Why? No one knows for sure, but we wanted to see to it that Carl had a good internal medicine doctor who would maintain consistent evaluations of his heart, digestive tract, and joints. So the first thing I requested was that Carl go to his physician for a baseline screening of each of these elements.

Next, Carl needed consistent skin treatments to relieve and prevent itching. There are six types of treatments available: topical skin creams; light therapy, a treatment in which skin is exposed to UV light on a regular basis, slowing the growth of skin cells associated with the ailment; systemic oral medicines like cyclosporine, methotrexate, and acitretin; injected IV medicine to block TNF production; Chinese medicine; and nutritional treatment.

Carl had tried all the over-the-counter treatments for psoriasis with no relief. Topical steroids helped some but eventually the scaling came back with a vengeance. So we suggested that he consider light therapy with a competent dermatologist. Carl also was directed to an acupuncturist and Chinese herbalist who gave him gypsum, Imperatae, scrophulariae, paenae, rehmannia, Flos japonica, Artemisia, and Forsythia, among other herbs. And a nutritionist helped Carl identify which foods irritated his psoriasis—oddly, tomatoes were one that did. Carl also began taking DHA.

In addition, he started incorporating small bits of spontaneity and controlled chaos into his life. And he worked to change his thoughts with the affirmations for general skin health (I feel safe to be me); general skin problems (I lovingly protect myself with thoughts of joy and peace. The past is forgiven and forgotten. I am free in this moment); rash (I lovingly protect myself with thoughts of joy and peace. The past is forgiven and forgotten. I am free in this moment. I feel safe to me be); and psoriasis (I am alive to the joys of living. I deserve and accept the very best in life. I love and approve of myself). With all the changes Carl had made, his skin cleared up . . . and he was simply thrilled.

All Is Well in the First Emotional Center

You have the power to strengthen your immune and musculoskeletal systems and heal skin disorders using medicine, intuition, and affirmations. When you learn to recognize the negative thoughts and behaviors underlying your physical problems and heed the messages your body is sending you in the form of first emotional center health issues, you can finally start to move toward true healing.

Establishing new thought patterns using Louise's affirmations will give you the foundation and strength to change the behavior patterns that add to first emotional center illnesses. You'll learn to balance your individual needs with those of family, friends, and community.

The world is a safe and friendly place. All is well.

Chapter 5

IT TAKES TWO

The Second Emotional Center: Bladder, Reproductive Organs, Lower Back, and Hips

The second emotional center is all about love and money. If you aren't able to bring balance between these two areas of life, you will be prone to health problems of the bladder, reproductive organs, lower back, or hips. So the key to mastering health in this emotional center is learning how to manage your finances without sacrificing your love life and vice versa. Easy enough, right? Wrong. There are very few people who are naturally good at this, so let's get started.

Just as with all other emotional centers, the part of your body that is affected will depend on what type of thought pattern or behavior is causing the imbalance in this area of your life. For second emotional center problems, we find four types of people: those who would rather focus on love than money, those who focus on money rather than love, those who have an unbridled drive to move forward in money and love, and those who can't responsibly handle either love or money. We will get more specific as we work through the body parts, but in all cases it is important to listen to your body. Remember, your body is an intuitive machine, and it will alert you to problems in your emotional health by yelling out physically.

The negative thought patterns associated with the second emotional center involve anxiety, anger, or sadness about gender identity and sexuality, as well as relationship struggles and financial concerns. This, of course, makes sense because when we leave the safety of our family (the first emotional center) and strike out on our own in the world, the first challenges we have to handle on our own are love and money, relationships and finances.

So what is standing in the way of *you* making the critical changes in your finances and relationships to create better health? Are you holding on to anger at your partner? Do you always let other people handle your money? Are you irresponsible with your money? Do you feel stifled?

These are just a few of the types of emotions and behaviors that lead to second emotional center health problems. If you can identify the thought patterns that underlie your health problem, you can begin to make the necessary emotional, behavioral, and physical changes to improve the health of your bladder, reproductive organs, and lower back and hips. Identifying the root cause is the first step. The next step is to transform these negative thoughts and behaviors into new ways of thinking to create health.

Second Emotional Center Affirmation Theory and Science

As with all other illnesses, Louise's affirmation theory looks at the emotional nuance behind the health problems in the second emotional center. For example, the health of the menstrual cycle as a whole and a woman's capacity to be free of amenorrhea, dysmenorrhea, or fibroid tumors depends on whether or not she has a healthy sense of her femininity. Rejection of femininity is a negative thought pattern associated with female problems in general. Sexual guilt and anger at a mate are associated with vaginitis and bladder infection.

Alternatively, the prostate represents the masculine side of the principle. Sexual pressure and guilt, as well as a person's attitudes about aging, are associated with prostate problems.

Power struggles in relationships set the scene for sexually transmitted diseases. Whether it's gonorrhea, herpes, or syphilis, beliefs that genitals are "sinful" or "dirty," sexual guilt, and a feeling that you need to be punished are all thought patterns that are connected to venereal disease. A belief that sex is bad or the experience of sexual pressure creates thought patterns connected to impotence.

Looking at fertility through the lens of affirmation theory, we see that if you have trouble conceiving, you have concerns about the timing or the need to be a parent in general.

And, finally, who hasn't had a lower-back problem when they were concerned about money? Fear of money and the future are negative thought patterns associated with lower-back pain and sciatica.

So what does science tell us about the mind-body connection behind negative thoughts and emotions affecting the organs of the second emotional center?

Studies have found that the rate of infertility and menstrual cycle irregularities is higher in women who have inner conflicts about being a mother and who are worried about changes in their bodies.[1] While they feel social pressure to have children, motherhood may not fit in with their long-term goals. The emotional stress surrounding this issue increases cortisol and decreases progesterone, which hurts successful implantation of the embryo into the uterus. It also decreases oxytocin and increases norepinephrine and epinephrine; all of this works together to suppress sex hormones and turn off the mechanism that pulls sperm up into the uterus.[2]

If a man is under a lot of pressure, the anxiety he experiences causes his body to produce antibodies that make sperm "impotent," as they say. The stress and sadness also cause the testes and adrenal glands to produce more cortisol and less testosterone, which decreases sperm counts. Both of these problems can lead to infertility.[3]

There is a lot of scientific literature that shows how relationships affect the health of the pelvic organs. Depression and anxiety stemming from relationship trauma have been shown to affect female reproductive health by making the adrenal glands produce too many steroids. This changes the levels of cortisol, estradiol, and testosterone in the body. The imbalances between these three hormones can cause everything from irritability to pain to fibroids and ovarian cysts, not to mention weight gain.[4] In fact, one group of studies showed the connection between chronic pelvic pain and sexual abuse. Sexual trauma, especially in childhood, is known to help set the scene for pain in the genital and urinary tract, as well as the third emotional center issues of eating disorders and obesity.[5]

Women with cervical dysplasia and cervical cancer are likely to have had more sexual relationships at an earlier age, a higher number of premarital sexual experiences, extramarital affairs, or several marriages and divorces. More than half of these women grew up in homes where the father died young or deserted the family.[6] Essentially, these women never had adequate love from a man as children. It's quite possible that their later sexual behavior is a cry for love, an effort to find what they couldn't find at home. Without an internal representation of love, they constantly try to fill up the empty hole inside with an abundance of unbalanced relationships. Very frequently these women enjoy the sex they are having, yet they tend to be selfless and do whatever pleases the man, physically and emotionally.[7]

The influence of financial struggle and a poor economy can be seen as a burden on the backs of the country's workers—literally. A number of studies have shown that backache and increased muscular tension occur when people become depressed or unhappy about their finances, especially if they hate their jobs.[8] For example, one study found that job dissatisfaction increased the risk for back pain nearly sevenfold.[9] Lower-back pain is the number one cause of workplace disability in the U.S., not just for furniture movers or dock workers, but also for white-collar workers. And the incidence of lower-back pain doesn't necessarily decrease even in ergonomically appropriate conditions. You know what I mean . . . all those pillows and devices that OSHA and companies have devised to protect our spines. A recent study showed that educating office workers in ergonomics did not significantly reduce cases of lower-back pain and disability.[10] Doing a job you enjoy may help, however, as it releases opiates that are in fact relievers of chronic pain.

Interestingly, lower-back pain has also been associated with problematic relationships. Improvement in a present marriage, for instance, can help alleviate chronic pain, especially in the lower back. When someone with lower-back pain and marital problems undergoes marriage therapy with his or her partner, the lower-back pain often improves significantly without the benefit of surgery or medicine as the relationship improves.[11]

Now that you know the science that supports Louise's affirmation theory, how do you actually heal health problems?

Bladder Problems

Folks who experience bladder problems are generally very emotionally sensitive when it comes to relationships, and this makes financial independence difficult. They are so focused on maintaining loving relationships that the skill required to maneuver a business deal or focus on the monetary bottom line isn't necessarily developed or used on a regular basis. These people are likely to put their finances on a back burner or cede all control to a partner. However, these actions often spawn bladder illness because they bring about feelings of anger and resentment—either by establishing complete dependency on a significant other or by the requirement to pick up some financial responsibility.

So let's look at a prescription to bring a little more balance to your love and money lives. We'll jump right in by looking at the affirmations that can help you change negative thought patterns that may be causing your bladder problems. Urinary tract–related infections—whether cystitis or the more serious kidney infection—correlate with being pissed off, usually at the opposite sex or a partner, and blaming others. So we have to get rid of that anger. A good healing affirmation for urinary tract infections is "I release the pattern in my consciousness that created this condition. I am willing to change. I love and approve of myself." Urinary incontinence (an involuntary leakage of urine) is associated with keeping emotions in check over a long period of time; the healing affirmation for this is "I am willing to feel. It is safe for me to express my emotions. I love myself." Affirmations will differ depending on the condition. For more specific affirmations, look up your particular ailment in the table on page 183.

Look at your past relationships with money. Did you ever become so utterly devoted to someone that you didn't pay attention to your finances? If you were in a relationship, did you cede all control of your money to your significant other? Do you feel out of control when it comes to money? If you answered yes to any of these questions, you are at risk of developing bladder problems.

If this sounds like you, the most important issue to address is your view of money and the importance it plays in life. This isn't going to be easy. To bring about this balance between love and money, you should start small.

If you currently have no financial independence, figure out a way to get some. For example, take control of paying just a few of the household bills: just write some of the checks. If you're feeling really strong and adventurous, look at your personal passions and see if you can find a part-time job around these interests. The important thing is to be responsible for something financial. You need to familiarize yourself with the language and beneficial power of money. This lessens your dependence on your partner and helps stem the resentment and anxiety that could come from being in a totally controlling relationship or being forced to step into a big financial role. No matter how much you love and trust someone in your life, you should always keep a hand in your financial outlook.

If moving toward financial involvement seems difficult, one problem could be a perception that money is not spiritual—maybe even the root of all evil—and that caring about it automatically makes you shallow or materialistic. To this, all I can say is, snap out of it. With the structure of our society today, money is necessary for life, just like food and water. While those with money and power can (and do) misuse them, this bad behavior is not intrinsic to their existence. You need to realize that being financially responsible means having a healthy independence. Nothing more. Nothing less.

So the goal is to find a way to balance money and love. Don't sacrifice your financial well-being to an important relationship. By taking control of your own financial situation, you are showing respect for yourself and the people around you.

From the Clinic Files: Bladder Disorders Case Study

Elise, 55, reported that she wasn't truly happy until she met her husband in her mid-20s. She had been completely focused on her career—attending business school and working as a bookkeeper—but she felt something important was missing. All of that changed when Elise met Gerald. They quickly fell in love and got married, and Elise finally felt at peace. Once headed to a career in business, she turned over management of all finances to Gerald, quit her job, and became a stay-at-home mom to their growing family.

Elise felt happy and fulfilled for a long time—until Gerald was laid off from his longtime job. He adjusted quickly to this unexpected early retirement, but it was a more difficult transition for Elise. After almost two decades as a stay-at-home mom, not dealing with any financial obligations, she was forced to go back to work as a bookkeeper to supplement their income.

Soon after Elise started her job, she and Gerald started arguing about money. She felt resentful and overwhelmed, at times angry. Work had at one time fulfilled her but now it only underscored how much she had changed and how much she had given up. She began having health problems. At first her symptoms seemed to point to premenopause—she developed urinary urgency, erratic menstrual cycles, and bladder infections. However, after months of suffering with urinary tract infections that would not be cured with antibiotics, she ended up in our clinic.

When we started helping Elise with her urinary and menstrual cycle problems, the very first step was to demystify this mysterious pelvic region. I feel that it's important for people to understand this because if we know what our equipment is and how it works, we are more able to visualize health there.

I explained to Elise that our urinary system consists of two kidneys, two ureters, one bladder, and one urethra. Kidneys filter toxins out of the blood, balance our sodium and water levels, and then produce urine, which is sent via ureters to the bladder and then out of the body through the urethra. Since the urethra opening is near the anus where bacteria are, infection can readily ascend, producing the common urinary tract infection. If you are immunocompromised, diabetic, or have a catheter or some other predisposing factor, the bacteria can climb from the bladder up the ureters to the kidneys and cause a dangerous kidney infection.

After we'd cleared up how her urinary system worked, we sent Elise back to her physician who had her get her urine checked, to verify that she actually had a bladder infection. When a bladder infection is present, white blood cells are present in the urine along with a very large quantity of bacteria. While it's normal to have a certain number of bacteria living in the bladder, this number skyrockets when an infection is present. In Elise's case, she had no white cells and minimal bacteria, so she didn't actually have a bladder infection. Then what was causing her pain?

The bladder is a muscular organ that can contain up to a quart of urine. So if you feel a sense of urgency to urinate every five minutes or so, yet you only produce a few ounces of urine, you have bladder or urethral *irritation*. This was the case with Elise, but her OB/GYN had to figure out just why. There were three basic reasons to consider:

1. Post-hysterectomy effects: After a hysterectomy there can be "stress incontinence," which means that surgery has "bruised" the bladder nerves that control urination.

2. Fibroid uterus: If a woman has large fibroid cysts in her uterus, these may compress the nearby bladder, making the bladder fill with smaller amounts of urine, which then leads to frequent urination.

3. Irritation from vaginal dryness and thinning: When estrogen levels drop during perimenopause, the vaginal and urethral tissue thins and gets irritated. This creates the same symptoms as a bladder infection, but you have no infection. You simply have urgency and pain during urination.

Since Elise hadn't had a hysterectomy, we knew this wasn't the problem, so the next stop was the gynecologist. Elise had been having heavy, erratic periods, and from the gynecologist she learned that she had two large fibroids—one of which was sitting directly on her bladder. At this point, Elise had two options for dealing with the fibroids. She could go to a fertility surgeon and have them removed. Or, if she didn't want surgery, she could choose to simply wait. The end of menopause brings with it a drop in hormones that often leads to the shrinking of fibroids. This would help relieve pressure on the bladder.

Elise's doctor also looked at the third possible cause for pain: irritation from vaginal dryness and thinning. Elise's periods had the erratic characteristics of perimenopause, and she had started to experience vaginal dryness and pain during intercourse.

Elise decided not to get the fibroid surgery and instead focus on treating the irritation to see if that would be sufficient to help her bladder problems. To address the dryness, Elise looked at a variety of lubricants that can help and found the one that was right for her. Her physician showed her both prescription and natural ways she could address the problem. Elise decided to start with the natural, using black cohosh to thicken the vaginal mucosa and desensitize this region, and dandelion leaves and oat to restore vaginal lubrication and decrease urinary frequency.

Unfortunately, these didn't help as much as she wanted, so Elise went back to her doctor, who suggested estriol cream and a vaginal cream that includes testosterone. These would help soothe the irritated vaginal and urethral region.

Finally, to address Elise's hormonally based urinary frequency and menstrual cycle irregularities, I suggested she visit a competent acupuncturist and Chinese herbalist. Elise was given an herbal combination called Lui Wei Di Huang, which contained rehmannia and Gui Ling Ji.

She also looked at the thoughts and behavior patterns that could have been adding to her problems. She worked with the affirmations for bladder problems (I comfortably and easily release the old and welcome the new in my life. I am safe) and urinary infections (I release the pattern in my consciousness that created this condition. I am willing to change. I love and approve of myself). She also began to address her relationship with money. By changing her perception of what money meant and changing her thought patterns to help with her anger, Elise began to heal.

Reproductive Organs

Men and women who experience illness in their reproductive organs generally have a mind-set where they have difficulty knowing how to create in a healthy way, focused, in part, by moving forward and creating at all costs. These people are typically driven to produce, produce, produce—whether it's job- or family-related, in essence it's all work. The love of a relationship is simply one of the tools they need to produce what they want, whether it's children, books, plays, technical manuals, or any other creations. This drive is only possible by managing all aspects of life with extreme organization and control. While this ability to focus and control is more obvious in the outside dog-eat-dog world of money and business, everyone knows that to run a home with a lot of kids or projects or pets involves a lot of organization and control. Whether they are in the rough-and-tumble world of finance or handling the juggling act of running a house, sometimes women and those unique men must turn off that innate feminine sensitivity (we all have some to one degree or another) to maintain a production schedule. If you tend to be hyperproductive, in business or at home, it may register as reproductive problems.

To become healthy in the reproductive organs, both men and women need to reevaluate their priorities—and change the underlying beliefs that lead to fibroids, infertility, prostate problems, or any other of the many possible reproductive ailments.

Female problems in general can be improved with the affirmation "I rejoice in my femaleness. I love to be a woman. I love my body." Uterine fibroids have to do with nursing a hurt with one's partner, and they can be improved with the affirmation "I release the pattern in me that attracted this experience. I create only good in my life." Sexual problems and impotence in women generally involve sexual pressure, guilt, or spite against previous mates, and even fear of one's father. These women often believe that engaging in sex or experiencing sexual pleasure is wrong.

Many women who are in menopause experience fears having to do with aging, not being wanted, and not being good enough. Menopause symptoms are improved with the statement "I am balanced and peaceful in all changes of cycles, and I bless my body with love."

For men, the first signs or symptoms of problems may be as subtle as a fleeting loss of sexual desire or slight imbalance in hormone levels. However, if these are not attended to, the warnings will get stronger and serious health issues will develop.

The negative thought patterns associated with prostate problems have to do with fears about masculinity and aging as well as sexual pressure and guilt. To promote prostate health, use the affirmation "I accept and rejoice in my masculinity. I love and approve of myself. I accept my own power. I am forever young in spirit." If the problem is with sexual potency, the negative feelings have to do with anger or spite, usually against a previous partner. The problem may even be associated with fear of the mother. To heal impotence, the affirmation is "I now allow the full power of my sexual principle to operate with ease and with joy."

For both genders, infertility has to do with being fearful, resistant to the process of life, and resistant to the parenting process. In this case the healing affirmation would be "I love and cherish my inner child. I love and adore myself. I am the most important person in my life. All is well and I am safe."

As in all the other sections, the affirmation you use will differ depending on the specific body location of the ailment. Go to the table of affirmations on page 183 and look up your particular ailment.

In addition to affirmations, you need to look to behavioral change to move away from reproductive problems. Your main goal is to learn to balance relationships and financial success in your life. Resist the urge to constantly strive for achievement in everything you do. If you usually feel compelled to control the finances in your home, let your spouse or partner handle the bills for a while. This can be tough to do, especially if you're better at the task, but grit your teeth and bear it. You can also let your children (if you have them) cook a simple dinner, even if you know they won't do it the same way you would. The most important thing you can do is attempt to let go of the need to control everything.

The goal is to bring love and joy back into your day-to-day experiences and learn to go with the flow of the world. You need to realize that it is possible to relax, take time off, and delegate and still be a success. There is reward in life other than the thrill of living at full throttle all the time. Try to surround yourself with people who seem to be happy with a more laid-back lifestyle. Look at them and ask yourself if you would consider them successful. Perhaps a reevaluation of your definition of success is necessary.

So work to bring yourself back to the joy of living. Take some time to bend the ear of a good friend. Talk about your feelings and dreams. Set aside a specific time when you can simply slow down. Another good thing to do is to try meditation, or simply sit in silence. This will bring your attention into the moment, interrupting the constant flow of thoughts about what needs to happen next. The goal is to live more fully in the moment, to see and appreciate what's around you. There is wisdom in the old saying "Take time to stop and smell the roses." Try to find the beauty in life as it currently stands. Soon you will find that control and constant striving aren't necessary for happiness. You, too, can learn to replace that fleeting adrenaline rush of pushing life forward with real peace, and enjoy better physical health while you are at it.

From the Clinic Files: Reproductive Organs Case Study

From a very young age, Geeta, age 29, knew exactly what she wanted from life: where she would live, what she would do for a living, the type of man she would marry, even how many kids she would have. And she set out to get it all. Throughout high school, Geeta pushed herself academically and socially. She also belonged to leadership groups, edited the school paper and yearbook, and was class president both her junior and senior years.

In college she was equally ambitious. In addition to a full academic load, she had a part-time job and started her own business. By the time Geeta got her bachelor's degree, she was engaged to a premed student and had been accepted into an MBA program. There was nothing she couldn't handle, nothing she couldn't do. She was obsessed with producing, producing, producing—ideas, money, goods, you name it. And then she wanted to produce the last thing on her list: a baby. But her body threw her a curveball. Geeta had planned to be pregnant by the time she was 30. But after months of trying, she grew impatient and had her doctor run some tests. They confirmed her worst fear: she had stopped ovulating. Geeta was devastated and felt that her body had betrayed her.

Her inability to become pregnant was a sign that she needed to reevaluate how well she was balancing the many aspects of her life.

We had to look at Geeta's problems from a bit of a different angle because, in essence, she was doing nothing wrong. She was eating healthy foods, exercising, and in general looking out for her well-being. Unfortunately, the conditions for getting pregnant often vary from the conditions necessary for living a healthy non-pregnant life. So first we had to help Geeta overcome her feelings of blame and shame. Many women experience these emotions when it comes to infertility—especially if their friends are getting pregnant and creating families without any problems. Geeta was holding on to this shame, believing that she was doing something *wrong* . . . that she was bad. She was questioning her own self-worth, and there is absolutely no reason for that.

Our next step was to look at any possible physical conditions that might be hampering Geeta's efforts. What we noticed about Geeta was that she was very thin. In fact, she was underweight: five feet four and 100 pounds. Often women with very low body fat stop menstruating and stop ovulating. Whether they are the classic long-distance runners or models who are hyperthin as part of their careers, they simply don't have enough nutrients to keep their bodies functioning in a way that can lead to pregnancy. So we had to look at Geeta's diet.

As we were discussing this, Geeta admitted that she didn't want to gain weight. She had worked hard to stay fit, and she felt healthy and strong. This brought to light another issue that we would have to face in Geeta's quest to get pregnant. Pregnancy requires that a woman give up control over the size and shape of her body. If a woman has a problem with this concept, she is likely to react in unhealthy ways when she sees her growing body in the mirror. This vision of herself can set off a whole host of obsessive thoughts and compulsions, and often cause her to restrict food intake in a way that would be harmful to a developing baby.

To work on these thought patterns, Geeta took two courses of action. She worked with the affirmations for general female problems (I rejoice in my femaleness. I love being a woman. I love my body); ovary health (I am balanced in my creative flow); general menstrual problems (I accept my full power as a woman and accept all my bodily processes as normal and natural. I love and approve of myself); amenorrhea (I rejoice in who I am. I am a beautiful expression of life, flowing perfectly at all times); and infertility (I love and cherish my inner child. I love and adore myself. I am the most important person in my life. All is well and I am safe).

She also started to visit a cognitive behavioral therapist to help her evaluate her anxious thoughts. Together they looked at how she could address her tendency to obsess about and control her weight. They came up with strategies unique to Geeta to help her tolerate the weight gain necessary to begin to ovulate again.

Geeta also began to meditate and incorporate some mindfulness into her day. Each day she set aside a little bit of time when she really tried to focus only on what was happening around her—not her to-do list or other future activities. She also made it a point to delegate some of the tasks she was handling to other people in her life. And after changing her thoughts and behavior—and her diet—Geeta was able to become pregnant and soon had a beautiful baby boy.

Lower-Back Pain and Hip Pain

People who experience lower-back and hip problems tend to be insecure when it comes to both money and love. Though they generally have the unwavering support of their families, they tend to have difficulties with finances and relationships—no matter what they do. This is partly because they don't trust in the competence or intentions of people around them. When these folks are part of something that fails, it's hard for them to see how their actions played into this outcome, but they can easily identify the fault of everyone else who was involved. After one relationship debacle after another, when one financial crisis is followed by another, these folks seize power to feel more in control. The idea of shared decision making in relationships and money transactions goes out the window as these people stop listening to the views or ideas of others. In reaction to constant disappointment, they end up feeling alone, stranded, and unable to move forward.

If you have lower-back problems and you recognize these negative thoughts and behaviors, consider what you need and how you can get it. If what you need is to get healthy, be free of pain, and feel strong and supported, you can reverse the effects of negative thoughts by using the affirmation "I trust the process of life. All I need is always taken care of. I am safe."

Specific affirmations help us take healing to the next level. Lower-back and sciatic pain has to do with fear about money, and hip problems have to do with fear about moving forward. If you have lower-back or hip problems, it's important not only to understand your thought patterns but also to practice the affirmations. So, for example, if you have hip problems that have to do with fear of making major decisions, use the affirmation "I am in perfect balance. I move forward in life with ease and joy at every age." If you have sciatica that stems from being highly self-critical and fearful of the future, the affirmation would be "I move into my greater good. My good is everywhere, and I am secure and safe."

As with the health of every body part, the important thing to focus on here is balance. If you suffer from lower-back or hip pain, it's time to look at your relationship both with yourself and with the people around you. Honestly assess your life and make some changes. Do you get support from your family that you're not getting elsewhere? Notice where you are getting support and openly acknowledge it and have gratitude for it. Do you tend to always blame others when things go wrong? Try to see the whole picture and see whether you are doing something that might be contributing to the problem. Do you feel out of control when it comes to finances? Look closely at any financial downfalls and try to pinpoint where things shifted from good to bad.

Your goal is to adopt a new view of the world. To really figure out what's going wrong in your relationships and finances, you must take a big-picture look at the reality of both. And to do this, you need to get a grasp of your emotions, be able to identify and address them.

The most powerful practices you can do to rebalance your life involve meditation and mindfulness. While those who are prone to reproductive issues need to use these practices to slow down and recognize the beauty in the world, if you have lower-back and hip pain, you need to get a handle on your emotions. Meditation teaches you to observe and describe, but not judge, your emotions while you're experiencing them. You will come to know that emotions are not reality, which means that they will not have so much power over you. Eventually, after practicing mindfulness and meditation, you will be able to detach from your feelings in a way that will help you take a more well-rounded view of the world and the people in your life. You will be able to interact with people in more respectful and productive ways that will ultimately lead to healthier finances and relationships.

Another important step you should take when it comes to healing lower-back and hip pain is to set up time to spend with people outside of your family or direct circle of friends. Widen your network of support. Even if it's only for a few hours each week, get out and experience life from a different perspective. Perhaps volunteer at a nonprofit organization. Offer yourself to this group as both a leader and a part of a team. This will help you learn how to balance your own opinions with the ideas of others.

With affirmations, a more positive mood, and some changes in behavior, it is possible to lead a rewarding life—financially and emotionally.

From the Clinic Files: Lower-Back and Hip Pain Case Study

Helen came to us when she was in her early 50s, at the encouragement of her family. Although she worked as a paralegal and had two healthy grown children whom she loved, both of her marriages had ended in divorce after both men left her for younger women. In the wake of her divorces, she found herself alone and in huge financial debt.

Helen struggled to get her love life back on track, but no man seemed to meet her high standards. As she watched friend after friend find a soul mate, Helen started to panic. What was wrong with her? Why couldn't she succeed on this very basic level?

Helen became depressed, and one day she woke up with severe lower-back and hip pain that made it hard for her to sit at a computer or even walk more than a few steps. An orthopedic surgeon ordered an MRI that showed a very mild lower disk bulge—nothing that would cause such disability.

Helen was in a lot of pain when I talked with her and very frustrated that her surgeon could not simply remove a disk or do a fancy fusion surgery to cure her.

What causes lower-back pain? Usually it's the overuse of the muscles, ligaments, and joints between the lower-back vertebrae caused by excessive weight, moving the wrong way, or injury. The repeated motion makes the soft mattresslike cushion between vertebrae, the disk, herniate—or slip. With more vibration and a lack of support from adjacent back muscles, inflammation occurs in the joints between the vertebrae, the "facet joints." The inflammation transforms into bony arthritis fragments that compress nerves, which in turn makes lower-back and leg muscles spasm, go weak, and become numb.

Unfortunately, lower-back pain can be aggravated by a number of other problems. Depression, with its concomitant changes in neurotransmitters, can make the pain worse. So can scoliosis, a lateral curvature of the spine, or spondylothesis, a condition in which the vertebrae slide forward. If estrogen and progesterone levels are going down in perimenopause, the resultant changes in neurotransmitter serotonin (estrogen) and GABA (progesterone) can exacerbate the pain and spasms.

Once Helen knew all the factors behind her lower-back pain, she could make a concerted effort with a treatment team to tackle her health problems. She figured out a way to put some more movement into her day. She bought an overstuffed chair with a hassock for her office and learned to get up and down several times an hour to keep her lower back supple and less arthritic. Next she aggressively treated her depression. Helen began with SAMe, and although it eased some of her back pain and depression, her mood and back were still bad. Despite the fact that she had some resistance to medication, she tried Wellbutrin and was delighted when her mood and back pain greatly improved.

Now with more energy, she was able to go to the gym to work out, but we made sure that she did this under the supervision of a physical therapist. Her goal was to rehabilitate her spinal muscles. From time to time she used Biofreeze cream to numb her sacral area so she could get through the exercise routine. Acupuncture and *qigong* also helped with pain control. Finally, Helen tried a form of neuromuscular therapy called Yamuna body rolling where you use a small ball the size of a cantaloupe to help stop the spasm of tendons adjacent to lower-back muscles.

Looking at other possible contributors to her back pain, we identified her shoes as a problem. She was wearing cheap shoes with no cushioning or support, so we recommended that she invest in better shoes—FitFlops, Nike Shox, and Asics Gel all help provide padding under the feet.

Over time, thanks to exercise and physical therapy, Helen noticed that even losing 10 pounds relieved a lot of pressure in her lower back. Surgeons note that for every 10 pounds of weight we gain we put 40 pounds of pressure on our joints. Helen followed her medical team's suggestions and lost a total of 25 pounds and could not believe the difference. Once her physician said it was safe, she began a regular yoga practice, which helped keep her spine flexible and strong.

We worked with her specifically to figure out what behavioral and thought modifications could help, asking her to make a list of all the risk factors that promote lower-back pain and put a checkmark next to the ones that applied to her. While we couldn't change things like genetic heritage or age, we could focus on her day-to-day activities and habits.

We discussed the importance of giving up smoking and keeping an eye on her depression. She decided to volunteer at her church—both as a youth group leader and a helper at the soup kitchen. She also started to journal in an effort to bring perspective to a number of chaotic situations in her life. To address the underlying beliefs that were making her ill, she started using the affirmations for various back- and hip-related issues. She focused on general back health (I know that Life always supports me); lower-back problems (I trust the process of life. All I need is always taken care of. I am safe); general hip health (Hip Hip Hooray— there is joy in every day. I am balanced and free); hip problems (I am in perfect balance. I move forward in life with ease and with joy at every age); and slipped disk (Life supports all of my thoughts; therefore, I love and approve of myself and all is well).

Helen worked with all of these methods, and she was able to bring her life to a wonderful, flexible, pain-free place.

All Is Well in the Second Emotional Center

People try to handle bladder problems, reproductive issues, and lower-back and hip pain by taking drugs or subjecting their bodies to surgery. In some acute cases this may turn out to be the most prudent course of action. But with more chronic illnesses and dysfunction, you may need to investigate other remedies.

In this chapter, we have explored the many ways you can create health in the second emotional center using a combination of medicine, your body's intuition, and affirmations.

When you learn to identify and examine the messages your body is sending you, you will be on your way to true healing. By balancing your attention to money and love relationships, you can remove the stressors that aggravate this health region. Acknowledge the negative thoughts and behaviors having to do with sexual identity, financial ability, and love and relationships. Then use Louise's affirmations to counter the negative thoughts in these areas and establish new thought patterns and behaviors by meditating on the phrases "I trust the process of life," "I know that Life always supports me and takes care of me," and "I am lovable and loved."

You are worthy of love. All is well.

Chapter 6

A NEW ATTITUDE

The Third Emotional Center: Digestive System, Weight, Adrenal Glands, Pancreas, and Addiction

Health in the third emotional center is all about an individual's sense of self and how they fulfill responsibilities to others. In this chapter we examine the many aspects of your third emotional center. Some of the discussion focuses on particular organs such as those that make up the digestive system, as well as the adrenal glands and pancreas, both of which regulate sugar and important hormones, and the kidneys, which regulate body chemistry. We also cover the broader, related themes having to do with weight problems and addiction. Just as with the other emotional centers, the ailment you experience depends on the type of thought pattern or behavior that underlies it.

People with health issues of the third emotional center generally fall into four categories: those who define themselves by focusing completely on the needs of others, those who bolster their sense of self by looking to career and material possessions, those who give up all concept of self and turn to a higher power for support, and those who avoid looking at themselves through feel-good distractions. These diverse people are affected in different ways when it comes to the health of the digestive system and issues with weight and addiction. We will get more specific later as we work through the actual body parts and individual ailments of the third emotional center.

For health in these areas of your life it is essential to develop a strong sense of self. If you don't cultivate your self-esteem and find a balance between how much time you spend worrying about pleasing others and the time you spend nurturing yourself, you may suffer from nausea, heartburn, ulcers, constipation, loose bowels, colitis, or kidney problems. You also may struggle with your weight, body image, or addiction. These health problems are messages from your body telling you that what you are doing is not working.

Third Emotional Center Affirmations and Science

According to Louise's affirmation theory, the health of the digestive tract, liver, gallbladder, and kidneys is associated with thought patterns that have to do with fear: the gut-wrenching anxiety you experience, especially in situations where you feel inadequate or overburdened. For example, digestive tract problems in general are associated with fear of new things and experiences. More specifically, spastic colon sufferers may have problems with insecurity. Colitis is associated with a fear of letting go, while colon problems in general are about holding on to the past.

Negative thought patterns associated with weight problems concern the need for protection. Addiction in general is a way of medicating emotions that you don't know how to handle: what Louise calls "running away from yourself."

Finally, metabolic problems with blood sugar are associated with responsibility and the burdens of life. Hypoglycemia is associated with being overwhelmed with the burdens in life, that despairing feeling of "What's the use?"

The health of the third emotional center is associated with having a strong sense of self-esteem, being able to handle responsibilities, and not escaping through substance abuse or addiction. The health of our gastrointestinal tract, weight, and body image depends on our capacity to have a healthy relationship with work and responsibility.

So let's see what science has to say about the effectiveness of this kind of approach to healing third emotional center disorders.

A large body of research shows that negative emotions—whether fear, sadness, or anger—can irritate the lining of our stomachs while love and joy can calm it down. In fact, the more we experience these negative emotions, the greater our chances of developing digestive problems such as GERD (gastroesophageal reflux disease), ulcers, and irritable bowel syndrome.[1]

Let's look at the ulcer as an example. Scientists attribute ulcers to an overgrowth of *Heliobacter pylori,* a bacterium that occurs naturally in the stomach.[2] This overgrowth is seen more often in people with heightened anxiety. This may be the result of an exaggerated immune system response in their digestive tracts, which makes their stomach and bowel lining more permeable to the bacteria.[3] Stress and anxiety can come from a number of sources, but this is especially prevalent in highly competitive work environments. Studies have shown that people who have to deal with significant stress on a day-to-day basis have an increased incidence of ulcers.[4] The same thing can be seen in animals. Studies found that when rodents are placed in situations where they have to constantly compete for mates and resources, they experience digestive problems and ulcers.[5]

Perfectionism is also closely associated with stomach and bowel problems.[6] This personality trait leads to persistent feelings of not being good enough, and it lowers self-confidence. Studies have shown that knocks to our sense of self-worth cause a drop in blood levels of somatostatin, a hormone that inhibits the production of a number of other hormones. If hormones are out of balance, the stomach and intestines don't function properly. This can result in ulcers and irritable bowel syndrome. Ulcerative colitis, a chronic inflammatory disease of the bowels, is also associated with the need for perfection in some people.[7]

People who feel hopeless and helpless to escape stressful situations have higher levels of stress hormones in their blood, and this sets the scene for digestive problems.[8] One example of this can be seen in studies that have found a correlation between growing up in a home where there was physical abuse or constant conflict and the likelihood of developing ulcers or eating disorders as an adult.[9]

Stress can lead to problems with obesity. Studies suggest that stressful emotions affect a person's metabolism, or ability to break down food. When we are struggling under competitive, seemingly hostile circumstances, we also tend to eat larger and less frequent meals, an eating pattern that often leads to weight gain.[10] During a stressful day at work, who doesn't skip breakfast and lunch and then eat a big dinner as a reward? Unfortunately this seemingly trimmed-down eating schedule doesn't trim down your waistline. It does just the opposite: it increases abdominal fat.

Emotions such as worry over extreme life issues and increased responsibility also affect the way we break down sugar and can contribute to the onset of diabetes.[11] Emotional stress increases inflammation and the level of cortisol in the blood, which increases insulin, causing you to store more of what you eat as fat.[12] And researchers have observed that people with depression and anxiety may have disrupted neuropeptides that affect both their emotions and their digestion. So it makes sense that affirmations that help mend your attitude can also heal your waistline.

The link between addiction and feelings of low self-worth and self-esteem is evident in many studies. Time and time again research has shown that people overeat, smoke, drink too much alcohol, and engage in other forms of escapism to cover up anxiety, depression, anger, or feelings of inadequacy and to escape responsibilities they can't handle.[13] These are simply diversionary tactics, and it makes sense that people use them. Alcohol is an antianxiety drug that many people use to numb themselves and avoid facing their true identity. While it is unhealthy, nicotine can help people deal with anger, impatience, and irritability. It has been shown to give us a temporary feeling of happiness and relaxation. The same is true for certain foods—specifically carbohydrates and chocolate.

A strong sense of self—the focus of the third emotional center—can help us simultaneously avoid and deal with feelings of stress, hopelessness, and helplessness that lead to many of the digestive, obesity, and addiction problems we've just explored.

So now that we know the affirmation theory and science, how do we actually create health in the third emotional center?

Digestive Problems

The organs that make up the digestive tract are the mouth, esophagus, stomach, small intestines, large intestines (or colon), rectum, and anus.

People who tend to have digestive tract–related issues are generally focused on getting more, more, more of everything. Excess is stimulating, and we thrive on adrenaline because it makes us feel bigger than we actually are, so these people search for this rush. They work too much, party too much, and simply keep going and doing until it nearly kills them. They amass power and material wealth in an effort to fill a void in their souls. So while it may look like these folks have everything figured out, this constant hunger is born from a low sense of self-worth. They have yet to find contentment and joy in who they are. Their lives are all about appearance, and they search for bigger, better cars and houses, believing that this will make them feel bigger and better, pumping up their self-esteem. But bigger isn't necessarily better. It's important to have a healthy self-esteem that's based not only on your outside but your inside as well.

There are plenty of effective medical options available for digestive disorders you may experience, including heartburn, reflux, ulcers, abdominal distension, bloating, Crohn's disease, and irritable bowel syndrome. But in most cases, medical treatment works to address the symptom rather than the root cause of the problem. If you are experiencing chronic digestive tract problems, you also will have to address the thought and behavioral patterns that underlie these health issues.

All digestive problems stem from the same basic emotion—fear. For example, people with general stomach problems fear what is new and believe that they are not competent enough to handle what life sends their way. They are often controlled by fear, anxiety, and uncertainty. If this sounds familiar and you want to banish the fear and face new experiences head-on, the healing affirmation is "Life agrees with me. I assimilate the new every moment of every day. All is well." If you suffer with ulcers, the negative thoughts likely have to do with the fear that you are not good enough, and the affirmation would be "I love and approve of myself. I am at peace. I am calm. All is well." Colitis (inflammation of the colon) is associated with deep-seated insecurity and self-doubt, and the appropriate affirmation is "I love and approve of myself. I am doing the best I can. I am wonderful. I am at peace." Remember that the specific affirmation will depend on the condition. For more affirmations to heal specific disorders, see the table in Chapter 11.

In addition to the affirmations, you must also evaluate your life and your priorities. Check out your current situation. Are you always on hyperdrive? Do you live and work in a very competitive environment? Do you take any time to get to know yourself outside these external pursuits? The answers to these questions will help clue you in to where the imbalances in your life exist. If you are all work, you need time to play. If you are all about speed, you need to slow down. The human body cannot last at full throttle for its entire life. You may thrive on the rush of a good fight, the adrenaline that pours into your system when you face a challenge, but soon your body starts to sense that you need more peace. It clues you in with stomach problems, hinting that you simply can no longer stomach this fast-paced life. Your body is screaming out for rest and relaxation.

When looking at changing thought patterns and behaviors that could be adding to your digestive problems, the most important change you can make is to realize that you have innate goodness—you are more than your net worth. The low self-esteem that causes people to go, go, go will manifest in pain. It's not easy to build up your sense of self but it can be done.

Look at your life honestly. Ask yourself if your material goods really bring you joy or if they're simply a cover—a protective shell—that hides you from the world. You need to get your consumer tendencies under control. Try to take a spending vacation one day each week, meaning you don't buy anything. Put the credit cards away. Stash your cash somewhere hard to access. If you can manage it, don't handle cash or finances at all—even if they're not your own. And at the end of the day, evaluate the feelings you had from living simply. If you find it too hard to step away from money for one day per week, you might want to look into counseling to help you find a way to let go of this obsession.

Along the same lines, take a day during the week where you don't primp. No makeup. No hairstyling. No fancy labels or accoutrements. Note your mood throughout the day. If your mood plummets, this will clue you in to the amount of importance you place on external appearances—the appearances that hide who you are.

Take time out of your busy schedule to try some new activities. Try to find something that you enjoy for its own sake, not because it will make you richer, smarter, or more attractive. The goal is to build up your true identity and realize that it has value. You can schedule time once a week or even a little time once a day. The important thing is to spend some time with yourself—without the distractions of the world. Tune in to your thoughts. Get to know who you really are and this will guide you to better self-esteem and better health in the third emotional center.

From the Clinic Files: Digestive Health Case Study

By the time I met Ken, age 27, he already owned a successful cowboy boot business and was living the high life in every sense of the word. He had a home in Nashville and a farm in its suburbs. Ken loved the rush he got from spending money, eating, drinking, smoking, driving fast cars, and chasing women. To maintain his extravagant lifestyle and win the admiration of the many women in his life, Ken worked day and night—fueled by copious amounts of caffeine. Ken's motto in life was "Nothing succeeds like excess."

This lifestyle worked for Ken for many years, but when he came to me he was finding it hard to keep everything together. He struggled to pay his bills. He was stressed and anxious about everything, and it seemed that his stomach was equally anxious. The stress of trying to keep his head above water financially registered in constant heartburn that he tried to medicate with daily antacids. However, rather than downsize, Ken tried to keep his extravagant lifestyle going by spending money he didn't have.

He eventually ended up in the emergency room with diagnoses of esophageal reflux, gastritis, and a small bleeding stomach ulcer.

When we talked to Ken, he just didn't understand why all those antacids he was taking didn't prevent the burning feeling in his stomach. To achieve digestive health and understand why antacids weren't his gastrointestinal salvation, he first needed to understand the relationship between his esophagus, stomach, and normal acid production.

When we swallow food, it enters into the esophagus, which dumps the food into the stomach, where it begins to be broken down by gastric enzymes, one of which is acid. There is a one-way trapdoor between the esophagus and the stomach so these acid enzymes don't back up or "reflux" into your esophagus and mouth, causing burns and erosions. But this trapdoor can weaken and thus not shut fully to prevent the reflux. If this happens often, the diagnosis could be gastroesophageal reflux disease, or GERD. This was Ken's first problem.

His next problem was his stomach ulcer. Like a football team, stomach problems involve a balance between the offense (the elements that break down the food, the amount of acid, and other stomach enzymes) and the defense (elements that protect the inner stomach wall). When people have stomach pain, almost everyone thinks about lowering acid with antacids but not about helping protect the stomach lining's mucus, bicarbonate levels, blood supply, prostaglandin inflammatory mediators, and appropriate bacterial levels—all of which defend your digestive tract from getting ulcers.

To reduce Ken's digestive issues, we advised that he make a number of changes in his life. He needed to reduce the size of his meals, lose 20 pounds, and stop wearing his standard uniform of tight jeans, which put pressure on the abdomen and physically compress the bowels and lower esophageal sphincter. He also needed to stop smoking. In addition, we changed his diet so it didn't include food that added to the acidic base of his stomach. We recommended that he stop eating chocolate, tomatoes, caffeinated beverages, fatty and citrus foods, onions, peppermint, and alcohol—at least for a while. Once his ulcer healed, he could have one alcoholic drink per day. We also put Ken on an eating schedule and had him angle his bed in the best way to prevent the effects of stomach acid on his esophagus. We put him on a schedule that required him to not eat during the three hours prior to going to sleep. This would allow his food time to digest, and it would mean that he was upright during this process—lying down makes it easier for the acid to move up toward the throat. For the same physical reason, we recommended that he sleep with the head of his bed raised or with his body propped up on pillows.

The very straightforward changes we recommended to Ken would help get him on the right track, but he also decided to take a bit more dramatic action. He began taking antibiotics to lower the corrosive bacterial levels of *Helicobacter pylori* in his stomach. Then he was given a choice of three types of drug therapy: antacids (Maalox, Mylanta, Rolaids, and Tums), which neutralize stomach acid; H2 blockers (Axid, Pepcid, Tagamet, and Zantac), which lower acid production; or proton pump inhibitors (Nexium, Prevacid, Prilosec, and Zegered), which block acid production and help heal the esophagus wall. All of these medications have side effects. For example, long-term use of proton pump inhibitors in people over 50 can be associated with hip, wrist, and spine fractures.

To help stabilize his body and prevent as many side effects as possible, we recommended that, in addition to his medical care, Ken consider an integrative medical approach to his treatment.

I suggested that Ken see a reputable Chinese herbalist and acupuncturist and work with this expert to figure out which of the common herbal blends recommended for digestive problems would be best for his unique case: Shu Gan Wan, Aquilarie, Saussurea, Sai Mei An, or Xiao Yao Wan.

In the behavioral changes category, we recommended that Ken take some time to look honestly at his life. To do this, he took the recommendations we outlined earlier regarding his appearance and financial matters, and wrote out the feelings that each brought about. His goal was to reduce his anxiety levels and revise his motto to "I can succeed without excess" in work, smoking, drinking, and eating. We set him on a schedule of aerobic exercise, 30 minutes every day, to get his excess energy out and weekly massages, aromatherapy, and lessons in guided imagery to help him relax and de-stress his muscles. This relaxation would eventually sink in all the way down to his digestive tract.

Ken needed to work with affirmations to help change his underlying thoughts. He used affirmations for general stomach health (I digest life with ease); general stomach problems (Life agrees with me. I assimilate the new every moment of every day. All is well); ulcers (I love and approve of myself. I am at peace. I am calm. All is well); and anxiety (I love and approve of myself and I trust the process of life. I am safe).

The many changes we helped Ken implement in his life brought him to full recovery—his digestive tract and his life were on a much healthier course.

Weight Issues and Body Image

People with weight and body image problems are givers and doers and are often excessively generous. On the face of it these are all good qualities. However, as with those who suffer from other third emotional center health problems, people with health issues related to weight are usually governed by fear and low self-esteem. They expend all their energy on others and have little left over for themselves. Who they are is defined by how much they do for others.

Weight gain and weight loss can be signs of an underlying health problem such as thyroid or hormonal imbalance, but they can also be the *cause* of health problems such as heart disease. So first address the physical problems that are triggered by being overweight or underweight, or by certain body image disorders, such as anorexia and bulimia. Once you have a handle on the most serious of these, it's time to face the emotional issues that are contributing to your weight issues.

Once again it is all about balance. I am not suggesting that you stop doing good deeds or helping others, or become self-centered. The point is to examine *why* you are running yourself ragged helping others while your own needs remain unmet. Once you have done this, you can begin to alter the negative thoughts and behaviors that are adding to your health problems by listening to what your body is telling you and incorporating affirmations into your life.

Louise Hay's affirmation theory demonstrates how weight is a reflection of our self-image. So for example, being overweight or having an excessive appetite is a result of low self-esteem and avoiding your feelings. According to Louise, fat in general is a protective shell created by people who are overly sensitive and feel they need protection. To begin to remove this shell and promote weight loss, the affirmation would be "I am at peace with my own feelings. I am safe where I am. I create my own security. I love and approve of myself."

Anorexia has to do with extreme fear and self-hatred. The affirmation to begin the process of valuing yourself is "I love and approve of myself. I am safe. Life is safe and joyous." Bulimia is about stuffing and purging caused by self-hatred, hopelessness, and terror; the healing affirmation is "I am loved and nourished and supported by Life itself. It is safe for me to be alive."

Louise's affirmations will vary depending on the thought pattern and the body part that is experiencing illness. For example, weight in the belly area is associated with anger over being denied nourishment, whereas being overweight in the thighs has to do with childhood anger—possibly at a father. (For more specific affirmations that Louise recommends, refer to the table on page 183.)

Eradicating old, negative thought patterns is a particularly important step for people with weight problems. Low self-esteem can lead to an overflow of self-destructive thoughts. Change these thoughts with a positive, self-esteem-boosting affirmation such as "I love with wisdom. I nurture and support others as much as I nurture and support myself."

If you are a charitable, kind, and generous friend, good for you! But remember to be equally devoted to yourself. It is not selfish to focus on your own needs, appearance, and happiness. In fact, doing so is the only way to be a true friend, partner, or parent. If you don't take care of yourself, at some point you won't have anything left to give.

So the first thing to do is to look at why you keep doing for others at your own expense. Do you have a belief that you are only worth something if others need you? Can you think of a relationship or situation that would have brought this belief about? Try journaling about this. See if you can establish why you feel this way.

You must work against this false belief, and the best way to do that is to take a responsibility holiday. Take one day a month, or a few hours a week, to not do anything for anyone. This is time to focus solely on yourself. Take a class or find a hobby you enjoy. Nurture your self-esteem. Realize that you have innate worth and that you cannot judge yourself solely on what you do for others. If you don't change your current mind-set, your body will signal you that it is feeling deprived and weight issues will emerge.

From the Clinic Files: Weight Issues Case Study

Isadora, age 28, was dependable, prompt, and quick to volunteer her time at work or for a worthy cause. Similar to many people who suffer from weight problems, she was more than willing—she was thrilled—to help others. Isadora told me it gave her life purpose and direction. But in spite of her many good deeds, her self-esteem was so low that she could barely look at herself in the mirror.

Isadora had two sisters who both worked as professional singers, and their appearances were very important to them. Isadora did their hair and makeup. She took great pride in how polished and beautiful she made them look for their performances and said she didn't mind being the "unsung" sister—their success was enough for her. You would never guess that Isadora was a hair and makeup artist judging by her own appearance. She went for comfort rather than fashion, wore a baseball cap over her unstyled hair, and usually didn't bother with makeup. She was also 80 pounds overweight when I met her, and she admitted that she had given up on exercise and any other attempts at self-improvement.

When we work with someone who has a weight problem, it's important to figure out the medicinal, nutritional, environmental, and hormonal causes of weight gain that are unique to each case. Then we create a plan directed at transforming these causes to help them lose weight.

Weight gain can come from any number of factors:

- Medicine: One of the side effects of some common medicines is weight gain. Included in this list are oral contraceptives (the pill); steroids; older tricyclic antidepressants such as Elavil; some newer antidepressants, including Paxil, Zoloft, and Zyprexa; the mood stabilizer Depakote; the diabetes drug Diabinese; and heartburn medications like Nexium and Prevacid. While not all of these drugs necessarily cause weight gain, they have been known to do so.

- Nutrition: One of the most common causes of obesity is simply nutritional habits. What and when people eat has a huge effect on the amount of weight they put on.

- Environment: This takes into account such issues as how often you move during the day and with whom you surround yourself. It can play a huge role in how much you weigh.

- Hormones: If you are stressed, stressed, stressed, you are going to gain weight no matter how much you exercise and limit your diet. Sadness, depression, and anxiety all cause the number to go up on the scale, but anger is the most weight-o-genic emotion. Being constantly angry and frustrated causes your adrenal glands to produce the hormone cortisol, which causes the pancreas to produce insulin—and voilà!

When we started to explore Isadora's unique situation, we saw that she regularly took three medications that have the known side effect of weight gain. She was on the pill, and she often took Nexium and Prevacid to help with stomach and reflux discomfort. As for her eating habits, we found that Isadora had a pretty off-kilter eating schedule. She didn't eat a regular meal during the day but snacked a lot, and on unhealthy things. Her only meal was a giant dinner at about 8 P.M. And this meal was never very well balanced—Isadora often just loaded up on carbs rather than making sure her plate had a nice array of each food group. She was not aware of how important it is to match carbohydrate intake with protein at every meal to help stabilize blood sugar and control hunger.

The environmental factors affecting Isadora included very little movement and an unsupportive office environment. While she worked on the second floor, Isadora never used the stairs. She sat at her desk all day, with her only breaks being trips to the bathroom—or perhaps to the candy dish sitting on the receptionist's desk. Her office was also right next to the conference room, where most days there were fresh pastries and baked goods for employees to munch on, and there was a machine with free soda anytime she wanted it.

Between her out-of-control weight and her busy life, Isadora also experienced a lot of stress, frustration, and anxiety. She disliked her body, which led to feelings of shame and anger. Unfortunately, these feelings just added more fuel to the fire.

To help Isadora get her weight and life under control, the first thing to do was take care of the medically induced weight gain. I asked Isadora to go to her physicians and ask for an alternative form of contraception that wasn't as notorious for causing weight gain. In the process, she also found out that her stomach problems were the result of anxiety rather than acid reflux, so she was able to phase out the use of Nexium and Prevacid. To replace these drugs and give her relief from the very real upset stomach she experienced because of anxiety, her physician recommended lemon balm. She reported that this helped almost immediately.

Next we addressed the environmental factors affecting Isadora. She asked the receptionist to take the candy dish away—to put it somewhere less conspicuous—so she wouldn't be tempted to graze. In addition, she wore a rubber bracelet with the words HEALTHY WEIGHT written in bold black letters to remind her to avoid the food trays and soda at her office. When Isadora got the impulse to reach for these, she stretched the bracelet, which then snapped and stung her skin, grounding her to her own body. It helped her refocus her feelings and remind her of her goal to lose weight. As for upping her movement, Isadora not only started taking the stairs to her office, she also joined a women's fitness club and worked out for 30 minutes aerobically five days a week.

To add even more healing power, she used affirmations to address the underlying thought patterns that were leading her to hold on to her fat. So she used the affirmations for compulsive eating (I am protected by Divine Love. I am always safe and secure. I am willing to grow up and take responsibility for my life. I forgive others, and I now create my own life the way I want it. I am safe) and obesity (I am at peace with my own feelings. I am safe where I am. I create my own security. I love and approve of myself).

And last but not least, we recommended that she visit a nutritionist who could help her create healthy, delicious, and easy meals that fit within an eating schedule that they created together. To make her new eating regimen more fun, she invited her sisters along to learn with her. Together they supported one another in a new, healthy lifestyle. A new sense of closeness developed between Isadora and her sisters—one that had been missing when she was acting more as their employee than as a sister. And this closeness bolstered Isadora's self-esteem and made it easier for her to stick to her new eating regimen.

This shift of focus—from others to herself—helped Isadora recognize her own self-worth. She started to do more and more things to take care of herself. She even implemented the responsibility holiday we recommended. With her new view of the world and the help she was getting from the people around her, Isadora managed to lose a great deal of weight and feel healthier and happier for it.

Adrenal Glands and Pancreas

People who have adrenal gland, pancreatic, and blood sugar problems are often overwhelmed by their emotions and have lost their identity by being constantly in service to others. These people often feel better about their internal spiritual life than their external life of weight and looks and work. Spirituality becomes *the* outlet they use to build self-worth and self-love. It is literally how they define themselves. Because of this tendency, these people often let their physical appearance go and their digestive health plummets, leading to blood sugar problems and fatigue. To them, spirituality is the universe; advancing their career or caring for their appearance or well-being on Earth is not part of their skill set.

If you are one of the millions of people who suffer from the symptoms of adrenal gland and blood sugar problems, the first step is to take medical action. But as is the case with many emotion-centric disorders, medicine will probably only be effective for acute problems; chronic issues need a subtler approach to healing. You need to build your sense of self-worth and manage your responsibility to others.

If your mind is telling you that you are not capable or worthy and you are underachieving or sabotaging yourself, these are the negative thoughts and behaviors that cause a disruption in cortisol production, which is a precursor to many adrenal gland disorders such as Cushing's disease. In contrast, Addison's disease, which is an inability to produce enough cortisol, is related to severe emotional malnutrition. However, both come from the same negative mind-set. Louise's affirmation theory shows you how to change the thoughts and behaviors associated with general adrenal gland problems with the affirmation "I love and approve of myself. It is safe for me to care for myself."

Pancreatic disorders, including pancreatitis (inflammation of the pancreas) and pancreatic cancer, often stem from feelings of sorrow. If you have severe blood sugar problems such as diabetes, you may be dealing with disappointment about unattained lifelong goals or feel deep sadness about what might have been. In this case the affirmation would be "This moment is filled with joy. I now choose to experience the sweetness of today."

Whether the issue is cortisol problems from adrenal gland malfunction or blood sugar imbalances because the pancreas is producing inappropriate levels of insulin, your body's intuition will let you know that you need to reevaluate what you are doing. If you don't heed these warning signs, long-term cortisol and insulin problems will cause other conditions, including elevated cholesterol, high blood pressure, heart disease, weight gain, chronic pain, diabetes, renal failure, and stroke.

Changing negative thought patterns is key in eradicating painful and destructive feelings. But altering lifelong patterns is a process—a journey that takes time, dedication, and patience. Find some balance between your spiritual and physical selves. You can have part of your head in the spiritual clouds but at the same time, start addressing your physical appearance on Earth. Let's start with your weight and low self-esteem. We know you have great spiritual esteem, but you have to love yourself and your body, too. We're here to tell you that it's completely possible to attend to your own needs without being self-centered. So take some time to pamper yourself. Get a manicure. Get your hair done. Read a book. Go shopping. Try to do things that will help you come into your physical self. Try working out or dancing or doing yoga. Any of these activities will force you back to Earth.

While we know that it's important to focus on the needs of others, don't overdo it—even though you want to. Helping people out makes you feel good but it also depletes you, so try to limit the amount of time you spend offering your assistance. If you volunteer with a number of organizations, cut down your hours—perhaps only volunteer once a week. This will still give you the joy of helping but it will also leave time for you to care for yourself. All of these actions will improve your vision of yourself and help you keep a healthy spiritual focus.

As I've said before, you have innate worth on Earth and in the heavens. You are lovable and valuable, and you must remind yourself of this every day through affirmations and dedication to your physical health. A general, healthy affirmation is "My emotional fulfillment and satisfaction radiate to everyone around me."

From the Clinic Files: Adrenal Glands and Pancreas Case Study

As a teenager, Lorinda, now 57, discovered Eastern religions and was fascinated. She read about Buddhism, Zen, and Taoism and researched the Christian mystics. She was able to sense the "Divine" from an early age, and it gave her both peace and exhilaration.

Lorinda went to college and graduated with a double major in theology and biology. She eventually married a famous physicist and they had four children.

Lorinda was smart and well-read, and over the decades of their marriage she became a valuable resource to her husband, helping him write several books. Her marriage and family life with her children were happy and fulfilling—up to a point. But Lorinda had sacrificed her own ambitions and intellectual life, and now that she wasn't familiar with her individuality, she lived with a great amount of anxiety and fear. This wasn't healthy, and her body soon let her know it was time to change. She began to feel her body abandon her to fatigue. She walked slowly, talked slowly, thought slowly, and was tired of feeling heavy. It just so happened that levels of cortisol and insulin in her body were completely off balance.

The adrenal glands and pancreas—the organs that control cortisol and insulin production—are mysteries to most people. All people have two adrenal glands. Think of these as oranges. The inner pulp produces epinephrine, a caffeine-like, stimulating substance that is released when you need short-term bursts of energy. The outer layer of the adrenal gland, the "peel," produces an array of hormones from your body fat for long-term energy. The most infamous of these is cortisol. However, adrenal glands also produce other hormones, including progesterone, DHEA, testosterone, and estrogen, from body fat.

If you are suddenly anxious, under threat, or furious about something, your brain via your pituitary gland tells your adrenal glands to pump up production of epinephrine, cortisol, and other hormones to put your body into high alert. Once the threat goes away and you "cool off," the adrenal glands stop their escalation of hormones. However, if your mind ruminates about the anxiety and threatening events, with such thought patterns as "It's hopeless"; "My life is a disaster"; "Things should be different!"; and "This is unfair!" your adrenal glands continue to overproduce cortisol and estrogen. This leads to your pancreas secreting more insulin, and you get symptoms of what is commonly known as "adrenal gland exhaustion."

Adrenal gland exhaustion is tricky because it is not always clear whether you have too little cortisol or too much. However, your symptoms and blood and urine tests will reveal the direction of your adrenal imbalance. This is very important to know because if you medicate for the wrong condition, you will feel no relief—in fact, the symptoms could get worse.

So in Lorinda's case, we sent her to an endocrinologist, who would look at her symptoms. The symptoms of low cortisol include vague weakness, discoloration in the pigmentation near the mouth and other mucous membranes, nausea and vomiting, diarrhea, low blood sugar, and low blood pressure. These symptoms are subtle.

Excess cortisol leads to weight gain in the abdomen and face, increased blood pressure, erratic blood sugar levels, strange hair growth, acne, depression and irritability, bone thinning, muscle weakness, and irregular menstruation.

After a trip to visit her physician, Lorinda came back with the full report. The doctor had explored all the possible symptoms and determined that she was producing too much cortisol. Lorinda was five feet four and 180 pounds, with most of her weight clustered around her abdomen. She had some hair thinning near the crown of her scalp, and she had some hair growth on her upper lip and chin. Her blood pressure was 140/85 and her blood sugar was 130, both of which are mildly elevated levels. She had acne on her shoulders, back, and face.

After determining that her symptoms resulted from excess cortisol, her physician wanted to do a test to verify that she didn't have Cushing's syndrome, a disorder of the adrenal glands. Luckily, the results of blood tests and a dexamethasone suppression test were normal.

Finally, Lorinda went to an endocrinologist, who ran further tests for adrenal enzyme abnormalities, all of which came back normal. So Lorinda was dealing with run-of-the-mill adrenal fatigue.

The solution? She needed to lose some body fat so her adrenal glands would have fewer building blocks from which to make cortisol and the other hormones that were driving up her blood sugar, blood pressure, and hair growth.

To help give her the energy she desperately needed to make changes in her life, we started her on chromium. This would not only give her energy but also help regulate her blood sugar. She started taking green tea extract, which has been shown to give people a great deal of energy, and began with a pharmaceutical-grade multivitamin with folic acid, pantothenic acid, vitamin C, iron, magnesium, potassium, and zinc because any deficiency in vitamins can lead to fatigue.

Next we had to address Lorinda's anxiety. Because she wasn't taking serotonin medicine, I asked her to find out from her physician if it would be okay to add 5HTP to her supplement regimen.

This natural serotonin supplement is often used to calm anxiety, which could be a contributing factor in the overproduction of cortisol. However, she also needed to talk with a counselor to help her get a handle on the sources of her anxiety.

Our last integrative medical recommendation was for Lorinda to visit an acupuncturist and Chinese herbalist. There are a number of herbs—astragalus, licorice, Siberian ginseng, Cordyceps sinensis, Rhodiola extract, banaba extract, wild oats, and schisandra—that are said to be helpful in managing adrenal gland hormone production imbalances. A skilled practitioner would help her figure out the best combination to use.

While Lorinda needed to lose weight, her problem wasn't necessarily only one of bad nutrition. She ate poorly at times, but this was generally because she was so busy with her responsibilities to her family and friends; it was not that her instinct was to eat badly. So instead of focusing on a food diet, I put Lorinda on a variation of the responsibility holiday we discussed in the weight section. She didn't have to go an entire day without helping people, but she was forced to ration her efforts toward others. She had always put her husband's career first, so we decided to institute a system devoted to her own career development. For every hour she spent on his work, she would spend an hour on her own career. Lorinda winced when I talked about this diet but she made it happen.

Lorinda also learned tai chi and *qigong* to help her manage her energy rather than shunting it into other people's projects.

And finally, to change the underlying thought patterns that were perhaps contributing to her illness, Lorinda worked with affirmations for adrenal problems (I love and approve of myself. It is safe for me to care for myself); fatigue (I am enthusiastic about life and filled with energy and enthusiasm); and pancreas health (My life is sweet).

Lorinda's work to heal her adrenals inspired self-confidence. She was able to find solace not just in spirituality but also in the earthly realm.

Addiction

People who are prone to addiction—aren't we all to some extent?—often have a strong desire to feed their sense of self-worth. They want personal and creative satisfaction, peace, and clarity, but they often lack the discipline to follow a diet and exercise regimen or even a work schedule. They are so controlled by cravings for something that gives them pleasure—the food, the alcohol, the credit card purchases—they have trouble finding the time or interest to care for themselves or, in some cases, others. Everyone has their own unique recipe for addictive behavior. The quest for self-worth and satisfaction can be exhilarating, but it can also be tiring and frustrating. And the stress and anxiety that come from knowing you are avoiding healthy levels of responsibility can be overwhelming. We often turn to things that make us feel good—alcohol, prescription drugs, sex, gambling, food—to deal with these strong emotions.

So what is the prescription for beating addiction? Your ability to renounce addictive behavior and rescue yourself from irreversible damage to your health depends on changing the thoughts and behaviors associated with addiction. One good place to start is by making use of tried-and-true treatments for addiction such as 12-step programs and other recovery groups. The next step is to take a good look at what your body is telling you about the connection between your behavior and your health. Once you have identified what your issue is and what emotions are causing it, you can begin to incorporate affirmations into your daily life.

Louise Hay's affirmation theory demonstrates how addiction originates from fear and low self-esteem. More specifically, those with addictive personalities spend their lives running away from—and not being able to love—the person they are. A good affirmation for addiction in general is "I now discover how wonderful I am. I choose to love and enjoy myself." Alcoholism specifically is associated with guilt, inadequacy, and self-rejection. To counter these negative emotions and turn self-hatred into self-love, Louise recommends the affirmation "I live in the now. Each moment is new. I choose to see my self-worth. I love and approve of myself."

At one time or another, most people have fed their self-worth artificially through addictive behaviors or have medicated emotions they couldn't handle. What we've learned is that when life becomes too confusing, people are more likely to escape into addiction because reality is just *too* painful. People can develop addictions to very specific things such as alcohol, cigarettes, eBay or Facebook, computer games, or sex. All addictions—whether to a drug or a food or a behavior such as gambling—release opiates that numb physical and emotional pain. However, eventually the substance wears off or the behavior no longer provides an escape and reality returns—along with the pain.

The most important thing you can do if you have problems with addiction is to admit that you have a problem. I know it sounds simplistic, but this admission sets the stage for everything else you will do. If you're unsure about whether or not you have a problem, ask a dear friend or family member. Then, with their assistance, ask yourself the following questions: Are you unable to control how much you drink, eat, gamble, or engage in sex? Do you feel guilty about your behavior? Are you unable to stop even in the face of serious health problems? Do these behaviors affect your job or family life? Do you have family members who have struggled with addiction? Have you been told you need to stop? Do you make excuses or try to hide what you are doing? If you answer yes to two or more of these, it's time to step back and take a serious look at your addiction.

And remember, fighting an addiction is hard. You should employ the help not only of a professional who can help you get in touch with your strength and emotions but also of your friends and family. Go for help now. There are support groups for nearly every addiction out there. Find people who relate to your problem. They will be able to bolster your courage and provide advice you may not think of. Between the help of a professional counselor, your family and friends, and any other support group you find, it is possible to stop your addiction. These people are important in your healing because they can be essential to your ability to come out on the other end of addiction with a strong sense of self.

There are also some things that you can do on your own to address the feelings of despair that your addiction is trying to help you avoid. Try to institute a meditation practice. Sitting silently—even for a minute—will help you get a better grasp on your thoughts and emotions. Your thoughts come and they go. They are impermanent and they can be changed. These are just attitudes that have been etched in your brain. They are not reality. By creating a new way to look at your thoughts, you can make them more tolerable and even transform them into healthier attitudes by using affirmations.

You might also want to think about taking up journaling. Sometimes simply putting your thoughts into words helps you see them in a new light.

The important thing with all of these actions is to become more secure in who you are. Learn about your innate strength. We were all built to survive and thrive on this planet. You have just as much power to do so as the next person. You just have to take hold of it and make it work.

From the Clinic Files: Addiction Case Study

Jenny, now 49 years old, was always sensitive and nervous. When she was a child, her father was a businessman and traveled frequently for work. Jenny often felt lonely. She turned to food, which became her faithful companion. Jenny's other passion was to be a ballet dancer, but when she applied to ballet school she was told she was too heavy for a serious career in ballet. Although she continued to dance, she struggled with her weight and was often injured. After a particularly bad knee injury, Jenny's doctor prescribed Oxycodone for the pain and Xanax for the related anxiety. However, even after her injury had healed, she continued using the Xanax and Oxycodone and other prescription medicines to manage her anxiety and fears. Finally Jenny quit ballet altogether.

Jenny eventually got married and life was better; she felt happier and was able to wean herself off the drugs. But after her second child was born, her depression and anxiety returned, and once again she turned to prescription drugs to deal with her stress.

Jenny soon developed symptoms that different practitioners diagnosed as various illnesses ranging from chronic fatigue to irritable bowel syndrome to attention deficit disorder—all of which led Jenny to medicate these new problems with medicine, at escalating dosages. At this point, one physician, recognizing a problem, refused to write her prescriptions and told her she had to deal with her addiction problem.

Addictions to drugs, food, sex, gambling, rescuing, or, in Jenny's case, prescription medicines are used to cover up emotions we can't handle, whether they're sadness, anxiety, anger, lost love, boredom, or low self-esteem—the list is endless. Addictions also block intuitive messages that we don't want to hear. The substances fill a spiritual void, a "nameless emptiness" that we don't even know exists.

But addiction isn't simple use of substances. It's a dominant use that has led to problems with work, school, home, or other relationships. Addiction causes us to be late, absent, or fired as we neglect our responsibilities to everyone, including ourselves. Sometimes addiction can escalate to the degree that it becomes physically hazardous, resulting in accidents or worse. But we can't stop the compulsive behavior despite its adverse consequences.

Jenny took Oxycodone and Xanax to get to sleep, to be free from anxiety, and to handle the chronic pain from old ballet injuries in her feet and spine. So the first thing we did was try to identify whether any of her "new illnesses"—the fatigue, bowel complaints, and attention deficit disorder—could stem from this drug use.

Oxycodone side effects include drowsiness, fatigue, impaired attention and memory, and constipation, among others. Xanax and other "benzodiazepines" cause problems with attention and memory as well. When I suggested to Jenny that the very drugs she was taking for sleep, anxiety, and pain could be causing all of these new health problems, she told me it was worth it. She didn't feel that she could handle the pain without the Oxycodone, and she got very defensive about it, asking me why I didn't "get it." After she calmed down, she told me she was at a crisis point in her life. She had already lost her driver's license for driving impaired, and her husband had threatened divorce because her use of drugs had so affected their marriage and family life.

I told Jenny that she was not alone and there was nothing to be ashamed of, since problems with opiate addiction were escalating across the world. Morphine, codeine, Dilaudid, Demerol, heroin, and Oxycodone are all opiates that affect the "opioid" receptor, the same brain/body receptor for mood, self-esteem, spiritual fulfillment, pain, and sleep. If you use these medicines, whether they are prescribed by a physician or you get them "off the street," you quickly build up a tolerance, meaning that you need more and more of the medicine to feel the desired effect. Xanax, Ativan, Valium, and Klonopin hit a different receptor—the GABA receptor. This is the same one that is affected by alcohol. The power of these drugs is so intense that you can't just stop, as sudden withdrawal can cause seizures and death.

I told Jenny that she needed support to get off Oxycodone and Xanax. In addition to going into rehab to help her body slowly wean itself off the drugs, she would learn new skills to manage her anxiety, sleep, and old athletic injuries.

Although she had a lot of reservations, after a month Jenny went into a drug addiction recovery unit that helped treat her addictions to the prescription drugs. The physicians very slowly weaned her off the drugs she had been taking, and then she received the nonaddictive drug clonidine to treat her racing heart. In team meetings with her husband, she was offered a variety of drug maintenance programs to help prevent her from going back to Oxycodone when she was discharged.

A pain treatment team evaluated her spine and feet and diagnosed her with arthritis from her ballet years. To address this, Jenny decided to go aggressive with high doses of vitamin C, grape seed extract, and glucosamine sulfate. These supplements, along with weekly yoga, acupuncture, and Yamuna body rolling treatments, helped her tap into her natural healing powers. If things got too bad, she could always use methadone, levomethadyl (LAAM), naltrexone, or buprenorphine but only under the strict supervision of her treatment team.

In the rehab unit, Jenny took part in a therapy program called dialectical behavior therapy (DBT), which is tailored for people with substance abuse problems. DBT is a form of mindfulness training that helped Jenny learn how to regulate her anxiety. She worked with a psychiatrist who was skilled in the science of combining pharmaceutical medicine with complementary medicines. So along with passionflower, lemon balm, and 5HTP, Jenny was prescribed Zoloft and Remeron.

Finally, Jenny was required to create a strong long-term plan with a vocational counselor and coach. She began to see that much of her drug use, pain, anxiety, and insomnia came from a lack of direction after her ballet career was cut short. Her vocational counselor helped her identify some alternatives that would allow her to continue being involved in what she loves, including the possibility of starting a dance school for children.

In addition to the help Jenny got in learning about herself and cementing her self-confidence, she worked on her own to address the emotions that were contributing to her addiction. She used affirmations for anxiety (I love and approve of myself and I trust the process of life. I am safe); depression (I now go beyond other people's fears and limitations. I create my life); panic (I am capable and strong. I can handle all situations in my life. I know what to do. I am safe and free); and addiction (I now discover how wonderful I am. I choose to love and enjoy myself).

Bringing all these treatments together to create a strong, integrated plan helped Jenny find herself. She was able to face the uncertainty and pain in her life and heal her addiction.

All Is Well in the Third Emotional Center

The third emotional center encompasses a broad spectrum of health problems, including mild or serious digestive disorders, blood sugar issues, and weight and addiction troubles. But at the heart of all of these is a lack of self-esteem and an inability to balance inner needs with outer responsibilities. When you feel good and you have a healthy sense of self-esteem, you can create lasting health in the third emotional center. Look to the messages your body is sending you about how healthy you are emotionally and physically. Identify the stressors that contribute to your imbalance. Your body will tell you if you listen and heed its warnings.

Once you change the negative thought patterns and behaviors that stand in your way and learn to define yourself not by family, work, or what you do for others but by who you are, you will find health. Know your weaknesses but do not dwell on them or run from them. Feed your self-worth and realize that you have innate goodness. Resist any negative thoughts about who you are with the assertion "I am good enough. I don't have to overwork to prove my worth."

Love yourself and all will be well.

Chapter 7

SWEET EMOTION

The Fourth Emotional Center:
Heart, Lungs, and Breasts

The fourth emotional center is about balancing your needs and the needs of someone else with whom you're in a relationship. If you aren't able to do this, your body will let you know by creating health problems related to your heart, breasts, or lungs, such as high cholesterol, high blood pressure, heart attack, cysts, mastitis or even cancer, pneumonia, asthma, coughing, or shortness of breath. The secret to mastering health in your fourth emotional center is learning how to express your own needs and emotions while also taking into consideration the needs and emotions of others. It's a matter of give and take.

Just as with the other emotional centers, the part of your body that is affected will depend on what behavior or negative thought pattern is causing the imbalance in how you deal with emotions in a relationship. Those who are not in touch with their emotions tend toward heart problems; people who are overwhelmed by their emotions often experience lung issues; and people who express only the positive side of their emotions develop breast problems. We will get more specific later when we address each body part. However, generally speaking, the negative thoughts and behaviors that are associated with fourth emotional center health tend to come from anxiety, irritability, depression, and long-term emotional problems. People who have fourth emotional center health problems fear life and don't feel worthy of living a good life—they have an apparent lack of joy. They also tend to overmother and put others' emotions before their own.

If you have heart, breast, or lung issues, your body is telling you that you need to examine how you maintain your own emotional health while nurturing the emotional health of a relationship. The signs may not be as severe as a heart attack or breast cancer; they may be as subtle as breast tenderness, slightly elevated blood pressure, or lung tightness.

Taking note of these slight changes in your health is the first step. As always, seek medical help for any serious health problems, but also make sure to look at the emotional aspects of these health problems. Your goal is to transform your behaviors and thoughts so you can find a comfortable balance between the effort you expend to help others and how much energy you invest in yourself.

Fourth Emotional Center Affirmation Theory and Science

Louise's affirmation theory explores the subtle emotional differences behind the health of fourth emotional center organs. Health in these areas depends upon your ability to fully express all emotions and to develop the capacity to experience anger, disappointment, and anxiety—the so-called negative emotions— without becoming overwhelmed by them. Only then is it possible to truly move through anger, find a way to forgive, love, and experience joy again. Knowing, feeling, and expressing all of your emotions, whether love and joy, fear and anger, is good for your health. These emotions keep you moving steadily through life and, as Louise says, this helps keep your blood flowing through your heart and blood vessels. In fact, the word "emotion" comes from the Latin word meaning "to move."

The ultimate goal is to use affirmations to transform negative thoughts and behaviors into positive ones and actually effect physical change, such as lowering blood pressure and cholesterol, easing asthma symptoms, or balancing hormone levels that increase the risk of breast cysts and other breast problems.

The heart represents the center of joy and security, so heart problems and high blood pressure are associated with long-standing emotional problems and lack of joy. Therefore, the health of the heart as a whole, and more specifically in terms of diseases relating to high blood pressure and high cholesterol, depends on your ability to find joy in life and express that joy in terms of emotions. Resistance and a refusal to see what is in front of you are associated with arteriosclerosis, a disease in which arteries become narrow and hardened, making them resistant to blood flow. Squeezing all the joy out of the heart in favor of money or position is related to heart attacks. If we look at respiratory or lung problems through the prism of Louise's affirmation theory, we see that if you have trouble breathing, you are afraid or refuse to fully take in life. And, finally, a tendency to overmother others, put your partner's emotions first, and fail to nourish yourself is connected to breast problems, including cysts, tenderness, and lumps.

So what does science tell us about the mind-body connection between negative thoughts and behaviors and the fourth emotional center? Does medical science support the theory that affirmations can help the health of our heart, breasts, and lungs?

Yes, it does! By transforming our anxiety, frustration, depression, and the "heartache" of lost love, we can change the health of our heart, lungs, and breasts.[1] In fact, study after study has shown the connection between how emotions are expressed and illness in the organs of the fourth emotional center.

Just looking at heart ailments, we can see an example of this in the ways men and women experience heart attacks. Women, as a whole, experience illnesses in the heart differently from men. When having a heart attack, men tend to have a more distinctive pattern of symptoms: the classical left-sided chest pain that radiates to the jaw and down the left arm. Not so with women. When having a heart attack, women do not have one stereotyped pattern of symptoms. They may have a sudden onset of digestive distress under their rib cage accompanied by anxiety as well as a host of other symptoms.[2]

Science has shown that there is a link from brain to heart, so perhaps this difference in the expression of heart attacks between men and women is associated with their brain wiring. With this in mind, we can look at the styles of heart attack and see that they mirror the way emotions are handled in the brain. Women's brains are structured to constantly use the information from both fact and emotion, while men tend to try to brush emotion aside and use mostly the logic area of the brain. Because women's brains tend to be more integrated, women have a much easier time putting their emotions into words and thus want to engage in a discussion about difficult issues. Men have a much harder time doing this, and as a result these emotions are likely to be shunted into physical or physiological reactions.[3] Maybe men's explosive heart attacks occur because emotions finally have to come out in some way—they work their way out in a more abrupt and overt fashion. I don't know . . . and neither does science. But when it comes to heart attacks, it seems that men's hearts tend to boil while women's hearts more or less simmer; the emotions and the heart attack symptoms seem to relate.

There are other important connections between heart attack and emotions that are borne out by science. For example, people who have difficulty handling a major loss, such as the death of a loved one, are more likely to die of heart attacks and heart disease in the first year of their bereavement. We also often see heart attacks directly following retirement or the loss of a career.[4] The feelings of hopelessness and failure that come with both of these losses can be very powerful and affect your heart health.[5] In fact, in one study they were shown to have the same risk for causing heart disease as smoking a pack of cigarettes a day. Not one or two cigarettes—an entire pack![6]

Other studies have linked heart disease and heart attacks with the personality traits of people considered to be "Type A." These people tend to thrive on being aggressive and overly competitive. To maintain this state of being, their bodies require a constant drip of stress hormones and this drives up blood pressure and clogs arteries.[7] But we can change our thoughts and positively affect the health of our heart. For example, one study followed a group of men, all Type A personalities who had suffered heart attacks. The men who were counseled on how to change their thoughts and behavior, especially about their long-standing emotional problems connected to expressing and moving beyond their hostility and anger, had a lower recurrence of heart problems than those who received no counseling.[8]

Scientists have also found that suppressed emotions—especially anxiety, depression, and anger—play a role in creating hypertension, a hardening of the blood vessels. So what's the domino effect that takes us from depression to hypertension? Depression causes the brain to release norepinephrine, which stresses the adrenal glands. This in turn causes the adrenal glands to release too much cortisol, which starts a cascade of inflammatory substances, including cytokines. These cytokines cause oxygen to become "free radicals," which make any cholesterol in the blood harden and cement onto the arteries, causing them to clog and making blood pressure rise into hypertension range. So there you go. The domino effect of depression to hypertension, emotions moving from the brain to the heart. And it just shows that roadblocks to emotions can cause roadblocks in the flow of blood. A similar inflammatory response is seen in people dealing with chronic frustration.[9]

The connection between suppressed emotion and the health of blood vessels has also been shown in numerous studies that looked at a syndrome called stress cardiomyopathy, also known as "broken-heart syndrome." This condition can occur following a variety of emotional stressors such as grief (for example, after the death of a loved one), fear, extreme anger, and surprise. Studies found that patients who stuff their anger deep inside, leaving it unexpressed, experience a higher rate of blood vessel tightening, which drives up blood pressure and reduces blood flow to the heart.[10]

In general, science supports the claim that suppressed emotions, especially anxiety, depression, and anger, play a role in blood pressure problems.[11]

The same connection between expressing emotions and health is true for our lungs.[12] In one study, asthma sufferers were taught "emotional intelligence," or mindfulness therapy, and it successfully improved their respiratory symptoms. The study taught them how to name the emotion they were experiencing; indicate what scenario precipitated it; and choose a healthy, balanced response to soothe the emotion. This practice of acting with emotional intelligence decreased their tendency toward bronchial asthma attacks and improved their quality of life.[13]

Scientific research has also shown that emotional health affects the health of the breasts. Specifically, there is a relationship between lifelong overnurturing of others, an inability to express anger, and risk for breast cancer. In fact, women who depend on child rearing as a source of self-esteem and a feminine identity are at greater risk for breast cancer.[14]

Perhaps women with breast concerns (and I am one of them) think they are taking care of other people by holding in their emotions. But in reality, martyrdom really doesn't nurture anyone and it's bad for your breasts. Long-term unhealthy expression of anger, depression, and anxiety disrupts the normal levels of the stress hormone cortisol, which may dampen the body's immune capacity to prevent cancer.[15] One study showed that 75 percent of the women who had breast cancer tended to be self-sacrificing and nurtured others more than they nurtured themselves.[16] And when it comes to recovering from breast cancer, it has been shown that receiving loving support is as important as the love and nurturance you give to others.[17]

So now that we understand the science behind the fourth emotional center affirmation theory, what do we actually do to heal these illnesses?

Heart Disorders

People who suffer from heart-related health problems—whether chest pain, heart palpitations, high blood pressure, fainting spells, or blocked arteries—have difficulties expressing their emotions. They have a huge backlog of bottled-up emotions just waiting to break out—and they do every once in a while, in wild, passionate fits of anger or frustration or an unexplained and unexpected sudden retreat. The swings between emotionlessness and fiery passion make it hard for these folks to relate to the people around them, and they sometimes become loners rather than deal with the anxiety that relationships bring with them.

Heart-related symptoms—even those that seem benign—can be serious, so see a doctor if you experience any signs that your heart health may be in trouble. But it's also important to take a longer-term approach to health by changing your behaviors and thought patterns.

Listen for the messages your body is sending you about the emotions underlying your health problems, and then work to change your mind-set through affirmations. For example, heart issues in general stem from long-standing emotional issues that have hardened the heart and blocked happiness and joy. So we need to open the heart and let joy in. A good general affirmation to counter the negative feelings is "Joy. Joy. Joy. I lovingly allow joy to flow through my mind and body and experience." Hardening of the arteries, or arteriosclerosis, comes from a resistant intention, hardened narrow-mindedness, and a refusal to see the good in life. If you have these problems, help yourself with the affirmation "I am completely open to life and to joy. I choose to see with love." Cholesterol concerns have to do with a fear of or inability to accept happiness. To open the clogged channels of joy related to cholesterol, you would use the affirmation "I choose to love life. My channels of joy are wide open. It is safe to receive." To lessen unresolved and long-standing emotional problems that are associated with high blood pressure, use the affirmation "I joyously release the past. I am at peace." These are a few of the most common heart issues. For more specific affirmations Louise recommends, look up your specific ailment in the table on page 183.

The important work you need to do to protect your heart health is to become more in touch with your emotions and learn to express them in ways that will help you move through them. Make sure to pay attention to your feelings—but don't judge them. Try to pinpoint what brought on the emotion. By putting your analytical skills to the test and dissecting your feelings to determine their origin and character, you are connecting your problem-solving left brain to your emotional right brain. This will help you learn to express those tricky emotions: first to yourself, and then to the people around you. Paying attention to your emotions will also help you chart your progress. If you are still having trouble managing your feelings around other people, you might notice a panicky or irritable feeling in certain situations. It is important to work your way into these situations slowly so you don't get overwhelmed and have to retreat or explode.

You may also want to work on getting in touch with your emotions through practices such as meditation and journaling. There are even sources online that give lists of feeling words. Check out these lists and become familiar with them. Just being able to recognize and define the words that people around you are using will help increase your emotional vocabulary.

Once you are able to express yourself, cultivating relationships will become easier. And this is important. You must do all you can to keep yourself from living a solitary life. Try to plan various activities throughout your week that force you to interact with people. Perhaps you can even use some of this time to interact with adolescents through a volunteer position. These kids are trying to develop their interaction skills—just like you. You can learn a lot from observing their successes and failures.

If you can learn how to identify your emotions and skillfully express them in a healthy or constructive way, you will reduce your tendency toward heart problems. Otherwise, your frustration, anger, sadness—even love—will boil over and be transformed into high cholesterol, high blood pressure, and cardiovascular disease.

From the Clinic Files: Heart Disorders Case Study

Paul is a 47-year-old computer engineer who was very comfortable at home, with his family, and in his cubicle at work. But if you asked him to step outside his comfort zone to attend a cocktail party or other social occasion, he would become anxious and introverted. His natural talents steered him toward a life that required little human interaction; even when he was home with his family, he spent most of his evenings at the computer.

Things were great until Paul's children grew up and moved out of the family home. At this point his partner began to reach out for more emotional connection. But Paul was unable to respond, becoming more apprehensive and withdrawn than usual. Soon his blood pressure shot up, he began to have palpitations and chest pain, and he was diagnosed with a blocked coronary artery in his heart.

To help Paul create a long-term plan to heal his heart and blood vessels, we helped him first realize what a healthy circulatory system looks like.

The heart is a muscle that sends oxygenated blood through all the arteries to all the body's tissues. If the arteries get clogged with cholesterol and become stiff and hardened via a disease called arteriosclerosis, people develop hypertension, or high blood pressure.

Among the body's vast network of arteries, we have coronary arteries—the arteries of the heart itself. If these arteries get clogged from high cholesterol levels and arteriosclerosis, the heart can't get enough oxygen, and this causes chest pain, or angina. If the clogged coronary arteries become extensive, the muscle of the heart dies in a process called a heart attack, or a myocardial infarction.

Paul's first problem was arteriosclerosis. But he also had coronary artery disease. He had a single blocked coronary artery, and the chest pain he was experiencing was angina. He was lucky in that he had not had a heart attack. Paul elected to have an emergent cardiac catheterization to remove the 90 percent blockage from his coronary artery. However, he learned that if he didn't change his lifestyle, other coronary arteries would soon become clogged. Fortunately for Paul, many of the solutions to addressing arteriosclerosis—lowering cholesterol levels and trying to relax the stiffness in the artery walls—also treat coronary artery disease.

But what about Paul's heart palpitations? Paul was diagnosed as having ventricular tachycardia, a heart rhythm disorder. Inside the right side of the heart is an intricate series of nerve fibers, called the SA node and Purkinje fibers, that control the heart rate and rhythm. If the coronary arteries nearby get clogged, the normal heart rhythm is disrupted and becomes an arrhythmia, like tachycardia or fibrillation. Here, the solution was not merely opening arteries but fixing the damaged nervous system that created an abnormal rhythm.

To bring about freedom from the heart palpitations, Paul had to employ both lifestyle changes and medicine. Paul's cardiologist gave him a strict short-term medication regimen including sublingual nitroglycerin (only if he experienced chest pain), baby aspirin, a prescription calcium channel blocker called verapamil, a beta blocker, and Lipitor to lower his cholesterol. He was also warned not to use impotency medication like Viagra, which can cause fast or irregular heartbeats.

But this was only medication. He had to change his unhealthy lifestyle habits if he expected to avoid illness and even coronary artery bypass surgery. So the first thing we did was address his anxiety. He worked with a counselor to create an aggressive campaign that would help with his fears and help him step away from his one coping mechanism—smoking. Paul used cigarettes to calm his "nerves." This program Paul and his counselor set up included the short-term use of the medicine Klonopin and long-term use of mindfulness exercises and cognitive behavioral therapy to reduce his anxiety and blood pressure and help him quit smoking.

It was important for Paul to lose weight. As you already know, fat and cholesterol problems go hand in hand. So we worked with Paul to figure out an exercise routine that he could maintain. He lost 20 pounds by riding a stationary bicycle for 20 to 30 minutes per day.

He also went to see a nutritional therapist who put him on a pharmaceutical-grade multivitamin and antioxidant, which included folic acid, B6, B12, vitamin C, calcium, chromium, copper, zinc, selenium, and alpha-tocotrienol. It's important to work with a skilled professional when creating these supplement plans because they can alter recommendations depending on your unique case—including which prescription drugs you are already taking. For his blood pressure, Paul used stevia, Hawthorn, dandelion, and lycopene after checking with his physician.

One very important supplement that was prescribed—in addition to those listed above—was coenzyme Q10. This supplement was critical because Paul was taking the statin Lipitor. While statin drugs may lower your risk of heart disease, they also lower your body's coenzyme Q10 levels. This substance, which is naturally produced by the body, is essential for the basic functioning of all cells. So it is critical to replenish it.

If Paul's cardiologist decided that the adverse effects of Lipitor were too great, he could transition Paul to a more natural path. Red yeast rice is an alternative nutritional supplement that produces similar results to some of the major statins. In fact, Lovastatin—another popular prescription drug—is synthesized from red yeast rice. Astaxanthin carotenoid, an antioxidant found in microalgae, salmon, trout, and shrimp, also has statinlike effects on cholesterol.

Paul also began taking DHA to help stabilize his artery membranes as well as his mood. He took acetyl-L-carnitine to protect both his heart and his brain. Last, Paul started Siberian ginseng to improve his heart health and to aid in relieving depression. With his physician's permission, he also visited an acupuncturist and a Chinese herbalist, who started him on some herbal remedies to help with his cholesterol and blood pressure. These included herbs such as Eucommiae, ramulus, scutellariae, and Prunella.

Paul also considered hyperbaric oxygen treatment since the prolonged stress and hypertension injury to blood vessels may be improved by this treatment, but in the end he decided against it—simply because of the logistical problems of getting to a clinic where it was offered.

While also addressing the physical ailments he faced, Paul worked to change the behaviors and underlying beliefs that were likely adding to his poor health. He worked with the affirmations for general heart health (My heart beats to the rhythm of love); heart problems (Joy. Joy. Joy. I lovingly allow joy to flow through my mind and body and experience); artery health (I am filled with joy. It flows through me with every beat of my heart); and anxiety (I love and approve of myself and I trust the process of life. I am safe). He also worked to learn about emotion. He studied the lists of feeling words, and he practiced—starting slowly—expressing his needs to those closest to him. If he ever felt a sensation of being overwhelmed by emotion, he was able to stop and look at what was happening rather than just running away or exploding.

By changing his thoughts and actions, Paul was able to bring about a healthy and happy future that included other people. He learned to express his emotions and hear the emotions of those around him.

Lung Disorders

People who have lung- or breathing-related issues such as bronchitis, pneumonia, runny nose, coughing, asthma, or hay fever have trouble engaging fully in life because they are trying to breathe through a cloud of emotions. Their emotional porousness and sensitivity are so great that they can downshift from the highest high to the lowest low in an instant, and their emotions are affected by everything around them. Just the opposite of those who have heart problems, folks with lung problems may be *too* immersed in, too saturated with their emotions. This makes it hard for them to function comfortably in society and in relationships without getting overwhelmed.

So how do you get past the sniffles, coughs, and wheezes? First, as with all acute physical problems, address your medical concerns with a physician or nurse practitioner. But as always, remember to pay attention to the subtle messages your body is sending you about how healthy you are.

Breathing problems indicate that you must look at your capacity to handle your emotions in your daily interactions with people you love and care about. If you are overly porous to other people's emotions—anger, irritability, sadness—you will be prone to asthma attacks, colds, flu, or other respiratory problems.

To complete the mind-body makeover for lung problems, we must conquer the negative thought patterns that have dictated our actions for too long. Louise's affirmations for lung problems in a broad sense address issues having to do with fears about engaging with and living life to the fullest. A good affirmation to combat colds and flu is "I am safe. I love my life." Coughing expresses a desire to bark at the world, *See me! Listen to me!* For the repetitive barking of a cough, Louise recommends the healing affirmation "I am noticed and appreciated in the most positive ways. I am loved."

Lung problems—such as pneumonia, emphysema, and COPD (chronic obstructive pulmonary disease)—are about depression, grief, and fear associated with not living life fully or not feeling worthy of life, so to counteract this use the affirmation "I have the capacity to take in the fullness of life. I lovingly live life to the fullest." Lung disease is all too common among those of us who have intense emotions we don't know how to handle. With emphysema, not only is there fear of taking in life but these people would rather not breathe at all. They should try saying aloud, "It is my birthright to live fully and freely. I love life. I love and cherish myself. Life loves me. I am safe." Pneumonia has to do with feeling desperate, tired of life, and having emotional wounds that are not allowed to heal. To start over and begin to heal old wounds, try repeating, "I freely take in Divine ideas that are filled with the breath and the intelligence of Life. This is a new moment."

Asthma is about an inability to breathe, feeling stifled or suppressed. If you have asthma and are feeling stifled, try meditating on the words "It is safe now for me to take charge of my own life. I choose to be free." For more affirmations Louise recommends, look up your specific ailment in the table on page 183.

Your negative thoughts and behaviors will begin to shift as you get more accustomed to this new way of thinking and become more adept at using affirmations. This is a critical time, so try to keep with it. It took years to develop your old habits, and it will take some time until you can break yourself of them. But we promise you can.

People with lung problems need to learn to control their emotions, to not be overwhelmed by them, and to not let the emotions of others affect them so extremely. Though it may seem counter-intuitive, one way to do this is to create a different relationship with your emotions—to tune in to them in a new way. Practices such as meditation can teach you to calm your mind. They can help you create a more stable relationship with your feelings. They can also help rewire your brain so you learn to control your emotions and not react so extremely to their presence.

Another practice that can help in regulating the effects of your dramatic emotions is to create a time-out structure. Look at your past emotional outbursts and try to determine why they happened. What triggered them? How did you feel leading up to them? What was the tipping point? If you are able to identify your triggers and your body's reaction to them, you will learn to recognize an emotional takeover in the moment—and not let it happen. This won't come naturally at first, but it will come. Once you recognize the signals of overwhelm occurring in your body, you will be able to react in a more constructive way. You will be able to take a time-out—whether this means physically leaving a heated situation or simply stepping away mentally to let your emotions become a little less intense. As you make mindfulness and positive thought patterns a part of your daily routine, you will find that you have to step away from your emotions less frequently.

These actions and affirmations will help you move toward a more emotionally balanced life. If you want to have healthy lungs, you need to learn to express your feelings in a calmer, more controlled way. It's possible to be calm, controlled, and in charge and still be exciting and emotional—the life of the party. Learn to balance your emotions with the needs of the important partners in your life, and watch your health in the fourth emotional center improve.

From the Clinic Files: Lung Disorders Case Study

My client Mary, 60 years old, describes herself as a "tornado of human emotion." She has always been thin-skinned, and her mood shifts depending on her relationship status, how much money is in her bank account, and even the weather. Mary says that she can be laughing one minute and crying the next.

Passionate at her best, and emotionally volatile at worst, Mary never does anything halfway, and that includes how deeply she feels each and every emotion. Mary's mood swings are exhausting for her friends, who never know what to expect from her behavior—there always seems to be a new drama. Mary started therapy to find out why she had so little control over her emotions. She was diagnosed with bipolar II (a less manic form of bipolar disorder) by one therapist, and borderline personality disorder by another. Neither the diagnostic labels nor their treatments were able to help Mary maintain stable relationships or keep a job.

Mary had suffered from asthma since puberty and noticed that her moods got worse when she had to take steroids to treat the most severe episodes of respiratory distress. By her late teens, even though she knew it was bad for her lungs, Mary took up smoking because it seemed to be the only thing that helped calm her mood swings. After one particularly tough breakup, she began smoking more than usual. One evening, she couldn't stop coughing and ended up in the emergency room. The doctor who treated her warned her to quit smoking: she was in the beginning stages of emphysema, or a lung disease called COPD (chronic obstructive pulmonary disease).

Mary had two medical problems, her mood and her lungs, and she had to address her moodiness in order to create pulmonary health. So that's where we began.

Mary wanted to know the name for her mood problem. Was it major depression? Was it bipolar II? Was it borderline personality disorder? Modern psychiatry has done much to ease our emotional suffering but unlike other medical specialties, it does not utilize blood tests, CT scans, MRIs, or other objective tests to give a person a definitive diagnosis. Instead, a psychiatrist, psychologist, nurse practitioner, or other caregiver will look at the symptoms and signs the client has and try to match these patterns with a condition listed in the *DSM-V,* the guidebook for psychiatric diagnosis. So there are no laboratory data to support or disprove a diagnosis.

That said, since Mary received three different diagnoses from three different psychiatric professionals, what was important for her was getting her mood treated adequately.

Mary finally committed to treatment with a psychiatric team that supported this focus and deemphasized her diagnostic label. Their main concern was to put together a plan with clear treatment goals. With the help of her counselor, Mary made a list of her emotional symptoms. Here's what she found:

- She had unstable moods every day.

- Her moods varied depending on what was going on around her, whether it was a "bad hair day," heavy traffic, or a crabby boss (called affective instability).

- She had problems with overeating, oversleeping, fatigue, low self-esteem, concentration, and hopelessness (called mild depression, or dysthymia).

- She experienced impulsive moments, including episodes of "road rage" and a couple of times when she became enraged and punched her spouse.

- She found that most antidepressant drugs have no effect on her symptoms.

- She experienced moments when after someone abruptly left, she felt like killing herself but the bad feelings quickly passed (transient suicidal thoughts).

Mary's treatment team quickly got her engaged in an emotional skills training class called dialectical behavioral therapy (DBT). Based in Tibetan Buddhism and mindfulness, DBT helped Mary learn techniques to stabilize her moods and regulate her daily activities so she was less prone to overeat and oversleep. She also learned to transform her rage and handle her transient suicidal thoughts through crisis chain analysis. In this process, she learned to break up a seemingly overwhelming crisis into understandable parts, identify the emotions associated with each part, and soothe herself through each step. She took weekly two-hour classes and a one-hour, one-on-one coaching session to introduce her to these very powerful methods.

To go along with her emotional skills training, a psychiatrist prescribed minimal amounts of medication that could help her stabilize her moods. Mary took Topamax, a mood stabilizer, and the antidepressant Wellbutrin XL, which helped her fatigue and concentration problems as well.

Next we turned to Mary's lung problems.

In asthma, the trachea and bronchial areas become very "irritable" for a number of reasons—allergies, side effects of medicines, mood, anxiety, and of course, cigarette smoke. When Mary's wheezing, shortness of breath, and coughing started to affect her, she learned (like everyone else) to pull out the classic inhaler with the stimulant Albuterol or Ventolin. A puff for relief. When that temporary relief didn't last, doctors upped the ante with an inhaler that has both the stimulant and a steroid that puts out the allergy/autoimmune fire underlying the asthmatic response. Mary tried a number of these enhanced inhalers—Advair, Pulmicort, and Flovent—but at times even these weren't enough.

By her bedside, Mary had a longer-acting inhalerlike device called a nebulizer that drove the medicine deeper into her respiratory tree. During particularly difficult times, Mary took oral steroids to put out the allergic fire in her body, but as she learned soon enough, these medicines have side effects, including moodiness, irritability, osteoporosis, and weight gain. Soon Mary began talking leukotriene inhibitors such as Singulair to help her asthma by knocking out yet another part of her immune system. Although these medicines all have side effects, they helped save her life because, at that time, she had no other options.

However, when Mary used mindfulness and affirmations in addition to her medicine, she was able to calm her anxiety and stop smoking, which greatly alleviated her asthma and lung problems.

Mary continued monthly—and then yearly—checkups with her pulmonologist. She also visited an acupuncturist and Chinese herbalist who helped her regulate her breathing problem with a variety of herbal blends, including respiryn extract, Crocody Smooth Tea Pills, Andrographis, and Bronchial Care remedy.

Even after Mary's official DBT classes ended, she kept up her mindfulness practice. She also used the affirmations for general lung health (I take in life in perfect balance); lung problems (I have the capacity to take in the fullness of life. I lovingly live life to the fullest); emphysema (It is my birthright to live fully and freely. I love life. I love me); respiratory ailments (I am safe. I love my life); COPD (I have the capacity to take in the fullness of life. I lovingly live life to the fullest); and breathing problems (It is my birthright to live fully and freely. I am worth loving. I now choose to live life fully) to help herself fully heal.

Mary changed her lifestyle, addressed her anxiety, and faced her negative beliefs to create a life without the pain of respiratory problems

Breast Problems

Women—and men—who have breast issues such as cysts, lumps, soreness (mastitis), even cancer, nurture and mother others often to the point of being overbearing. These people are much more comfortable solving other people's problems and comforting others' pain than handling their own. They hide their own emotions so they can keep stable relationships at all costs. In extreme cases, they'll never bitch, never moan, never complain. They are seemingly happy at all times.

If you are a nurturer by nature, it is hard for you not to take care of people in need. We're not saying you should give up being who you are—a loving, caring, involved human being. But you do need to examine why you are a compulsive nurturer of others and worry so little about yourself. You might also examine *how* you nurture and find slightly less imposing ways of caring for the people you love. So what is the prescription to bring a little more balance to your life?

As always, if you have an acute concern such as a lump or pain in the breast—especially if you have a close relative who has had breast cancer—see a doctor immediately. But you must also focus on your long-term breast health, which means changing the thought patterns and behaviors that are stressing your body.

Let's jump straight into Louise's affirmation system. Breasts have to do with mothering and nourishment. But nourishment has to go both ways—in as well as out. A good general affirmation to remind you to strive for equilibrium in this area would be "I take in and give out nourishment in perfect balance." Specifically, breast problems have to do with a refusal to mother yourself because you are putting everyone else first. To counter this imbalance in the way you nurture, try repeating the affirmation "I am important. I count. I now care and nourish myself with love and with joy. I allow others the freedom to be who they are. We are all safe and free."

Part of achieving balance in the fourth emotional center is giving voice to those thoughts that have been lingering beneath the surface. You may have no problem facing the emotional highs and lows of another person, but you can't address your own negative emotions such as fear, sadness, disappointment, depression, anger, or despair. So how do you learn to express these emotions? The key is to start slowly. Now that you know that voicing your emotions—good and bad—can be lifesaving, you can start to break through your wall of emotional stoicism, starting right this moment. And the best way into this is twofold: assess your own feeling about people in your life who show their less happy selves from time to time, and find yourself an emotional midwife.

The first of these steps is a hard realization for a lot of people. Assessing your feelings about others will help you get a better grasp on the reality of relationships. Your always being happy isn't the reason that people like you. They like you because you are you. And they accept that you are human. When your friends are experiencing disappointment, you want to help them. They likely want to do the same thing for you. And when they get upset, you tolerate and even understand their outbursts. Is it really wrong to assume that they will reciprocate when you show anger or frustration? Your friends will not discard you for not always being chipper. In fact, opening up and expressing your full range of emotions will help make your relationships deeper and more solid.

As for the emotional midwife, what we mean by this is to find someone—a friend, a therapist—who will provide you with a safe haven as you learn how to express negativity. Let them know that this is something you're working on, and ask for their help. Ask them to hold you accountable. If you can learn to speak about your sadness, anger, and disappointments in this environment, you will become much more comfortable using this language in the greater world.

And just remember: expressing negative emotions doesn't mean that you are nurturing a negative attitude. You aren't going to turn into a whiny old fuddy-duddy if you discuss legitimate complaints with those around you.

So work to incorporate this healthy affirmation into your life: "I express all of my emotions openly, willingly, and skillfully." Give your emotions a voice, and experience better health in the fourth emotional center.

From the Clinic Files: Breast Problems Case Study

Nina was a 33-year-old woman who was a mother to everyone who needed one. She could always be counted on to whip up a full meal for unexpected visitors or bake a delicious dessert when a friend was going through a rough time. She didn't just mother those closest to her. She volunteered her time helping the poor, counseling children and women in need, and teaching English to recent immigrants. Nina was upbeat and positive, even when faced with grim or dispiriting situations.

Long before the days of social media, Nina managed to stay in touch with friends from all phases of her life. In addition, Nina was married and had four children. People marveled at how she was able to juggle all the aspects of her life with little apparent effort. Then during a routine physical, Nina's doctor found a lump in her breast and diagnosed it as benign fibrocystic breast disease.

Fibrocystic breast disease is not breast cancer. In this condition certain areas in the breast have denser connective tissue. Many people think it's not a disease at all, but even with this consideration, it got Nina worried. Her mother had died of breast cancer, and she wanted us to help her create healthier breasts.

The first thing we did was refer her to our great friend and colleague Christiane Northrup's book *Women's Bodies, Women's Wisdom* because it has a whole section on how to create breast health. However, we also wanted to give her a program that was unique to her.

The first thing we discussed was her tendency to mother everyone around her. The lump in her breast was a sign that her life was out of balance. Her intuitive body was telling her that it was time for her to stop overcommitting herself to everyone and everything. Nina's lifestyle often led to adrenal gland stress and an imbalance in hormones that leans toward estrogen dominance. This hormonal state promotes cell overgrowth—including cancer cells.

Nina also needed to structure her diet in a way that would create the least estrogen possible. She had to minimize the amount of animal fat she ate since this may be connected to the body's ability to produce more estrogen. She moved to a high-fiber diet to help her body excrete estrogen through bowel movements. And she ate a great deal more broccoli, Brussels sprouts, and dark leafy greens, which, via Indole-3-Carbinol, change how your body metabolizes estrogen.

Her diet also needed to focus on losing excess fat, so in addition to the estrogen-focused eating changes, we instructed her to eat healthy protein (such as seafood, chicken, and low-fat dairy products) at every meal. She was also to set up an eating pattern that included a large breakfast and lunch and a tiny, carbohydrate-free dinner. And we limited her alcohol intake to one drink per day.

In further efforts toward weight loss, we helped her identify some aerobic activities that she could take part in for 30 minutes a day five to six times a week. She decided to alternate the elliptical machine and stationary bike at the gym with walks around the lake near her home.

We recommended that she take the antioxidants selenium and coenzyme Q10 to promote healthy cell function that would help prevent breast cancer.

Nina also needed to aggressively treat her depression and learn how to express the negative feelings she had. She started journaling and enlisted the help of a therapist to work through her grief. She also asked her best friend to be an additional emotional midwife.

To correct the imbalance in how Nina nurtured herself and others, she used the affirmations for breast health (I take in and give out nourishment in perfect balance); breast problems (I am important. I count. I now care for and nourish myself with love and with joy. I allow others the freedom to be who they are. We are all safe and free); and depression (I now go beyond other people's fears and limitations. I create my life).

After changing her lifestyle and thoughts, Nina managed to drop 20 pounds and is on the path of caring for herself and others while expressing all of her emotions—not just the happy ones.

All Is Well in the Fourth Emotional Center

When it comes to creating healthier hearts, breasts, and lungs, recognize that man (and woman) cannot depend upon medicine or nutritional and herbal supplements alone. Of course, it is important that you address acute health problems medically and under the supervision of a doctor. But for more long-term health in the area of the fourth emotional center, we recommend that you turn your attention to how well you balance your own needs with those of the other people in your life.

You are emotionally strong. All is well.

Chapter 8

SOMETHING TO
TALK ABOUT

The Fifth Emotional Center:
Mouth, Neck, and Thyroid

The health of the fifth emotional center indicates how well you communicate in your life. If you struggle to communicate—whether the difficulty is not listening to others or not expressing yourself effectively—you likely have health issues in the areas of the mouth, neck, and thyroid. The key to health in the fifth emotional center is finding a balance in how you communicate in your day-to-day interactions.

Remember, communication is a two-way street. Listening and talking both need to happen. Effective communication is about hearing and being heard. You have to be able to get your point across while also taking in the knowledge and opinions of others so you can alter your actions accordingly.

The area of your body that is affected by poor communication skills depends on the thought patterns and behaviors that create the problem. There are three communication problems that often lead to illness in this emotional center. Problems in the mouth—including the teeth, jaw, and gums—are often found in people who have a hard time expressing and dealing with personal disappointments. Problems of the neck are often found in people who—even if they have flawless communication skills on a regular basis—become inflexible and frustrated when they are unable to control the outcome of a situation. And finally, people with thyroid problems are frequently very intuitive but are unable to voice what they see because they too often struggle to keep the peace or win people's approval. We will discuss the specifics of each tendency as we work through the body parts later in this chapter. Just keep this in mind: if you have thyroid, jaw, neck, throat, and mouth problems, your body is telling you to examine your communication skills.

Fifth Emotional Center Affirmation Theory and Science

According to Louise Hay's affirmation theory, the health of the neck, jaw, thyroid, and mouth depends on having a voice. Specifically, throat problems have to do with an inability to speak up and a feeling that creativity is being stifled, while a peritonsillar abscess (an infection of the throat that grows near the tonsils) is related to a strong belief that you can't speak up for yourself or ask for what you need. Having a "lump in the throat" is associated with fear of expressing yourself.

Moving down to the neck, problems with the cervical spine have to do with being set in your opinion and having a closed mind. Refusing to see another's point of view can also set the scene for stiff neck and other cervical spine problems.

According to affirmation theory, thyroid disorders tend to occur when people are humiliated and don't get to do what they want to do. Not being able to assert your will can make you susceptible to hypothyroidism. People who feel "hopelessly sti-fled" have an increased risk for suffering from this disorder.

What does medical science have to say when it comes to the mind-body connection underlying fifth emotional center disorders such as neck, thyroid, and mouth problems?

The thyroid, one of the body's largest endocrine glands, is exquisitely reactive to all your hormones—and it's drastically affected by your ability to communicate.[1]

Women are much more likely to have thyroid problems than men—especially after menopause.[2] Studies done to figure out why often point to the difference in biology between the genders. Since thyroid problems often first kick in around puberty—when our bodies are flooded with new levels of testosterone, estrogen, and progesterone—and again when hormones in women's bodies are at their lowest around menopause, scientists have posited that difference in hormones correlates to thyroid function.[3]

However, hormones can't fully explain the different rates of thyroid problems between the genders. Speaking in general terms, men have higher levels of testosterone, which makes them perhaps biologically and socially predisposed to higher levels of assertiveness, especially when it comes to speaking.[4] Overassertiveness or an inability to skillfully speak up for yourself increase your chance of thyroid ailments.[5] Before women go through menopause, they have higher levels of estrogen and progesterone in their bodies. But there are other factors at play as well. These hormone levels, combined with a brain style that more constantly mixes emotion with language, lead to a tendency toward self-reflection. Women who have not yet gone through menopause innately tend to be less aggressive and impulsive in their communication, meaning they are more likely to not say what they really think in an effort to preserve relationships and family ties. This communication style often settles a tense situation but it doesn't necessarily address the personal needs of the woman involved, which can lead to thyroid problems at a young age.[6]

Women's communication styles—and their incidence of thyroid problems—change a great deal after menopause. In fact, the number of postmenopausal women with thyroid problems is higher than the number of men or younger women. As women enter into menopause, the ratio of estrogen, progesterone, and testosterone shifts, with the first two falling and the last one rising. At this point, women become more impulsive and less reflective, and this new communication style often creates new problems within their relationships and family. Then their incidence of thyroid disorders escalates. Women are then biologically predisposed to assert themselves by reacting, moving, and expressing more after menopause.[7] Whether it is a matter of not stating what you need or ineffectively expressing your desires, the inability to communicate well leads to thyroid problems. If you can't assert yourself effectively and you feel hopelessly stifled or are constantly getting in arguments, you are at an increased risk for thyroid problems.

Other studies have tied a subdued personality and an inability to speak up for yourself to thyroid disease. Specifically, people who have had a history of past trauma and often struggle with power dynamics in their later relationships tend to have problems with the thyroid. The experiences of their past conditioned them to be submissive, overly compliant, and unable to assert themselves. They don't "have a say" in their own lives and lack a drive for independence and self-sufficiency.[8]

Moving on to the throat, we again see correlation between communication and health. Feeling a lump in your throat when you don't know what to say is caused by a contraction in the neck muscles. In extreme states, anxiety and fear are shunted to the strap muscles in the neck that clamp down your throat, giving you a sensation of a lump. This occurs more frequently in people who tend toward being introverted, anxious, or likely to repress communication.[9]

The health of your mouth and jaw also relates to having a healthy ability to communicate and stand up for your needs. It has been shown that this ability—and finding ways to handle life's stressors—may actually lower a person's risk of periodontal disease. People with gum disease have disrupted cortisol and beta endorphin levels, the biochemical "fingerprint" of stress, in their bodies.[10]

So work to communicate better—both talking and listening—and you will have better health in the fifth emotional center.

Mouth Issues

People who are prone to health problems in the area of the mouth—such as cavities, bleeding gums, or related problems such as jaw pain or temporal mandibular joint (TMJ) disorder—have trouble with many facets of communication. These folks experience problems because they don't talk about and resolve their emotional disappointments. In places where they feel comfortable, they will talk, but they won't discuss what's bothering them in their intimate relationships. Such self-revealing conversations would embarrass them or hurt their pride. If they're in a situation that's uncomfortable or doesn't inspire a sense of passion, they can become aloof and quiet and would often rather seclude themselves. The problems of the mouth are all associated with not being able to effectively communicate your personal needs and disappointments.

If you suffer from problems related to the mouth and jaw, it's important to see a medical or dental professional but you must also attend to the thought processes and behaviors that have led to these issues. You must listen to the intuitive messages your body is sending or your underlying illness will come back.

Health of the mouth is related to communication, taking in new ideas, and nourishment. But communication can be blocked if you are angry. And because you are less likely to be open to others' point of view or able to make decisions if you are angry or resentful, you may develop troubles with your teeth. Reverse this indecisiveness and create strong, healthy teeth by using the affirmation "I make my decisions based on principles of truth, and I rest securely knowing that only right action is taking place in my life." Jaw problems or a locked jaw, TMJ, are about the desire for control or refusal to express feelings. For the anger, resentment, and pain underlying jaw problems and TMJ, the healing affirmation would be "I am willing to change the patterns in me that created this condition. I love and approve of myself. I am safe." People with tooth decay tend to give up easily and should try the affirmation "I fill my decisions with love and compassion. My new decisions support me and strengthen me. I have new ideas and put them into action. I am safe in my new decisions." People who must have root canal work because of tooth disease or decay feel their deep-rooted beliefs are being destroyed. They can't bite into anything anymore. Life feels untrustworthy. Their new thought pattern should be "I create firm foundations for myself and for my life. I choose my beliefs to support me joyously. I trust myself. All is well."

Once you have your physical body and emotional mind on the road to health, incorporate behavioral changes into your life going forward. It's important that you learn to speak about issues that are near and dear to your heart. Don't simply push those discussions to the side.

This is another instance in which it would be good to work with a counselor or another emotional midwife to create a safe space in which to express your emotions. While this will feel awkward at first, it's good to ease yourself into a healthy communication style.

It's also helpful for people to get a better handle on just how to identify their emotions. Search out literature—in print or online—that can help open your eyes to the minutiae of emotional language. Knowing precisely what these feeling terms mean can help you feel more comfortable talking about them.

Finally, it is important that you resist the urge to shut yourself off from the world. Make it a goal to create some real connections with other people—connections that allow you to express all aspects of yourself. If you learn to balance your communication skills in relationships, you will create a healthier mouth and jaw.

From the Clinic Files: Mouth Problems Case Study

By the time Sierra came to see us, she was 61 years old and in a lot of pain, with a bag of ice pressed to her cheek. Apparently some concerned friends had insisted she see a dentist when she showed up at church with a swollen jaw. Sierra admitted she had been ignoring some pain for a "few" months. The dentist diagnosed osteomyelitis, an infection of the bone caused by severe dental neglect—eight of her teeth had cavities and four others were infected.

Sierra told us that she was one of those rare people who had had a truly wonderful childhood and life. Her parents, sister, and brothers were all loving and supportive, as were her husband and children. Her life was everything she could ask for—until her husband died. Her children and grandchildren had all moved away and were so busy that they rarely called or wrote. Sierra didn't want to "be a burden," so she didn't visit them much because "they have their own lives now." For the first time in her life, she felt lost and alone. She immersed herself in church activities, which helped for a while. But she felt more comfortable sitting at home by herself.

The hint in Sierra's case was that her children never called or wrote. Without her husband or children, she had a communication stalemate in her life. Uncomfortable with her new widowed status, she didn't know how to integrate herself into the life of her children's families. And she didn't know how to fit into a life without her husband. Now that no one was making the first move, Sierra felt slighted and unwanted. She felt her dignity, pride, and self-respect would be injured if she made the first move, called her children, and asked them if she could visit. So dignity, pride, grief, and a heavy dose of resentment, grumpiness, and disappointment coalesced into infection in her mouth.

To create health for Sierra—and help remove the mystique behind her dental problems—we started by helping her understand what a healthy mouth looks like. We have 32 teeth, with 70 percent of each tooth being bone. The dentin core of the tooth, which has nerve sensation, is coated by enamel, the hardest material of the body. The dentin core blends into a tooth root that then juts into the bone of the jaw. The root area is where nerves and blood vessels connect the tooth to the body.

The rest of the mouth involves gums (gingiva), a tongue, and salivary glands. Bacteria always line the gums, but our body's immune system keeps them from overgrowing and creating inflammation called gingivitis.

Gingivitis was the first problem we decided to address for Sierra. Her severe dental neglect had made the bacteria grow out of control, producing plaque, an acid that erodes the tooth enamel and causes the gums to get inflamed and recede. This exposed her teeth roots and her jaw to even more bacteria. It was this bacterial buildup that led to her pain, tooth decay, abscess, and osteomyelitis.

In addition to neglect, we had Sierra review other habits that increased her risk of dental problems. She told us that she snacked throughout the day and endlessly sipped a number of sugary beverages. She also had GERD and had gone through a period of bulimia in her 20s, which brought her teeth into contact with stomach acid when she would binge and purge.

Based on this, we gave Sierra her marching orders. First, she set up an appointment with a reputable dentist whom she trusted to come up with a long-range plan to repair her mouth, jaw, and teeth. One major decision she faced was whether to get dental implants or have her teeth pulled and get dentures.

Sierra preferred the idea of dental implants, so she began to work with an alternative dentist to build up the immune system in her mouth so she would be better able to support the implants. The dental nutritional plan started with coenzyme Q10, lavender oil, calendula, Oregon grape, and a pharmaceutical-grade antioxidant. She also received an Echinacea cream to rub on her gums to improve the inflammation, soothe the soreness, and reduce bacteria numbers. Because her dental problems also led to bad breath, Sierra added parsley to her meals as a natural breath freshener and started using a homemade antiseptic mouthwash that was made by steeping 1 teaspoon of dried rosemary, 1 teaspoon of dried mint, and 1 teaspoon of fennel seed in 2½ cups of boiled water for 15 to 20 minutes and then straining it to remove the herbs and spices.

We also asked Sierra to get a bone density test. Bone loss causes the jaw to lose teeth and ultimately the remaining teeth become loose and more exposed to bacteria. From the test we found out that Sierra actually had osteoporosis, which she noted would explain her two-inch height decrease and the loss of a molar within the previous five years.

To help strengthen her bones—thus beefing up her jawbone—Sierra went to an acupuncturist and Chinese herbalist who worked with her internal medicine physician to put together a bone-health plan. They put her on a combination of supplements including calcium, magnesium, vitamin D, DHA, and a good-quality multivitamin.

Sierra had never made the connection between her bulimia and GERD and her tooth decay, but she did know that her snacking was part of the problem. Though she did try to snack healthfully—she carried organic raisins and dried fruit in her purse—this didn't help her tooth health. Any snack, if you have it often enough, can be bad for your teeth. In addition to snacking, she also had an addiction to Tic Tacs and other breath mints, which she used to mask her bad breath.

Sierra worked with an integrative nutritionist who helped her create a plan to deal with her emotional and physical eating issues. Instead of snacking constantly throughout the day, the nutritionist told her to make a conscious effort to eat every three hours and to rinse her mouth with water after eating. With a cognitive behavioral therapist, she learned how to identify her resentment about how her life had changed since her husband died. After working with her therapist, she got past her feelings that her pride would be hurt if she made the first move in the relationship with her family. Sierra reached out to her children and grandchildren, visiting them and inviting them back to their family home to stay with her. She also began to open up to socializing with old friends and even set up coffee dates and other outings with new people.

And finally, she worked to change the underlying thoughts that were likely contributing to her mouth and dental problems. Sierra used the affirmations for jaw problems (I am willing to change the patterns in me that created this condition. I love and approve of myself. I am safe); general inflammation (My thinking is peaceful, calm, and centered); health conditions that include the suffix -itis (I am willing to change all patterns of criticism. I love and approve of myself); general bone health (I am well structured and balanced); bone deformity (I breathe in life fully. I relax and trust the flow and the process of life), cavities (I fill my decisions with love and compassion. My new decisions support me and strengthen me. I have new ideas and put them into action. I am safe in my new decisions); and osteomyelitis (I am peaceful with and trust the process of life. I am safe and secure).

Sierra's new eating habits, medicine, behavioral modifications, and affirmations helped her overcome the pain and inflammation that were affecting her mouth—and in the meantime, she was also creating some healthy, lasting relationships.

Neck Problems

Neck pain, arthritis, and stiffness often come to those people who have amazing communication skills—both listening and speaking. Trying to see both sides of almost any story, they often become ill when their ability to clearly communicate things doesn't work as they expect it to. When an argument can't be settled by talking or when something in their lives goes wrong and they can't control it, they often become aggravated and stubborn, sticking to their opinion and refusing to consider other viewpoints. The frustration that leads to the breakdown in communication often creates illness in the neck.

If you are one of the millions of people who suffer pain, stiffness, arthritis, whiplash, slipped disks, and other neck problems, you have probably tried the gamut of treatments, including surgery, chiropractic, acupuncture, traction, yoga, or medications for pain. Any or all of these may offer temporary relief but probably won't provide a permanent cure. So what is the prescription for better and more balanced communication and lasting relief from painful neck problems?

In addition to medicine and behavioral changes, you must identify and change the negative thoughts that are triggering your health problems. In Louise's affirmation theory, the healthy neck and cervical spine represents flexibility and the ability to see both sides of a conversation. But turn this concept on its head by introducing an unbending mind-set or bullheadedness and health turns to illness and disease—in this case, a stiff or painful neck. People with neck problems, in general, tend to not be as good at the listening aspect of communication because they cling to set opinions and block out new ideas. They tend to be stubborn and inflexible and unable to see or understand other people's points of view. A good affirmation to counter inflexibility and the closed-mindedness associated with general neck problems is "I welcome new ideas and new concepts and prepare them for digestion and assimilation. I am peaceful with life." Although the general theme is communication, your affirmation will vary depending on the source of the pain and the underlying emotion. For example, a slipped disk in the neck is associated with feeling unsupported by life and also with being indecisive and not able to communicate your thoughts or needs clearly. So to heal, meditate on the words "Life supports all of my thoughts; therefore, I love and approve of myself and all is well."

As you incorporate affirmations into your everyday life, you should begin to notice a shift in the way you think.

Once your neck is healthier, some fundamental changes must occur to maintain equilibrium while moving forward. Learning to accept your emotional limitations in the middle of a discussion is one key to improving your neck problems. You do have an amazing skill for intuitively listening, understanding, and making logical arguments. However, you must accept where your intellectual power to reason and communicate ends. When you encounter conflicts that you can't resolve, don't push your opinion stubbornly, adding to the frustration of the situation. Instead remind yourself that there are multiple answers to every problem. Realize that your role is only one part of the solution. Finding balance between what you can control and what you can't and knowing when it is time to walk away from conflict will lead to better health in the fifth emotional center.

Important practices for those who might have neck problems are meditation and mindfulness. Meditation can help you become more in touch with your emotions, and living mindfully will help you understand how these emotions affect you in the moment. Once you are able to identify the sensations and emotions that indicate a shift in your communication style from diplomat to dictator, you can consciously make the choice to listen even more closely. You can work harder to keep an open mind. So when you experience a difficult conflict, you will be able to come to it with a new perspective and a sense of peace. It's important to realize that people can disagree on a point of view and still be in harmony, peace, and love with one another. What a concept.

We can create so many problems for ourselves by our attitudes. Stubbornness, inflexibility, and trying to fix other people against their will can all contribute to neck problems.

From the Clinic Files: Neck Problems Case Study

Raelynn, age 52, was famous in her family for her ability to settle a disagreement, often to the satisfaction of all parties. Every time there was a major legal dispute in the news, her family would joke that Raelynn could win it, no problem. Whether it was a family quarrel or a disagreement at work, Raelynn was truly a master negotiator—able to see both sides of the argument. But she could also be stubborn and willful, like a dog with a bone, not giving up but not listening either. On these occasions she became aggressive and angry and turned people off.

Raelynn mostly led by enthusiastic example throughout her life, raising her two children alone while working as a nurse practitioner. She believed in the power of positive thinking and taught her children as well as her patients that anything is possible if you set your mind to it. Raelynn's children, however, failed to thrive. Both ended up in trouble with the law at very young ages, and Raelynn worked tirelessly to help them.

As her adult-age children continued to struggle, Raelynn began to feel a sharp, shooting pain in her neck along with weakness, numbness, and tingling in some of her fingers.

To help Raelynn create a healthier neck, we needed her to know what a healthy neck would look like. Our spines are composed of a series of bones—vertebrae—stacked on top of one another and separated with puffy, shock-absorbing pillows called disks. The vertebrae and disks are critical in that they protect the spinal cord and its nerves, which run from the brain to every movable limb in the body.

The sudden onset of Raelynn's symptoms was scary to her, and even her doctors were quite concerned. When neck problems get worse quickly, as Raelynn's had, neurologists often suspect that a disk or something even more serious may be compressing nerves or the spinal cord. Even though Raelynn wanted to go out and "walk off the pain," we suggested she follow her neurologist's suggestion to get an MRI to better understand what was happening in her neck.

There were two possibilities for Raelynn. She could have a disk bulge, in which the shock-absorbing disk is slightly misshapen but there is still room for the spinal cord to move. This less-severe injury could be treated with over-the-counter pain medication such as aspirin or Advil. She could also implement acupuncture, *qigong,* and Yamuna body rolling to strengthen her muscles above and below the neck to prevent symptoms.

The other possibility was a slipped disk, and this ended up being Raelynn's problem. The MRI verified that she had a cervical disk prolapse in the C7 vertebrae of her neck. It also showed that the disk was compressing the spinal cord and pushing it against the vertebrae. Raelynn's doctors were concerned about this escalating into a neurological injury.

Given the rapid progression of Raelynn's symptoms and the fact that the disk was compressing her spinal cord, her medical team decided that surgery was her best option. Raelynn picked a neurosurgical team that she trusted and we made sure she met and liked her anesthesiologist before the surgery.

To prepare for her surgery, we suggested that Raelynn use imagery practices. Visualizations and imagery work have been shown to calm and relax patients and promote tissue healing during and after surgery. We helped Raelynn visualize exactly what the surgeon would be doing in her neck in the operating room, so she could "assist" with her own surgery even though she was anesthetized. Before she lay down on the pre-op table, Raelynn knew that the neurosurgeons were going to go in through the front of her neck, "decompress," or remove, some of her vertebral bone, remove the disk, and replace it with a metal prosthetic "cage" to make her neck more sturdy.

After the surgery, Raelynn was amazed; she was 100 percent pain free. But she wanted to keep her neck healthy. Exercise is a very important part of rehabilitation, but she wouldn't be able to work out for a few months following her surgery. We suggested that when she finally got back to the gym, she give up running and use an elliptical trainer instead. The Cybex arc trainer is specifically designed to prevent the neck-injuring lean-forward position. We also recommended that she buy high-quality shoes with great shock resistance. Nike Shox, Asics Gel-Kinsei shoes, or others with similar support would help put padding under her feet and thus under her spine.

Even though she didn't have a personality disorder, Raelynn bought the book *Skills Training Manual for Treating Borderline Personality Disorder* by Marsha Linehan and learned the communication skill exercise called DEAR MAN. This mindfulness-assertiveness exercise teaches you how to say something at the right volume and with the right words and inflections to maximize positive results. Through this, she would learn when and how to say something to her children, patients, or loved ones and when to let things go. She also tried to meditate daily to become more in tune with her feelings. With these skills she would be able to identify the frustration she felt in the heat of an argument and perhaps step back and not become so stubborn. Finally, Raelynn worked to learn *qigong* to ease her stress.

Raelynn also started working with the affirmations for general neck health (I am peaceful with life); neck problems (It is with flexibility and ease that I see all sides of an issue. There are endless ways of doing things and seeing things. I am safe); degenerative disks (I am willing to learn to love myself. I allow my love to support me. I am learning to trust life and accept its abundance. It is safe for me to trust); general pain (I lovingly release the past. They are free and I am free. All is well in my heart now); and general joint health (I easily flow with change. My life is Divinely guided, and I am always going in the best direction).

As with everything else in her life, Raelynn kept a positive outlook and worked to overcome her thought patterns and behaviors that led to her neck problems. She was soon back in the game, with a better perspective on life and communication.

Thyroid Problems

People who have thyroid problems are often so porous and intuitive that they can see what needs to happen in other people's lives to make them better. Unfortunately, their solutions are often unpopular, and these people frequently don't know how to give voice to what they know in a way that would be socially acceptable. They often try to express themselves indirectly, hinting at what they want or being very tentative—all in an effort to avoid conflict. However, if a situation gets too bad or their frustration gets too intense, they let loose with a flood of intensity that turns people off and makes them unable to hear what is being said. In either situation, the communication style of a person prone to thyroid illness is not effective.

Thyroid problems—whether hyper, as in Graves' disease, or hypo, as in Hashimoto's disease—are often ruled by two emotional centers. Because this communication pattern is very typical in family and friend groups that are not secure, the first and fifth emotional centers are often affected together. The first emotional center is involved because there is usually an immune component to certain kinds of thyroid issues. So looking at your immune system is helpful when you look at healing your thyroid. However, in this chapter we will focus solely on the effects your communication style has on the thyroid.

As is the case with all of the health issues we have discussed, the key is to identify the thought and behavioral patterns that are triggering the illness and transform them into positive, healing ones. For example, thyroid problems in general have to do with communication but also with humiliation—feeling that you never get to do what you want to or always wondering when it is going to be your turn. So if you have trouble balancing how much you talk with how much you listen, struggle with taking turns in a conversation, or are too passive during disagreements, you will have an increased risk of thyroid disorders. Alter the way you communicate by using the affirmation "I move beyond old limitations and now allow myself to express freely and creatively." The affirmation you use will depend on the slightly different thought patterns and behaviors that underlie your thyroid problem. So if you have hyperthyroidism (elevated thyroid function), you likely experience anger over being left out of a conversation. To temper the anger and remind yourself that you are part of the conversation, repeat, "I am at the center of life, and I approve of myself and all that I see." On the other hand, hypothyroidism (low thyroid) has to do with giving up and feeling hopelessly stifled. If this is you, your healing affirmation is "I create a new life with new rules that totally support me."

The goal is to seek balance in your life, especially in the way you communicate. There are moments in life when it makes sense to take a backseat and let others lead the way. Sometimes it is wise to keep your opinions to yourself. However, over time this lack of assertiveness can be destructive to your health, relationships, and financial security. You have to learn to stand up for what you think, and think in a timely fashion, even if you're just discussing where to go for dinner. You need to learn when to say nothing and when to say everything. Or something in between. It's tricky.

Clearly, stepping into this new communication style won't be easy. If you've been quiet for years, it's best to start expressing your opinion in small ways and in safe places. For example, even something as simple as saying no when you ask for Coke and the server says, "Is Pepsi okay?" can give you a taste of telling people how you feel. It's also good to get some supportive friends on your side. Ask your close friends to hold you accountable when decisions are being made. Request that they ask you what your opinion *really* is when you initially say you don't care what choice is made.

The people around you need to support you as you try to find your voice. Spend less time imagining how they might react and more time discussing ideas. But be careful not to swing too far in the other direction. People don't respond well to being bullied. Remember that with communication—as with most things—balance is key.

From the Clinic Files: Thyroid Problems Case Study

Ralph, 38 years old, was being groomed by his father-in-law, Sam, to take over the family business. Although he had planned to stop working earlier, Sam postponed his retirement because of the weak economy.

Ralph had been running the company side by side with Sam for years, but he was not an equal partner. Even when he disagreed with Sam's business decisions, Ralph did not have the power to overrule his father-in-law—he didn't even try.

After years spent suppressing his own opinions, Ralph's health began to suffer. He was exhausted and depressed; he had numbness in his extremities, gained weight, and was constipated. By the time we met, Ralph had been diagnosed with Hashimoto's disease, the most common cause of hypothyroidism. Ralph came to us because he was not feeling completely better even though he was taking his medication religiously.

We wanted to set Ralph up for complete healing, so the first thing we did was teach him all about his thyroid. The thyroid glands produce the hormones thyroxine (T4) and triiodothyronine (T3) that help regulate your basic metabolic rate. They also help with the cellular function of all the muscles, including the ones in your limbs and along the lining of your digestive tract and your heart. In addition, these thyroid hormones help the function of your brain, kidneys, and reproductive system.

So if thyroid hormone is low, as in Hashimoto's hypothyroidism, metabolism is slow and muscles are weak. Fatigue, lethargy, weight gain, chills, dry hair, dry skin, and in women, menstrual irregularities are often signs of a problem with the thyroid. With hypothyroidism muscle weakness comes in the form of constipation, stiff and cramping limbs, slow movements, and a deeper voice.

Hashimoto's hypothyroidism is caused by an autoimmune illness, so the first thing we had Ralph do was go to his internal medicine doctor to verify that he didn't have any other untreated autoimmune illnesses that would need to be treated in conjunction with the hypothyroidism. These other illnesses include such things as Sjögren's syndrome (chronic dry eyes), lupus, rheumatoid arthritis, sarcoidosis, scleroderma, and diabetes mellitus type 1. Luckily, Ralph had none of these other disorders; we could focus solely on the thyroid problems.

Next Ralph's doctor looked at all the possible physical causes that could be driving his thyroid hormone levels downward, including taking medicines like lithium, tamoxifen, testosterone replacement, interferon alpha, or large doses of steroids or estrogen. This could also be caused by a pituitary or hypothalamus disorder. Ralph wasn't on any of these drugs, nor did he have a pituitary or hypothalamus disorder, so his doctor looked at the medication he was currently taking for his thyroid problems to see if this would provide a clue. And it did.

Ralph was only replacing the T4 hormone. Some individuals will respond to this version of supplementation; however, some need both. More potent than T4, T3 is said to be more readily used by the brain. Ralph began taking both T4 and T3 supplementation.

Since it takes time for T3 to regulate brain serotonin function, we suggested that Ralph consider asking his physician whether it was all right for him to take a few supplements to help further boost his serotonin levels. Ralph started taking 5HTP. If this didn't give him enough relief, he could try SAMe instead.

Next, Ralph needed to address the autoimmune problems that initiated Hashimoto's disease in the first place. His hypothyroidism was caused by his body's immune system making inflammatory antibodies against his thyroid gland. This could be triggered by a number of things but the most common triggers are a virus or food allergies. However, Ralph told us he would not deal with any restrictive diets, so he didn't want to go for allergy tests.

We also had Ralph go to an acupuncturist and Chinese herbalist to get additional support in healing both his immune system and his abnormal thyroid gland. He started taking kelp, radix polygoni multiflori, Fructus jujubae, and pinelliae, all of which helped his constipation, fluid retention, fatigue, and weakness.

Finally, we sent Ralph to a coach who would teach him to be more assertive and skillfully have a voice, especially in heated business situations. Ralph also requested the help of his oldest and dearest friend, who took his task to heart, specifically putting them in situations where Ralph had to express his opinion.

Ralph started working with the affirmations for general thyroid health (I move beyond old limitations and now allow myself to express freely and creatively); hypothyroidism (I create a new life with new rules that totally support me); and depression (I now go beyond other people's fears and limitations. I create my life). We also had him use affirmations for some of the symptoms he was feeling as a result of his thyroid problems—fatigue (I am enthusiastic about life and filled with energy and enthusiasm); numbness (I share my feelings and my love. I respond to love in everyone); and being overweight (I am at peace with my own feelings. I am safe where I am. I create my own security. I love and approve of myself).

With a little training and some guidance from his health team, Ralph learned when to speak up and when to hold back. He got back on track with his health and his life, and he even started standing up for himself more at work, which convinced his father-in-law that perhaps it was indeed time to retire.

All Is Well in the Fifth Emotional Center

You have the power to create a healthy neck, thyroid, and mouth using medicine, intuition, and affirmations. If you have trouble with assertiveness—either being overly aggressive or too passive—you may already be suffering from health issues in these areas. By listening to your body and then altering your thoughts and behaviors, you can learn to hone your communication skills, heal your body, and change the way you approach relationships at the same time.

Figure out how to speak to your family, children, mother, father, and boss so that you are understood. If you are having communication problems, it's important to pinpoint just what they are so you can figure out how to address them and move on to have health in your fifth emotional center.

The world is listening. All is well.

Chapter 9

SUDDENLY I SEE

The Sixth Emotional Center:
Brain, Eyes, and Ears

The sixth emotional center is the center of the brain, eyes, and ears. And the health in this center depends on how well you are able to take in information from all realms—both earthly and mystical—and use this information in your life. It depends on how flexible your mind-set is and how you can learn from perspectives different from your own. To create health in your sixth emotional center, you need to be able to bend and sway with the winds of change, moving from a dig-in-your-heels, stay-the-course stance in some situations to a more exploratory, free-form mind-set in others. This balance allows you to grow and change with the times, focusing on what is happening in front of you instead of clinging desperately to ways that have passed, wishing you could turn back time.

The health issues related to the sixth emotional center span from ailments of the brain, eyes, and ears to broader themes of learning and developmental problems. As with the other emotional centers, if we are discussing a part of the body, the illness is often caused by certain thoughts and behavior patterns. However, when discussing the larger themes, the thoughts and behaviors do not stand as the cause; they are merely a factor that exacerbates certain tendencies, such as ADHD or dyslexia. We will get more specific as we work through the body parts and issues later in this chapter.

People who struggle with health in the sixth emotional center have an imbalance in how they see and learn from the world. Some are rooted in the earthly realm, with no connection to the greater universe, and others are totally connected to the mystical realm without a foot on the earthly plane. Finding a way to balance the input of both of these realms when facing life's ups and downs will bring health in the sixth emotional center.

Sixth Emotional Center Affirmation Theory and Science

According to the Louise Hay affirmation theory, the health of the sixth emotional center—the brain, eyes, and ears—involves a capacity to be receptive to information and a flexibility to think and reason your way out of situations.

The brain is like a computer, receiving information, processing it, and then carrying out the proper function. Information travels from every part of our body to the brain and from the brain to the body; however, the brain can be sidetracked in its job by its emotional components such as fear, anger, and inflexibility. For example, a person with Parkinson's disease may be ruled by fear and an intense desire to control everything and everyone.

The eyes and ears are the conduit from which you learn about the outside world, and health in each of these areas has to do with not liking the information you are taking in. For example, all of the eye problems have to do with fear or anger about the situation you're in. Children with eye problems are perhaps trying to avoid seeing what's happening in their families, while older people who are affected by cataracts are maybe afraid of what the future holds.

So let's see what medical science has to say about the mind-body connection underlying illnesses in the sixth emotional center.

There is a large body of literature proposing that personality style may predispose certain people to Ménière's disease or other ear disorders. Having a Type A personality gives people increased risk for this disorder. It has been shown that Type A personalities tend to hear only 20 percent of what is told to them when they are having a discussion in a relationship.[1] Despite having an external appearance of being calm and in control, Ménière's patients tend to have a lifelong problem with the outer world—they tend to experience anxiety, phobias, depression, and feelings of losing control.[2] In essence, people who develop this condition are more likely to be unable to handle the uncertainty of change.

Disorders of the eyes such as blepharitis (styes), dry eyes, and glaucoma have been associated with emotional frustration, anger, and irritability for thousands of years in the study of Traditional Chinese Medicine. It's interesting to note that scientific studies are now also seeing the psychological aspects of eye disorders. In one study, people with eye pain said they were actively "blotting out" feelings that they feared would be too painful to tolerate.[3]

People with Parkinson's disease tend to exhibit a lifelong pattern of depression, fear, anxiety, and a tendency to control both their emotions and environment. Scientific studies suggest that these patients may have been born with a low dopamine level to begin with, giving them a personality style that avoids risk and shies away from change. People with Parkinson's disease tend to be stoic and law abiding. They are trustworthy citizens, industrious, and belong to a lot of organizations. They are likely to be in charge and in control.[4]

Now that you've read the science behind illnesses in this region, what is the next step in healing your sixth emotional center problems?

The Brain

People who have brain-related issues such as migraines or other types of headaches, insomnia, seizures, memory problems, stroke, multiple sclerosis, Alzheimer's, or Parkinson's disease try to live with their feet planted firmly on the ground. They want to be good at activities that use both the creative right side of their brain and the structured left side. These folks often aim to be skilled in many areas of life, from geometry to history to painting or music. Living in this manner for a long time often leads to a crisis that forces them to start seeing the world from a new point of view. With a brain disorder, they are no longer able to count on the learning pathways they have always used and they must turn toward additional sources of intelligence and faith—information from a higher power.

If you have any of the brain problems above, see a doctor first, as there are effective medicines and therapies available. However, modern medicine and alternative remedies can only go so far. Once you have gotten the acute symptoms under control, take the next step in your healing. Your long-term health depends on changing negative thoughts and behaviors that are affecting how your brain is working and causing illness—in some cases very serious disease.

Learning new forms of intelligence and experiencing the world through the eyes of faith can decrease the chances of developing brain disorders as well as reduce symptoms that are already present. Most people who are diagnosed with a brain disorder feel a lot of fear and anxiety. Affirmations are *so* important because they help rewire the brain away from those thought patterns that aggravate your illness, help you acquire new ways of thinking, and bring you a faith in the universe. They actually do take your healing to the next level.

Rewiring your brain for new ways of thinking and finding faith in your experiences can help banish the thoughts that could be making your ailment worse. For example, in affirmation theory the thought patterns associated with epilepsy are rejecting life, constant struggle, and a sense of persecution. You can open yourself up to life and see the good in it with the affirmation "I choose to see life as eternal and joyous. I am eternal and joyous and at peace." Insomnia is associated with feelings of fear and guilt and not trusting the process of life. If you have trouble with insomnia coupled with anxiety, you can calm your nerves and sleep better with the affirmation "I lovingly release the day and slip into peaceful sleep, knowing tomorrow will take of itself." Migraine headaches, similarly, are about resisting life and also about fear of being pushed or driven. You can get relief from migraines by letting go and repeating the affirmation "I relax into the flow of life and let life provide all that I need easily and comfortably. Life is for me."

Alzheimer's and other forms of dementia are associated with a refusal to deal with the world as it is, being stuck in old ways of thinking, fearing new ideas, and feeling helplessness and anger. If this sounds like you, open your heart and mind to new ways of approaching life with the affirmation "There is always a new and better way for me to experience life. I forgive and release the past. I move into joy." If you are concerned about aging and memory loss and you feel like you are in a rut, release this judgmental mind-set with "I love and accept myself at every age. Every moment in life is perfect." With Parkinson's disease there are fear and an intense desire to control everything and everyone. Give up some of this control by meditating on the affirmation "I relax knowing that I am safe. Life is for me, and I trust the process of life." Multiple sclerosis is associated with inflexibility and mental hardness, an iron will. So we need to soften the rigid mind with "By choosing loving, joyous thoughts, I create a loving, joyous world. I am safe and free."

These are a few of the most common brain-related disorders. For affirmations that Louise recommends for other disorders of the brain, look up your specific issue on page 183.

In order to achieve the healthier mind-set required to heal sixth emotional center brain problems, you must work to bring other forms of intelligence and spirituality into your life. And when we say *spirituality*, we don't mean religion. We're talking about a connection to something greater than yourself. These issues will not be solved by study or logic; they will be solved through meditation and prayer. It is important that you understand that there is an indefinable power that connects all things—including you.

You must work to connect with the divine if you want to heal. How you do this is a very personal matter. You may want to set aside some time each morning to meditate. Or perhaps you can create space to walk in nature—not judging, or thinking, or figuring. Simply experience the beauty that exists.

If you are able to balance the input of the divine and a new intelligence in the earthly world, you will be able to live with health in the sixth emotional center.

From the Clinic Files: Brain Case Study

Vanessa, a 27-year-old freelance web designer, has an amazing memory and incredibly sweeping interests in everything from art to chemistry. Although she did not have the means to go to college full time after high school, she was determined to get an education, taking night classes at the local community college. Known for her brilliant mind and never at a loss for conversation, Vanessa was a popular party and dinner guest and she made friends easily.

Despite her lack of a formal higher education, Vanessa developed a thriving freelance career. She was making money and felt challenged creatively. But a few years after she started her business, she began feeling a prickling numbness in her arms and hands, was exhausted all the time, and had pounding headaches. Thinking it was a neck injury from all her long hours at the computer, she spent hundreds of dollars on ergonomic devices for her office. Nothing seemed to help. Then one day Vanessa woke up with blurred vision and found she was also unsteady on her feet. She made an appointment with her doctor, who referred her to a neurologist. To her disbelief, the doctor said that Vanessa might have multiple sclerosis (MS). He described this to her as "a progressive neurological disorder in which nerve fiber pathways in the brain and spinal cord are damaged." While he wanted to run more tests, she was too scared for a return visit.

When Vanessa came to us, the first thing we did was help her understand that an MS diagnosis is not the end of the world. With the correct treatment, many people are able to put themselves into remission and live productive, happy, comfortable lives. But to quote Dr. Phil, "If you can't name it, you can't fix it," so we encouraged Vanessa to follow up with a neurologist she trusted, to find out what was going on in her central nervous system, brain, and spinal cord. Within a month she met her physician and scheduled an MRI to look for damage to the brain or spinal cord, a lumbar puncture to test for specific proteins called oligoclonal bands, and a visual evoked potential (VEP) test to measure electrical activity in the brain. Vanessa's MRI and lumbar puncture suggested she did in fact have MS. Additional blood tests made sure her symptoms were not caused by another disorder such as Lyme disease, stroke, or AIDS.

Vanessa set up a varied medical team to look at her next treatment steps for MS.

To set up Vanessa's brain health program, we first helped her create imagery about what a healthy brain and nervous system look like. Our central nervous system, the brain and spinal cord, looks like an orange on a stick. Akin to an orange, the brain has an outer, tough, darker layer of cells that surround an inner, lighter area of nerve fibers. MS is an autoimmune illness in which the white blood cells produce antibodies that attack this light inner area. In MS these nerve fibers within the brain, and also those that proceed down the spinal cord, become scarred with white plaques and thus are not able to transmit signals normally between the brain and the body. With this knowledge, Vanessa could use visualizations to see her nerve fibers becoming healthy and unscarred. We helped her find audio versions of guided imagery, including a CD specifically for people with MS. The CD, *A Meditation to Help You with Multiple Sclerosis,* was created by Belleruth Naparstek, one of the pioneers of guided imagery who have helped prove the beneficial effects of this type of treatment.

Second, we sent Vanessa back to her neurologist, who showed her the drugs that were available to treat her MS. For this disease, physicians employ drugs for three reasons: to treat the symptoms, to prevent a relapse, and to modify the long-range course of the illness.

Vanessa's symptoms were numbness, tingling, and unsteadiness in her hands and feet (medically, this is called spasticity and ataxia). She also had fatigue, blurred vision, and pounding headaches. Vanessa's physicians offered baclofen, dantrolene, and physiotherapy for the limb symptoms, and amantidine and and other stimulants for fatigue. For her symptoms of a sudden nature—the intermittent headaches and blurred vision—her physician suggested a course of steroids. The doctors recommended beta-interferon, glatiramer acetate, or other drugs to mitigate the long-term effects of the disease. These drugs are said to reduce relapse rates by more than 30 to 60 percent, but they come with a chance of serious side effects. After much thought, since her symptoms were mild, Vanessa chose a short cycle of steroid treatment. For now, she wanted to avoid the other medicines, though she would stay in constant contact with her neurologist to monitor the level of her symptoms.

Next, Vanessa went to an integrative medical doctor and nutritionist who could also approach her illness from a symptomatic and illness-preventing point of view. The nutritionist worked to balance Vanessa's out-of-control immune system that was "attacking" her brain and spinal cord. Vanessa began taking DHA, calcium, magnesium, copper, selenium, and a pharmaceutical-grade B complex that included thiamine, B6, and B12. Vanessa cut out caffeinated beverages and any drinks or foods that contained aspartame or MSG, as these are known to affect people with MS. Vanessa also wondered whether a wheat intolerance made her symptoms worse, so she began to remove wheat from her diet.

Her next stop was an acupuncturist and Chinese herbalist who used certain points and herbs to reduce her limb spasticity as well as her headaches and fatigue. He suggested Boswellia serrata, which may decrease the autoimmune attack on the brain, and Ginkgo biloba, which has been shown to reduce the inflammatory response in the brain in MS patients. She also took horse chestnut, another herb that has an anti-inflammatory effect, as well as an anti-edema (decreases swelling) effect. He even suggested that she temporarily eat a macrobiotic diet in an attempt to "reset" her aberrant immune system.

The final member of Vanessa's team was a Tibetan herbalist, who helped her find an herbal combination that suited her individual needs. These combinations have been shown to increase muscle strength, and patients taking them have even shown improvements in some of their neurological tests.

In addition to these physical programs, Vanessa also started to work at changing the thought patterns that could be making her worse. She started to use affirmations to address both the multiple sclerosis (By choosing loving, joyous thoughts, I create a loving, joyous world. I am safe and free) and the symptoms it was causing—numbness (I share my feelings and my love. I respond to love in everyone); fatigue (I am enthusiastic about life and filled with energy and enthusiasm); headaches (I love and approve of myself. I see myself and what I do with eyes of love. I am safe); general eye health (I see with love and joy); and eye problems (I now create a life I love to look at).

And, of course, we stressed to her the importance of creating a connection with the divine. She was hesitant at first but decided to try it. She scheduled half an hour each morning to simply sit and meditate in the woods near her home.

Using these vast healing efforts, Vanessa was able to stem the symptoms of MS and continue to live a healthy and productive life. She was still a successful freelancer, and she was still the life of the party, but there was now also something more—a faith in the universe.

Learning and Developmental Problems

While many people classify learning and developmental problems as brain disorders, we look at them differently. All humans come into the world with their brains wired in a certain way. Some are prone to function more from the spatial, emotional right brain and others function from the logical, structured left brain. When it comes to learning problems, we find that these people live, learn, and work in environments that make their learning disordered. After repeated failures in school and work, they acquire an unhealthy mind-set, believing that they are stupid, lazy, and a failure. Many of the problems they experience come from being based more in one extreme of the mind—either the right or left side of their brain. There are pros and cons to each of these mind-sets. For example, those based more in the right brain are often able to see the big picture of a situation and perhaps see it from a completely new and exciting angle, but it's hard for them to deal with the details of our highly structured society. Those based more in the left brain are often brilliant at detailed things like math and science but they can't handle the emotional part of life. These conditions are not a matter of mere prominence of one side of the brain over another—rather, they are about an extreme imbalance of intelligence in one direction without the ability to tap into the characteristics of the other side.

There are therapies and in some cases medicines that can help with the symptoms of learning and developmental problems. To create a complete picture of health in the sixth emotional center, it is necessary to work with the behaviors and underlying thought patterns that may be exacerbating your problems.

When looking at developmental and learning disorders, we can see the extremes in dyslexia, ADHD, Asperger's, and others. People with dyslexia, a language-based learning disability, typically have a stronger right brain than left—they aren't able to focus on the details of language. People with Asperger's (a pervasive developmental disorder) have stronger left brains and tend to be obsessive and detail oriented, and have superior mathematical skills. Everyone's brain works slightly differently, with its own unique strengths and weaknesses. However, people with ADD, ADHD, Asperger's, and dyslexia have exaggerated developmental differences in how their brains are wired. This is why Louise's affirmation theory does not approach these issues as true disorders—because in most cases we all have aspects of these issues within us. The key is to be able to teach your brain to function in the best—the most effective—way possible. One way of doing this is to identify and change the negative thought patterns that are getting in the way of you acquiring all of your intellectual gifts.

To address the thought patterns underlying ADHD, Louise suggests the affirmation "Life loves me. I love myself just the way I am. I am free to create a joyous life that works for me. All is well in my world." But she also recommends you use other affirmations that address some of the common traits of the disorder. For example, the hyperactivity associated with ADHD is often accompanied by thought patterns that include feeling pressured and frantic. So if you tend to be hyperactive or unfocused, you may need a calming affirmation so you can let go of the anxiousness and worry. A good general affirmation is "I am safe. All pressure dissolves. I AM good enough." Stuttering, a behavior that can be associated with dyslexia, may develop from insecurity and a lack of self-expression. If you stutter, slow down and remind yourself that you have the strength and confidence to articulate your needs with the affirmation "I am free to speak up for myself. I am now secure in my own expression. I communicate only with love." Asperger's is often associated with depression, so if you suffer from this, you can use the affirmation "I now go beyond other people's fears and limitations. I create my life."

As you begin to incorporate Louise's affirmations into your life, you will see the past thoughts and behaviors that were weighing you down start to shift. You should feel less anxious and jittery and more calm and focused. It is natural to still have times when you fall back into old patterns. You probably have been this way for most of your life, so do not expect an immediate cure. Give yourself credit for the changes you have made and notice where you still need work.

As someone who is living with an extreme brain structure, you may need the freedom to pursue topics that really interest you. Unexpected change, rules, assignments, and requirements may shut you down. But a learning disability does not have to mean you will always struggle or that you will be unhappy in life. People with attention problems and other learning and developmental issues who follow this mind-body makeover will be amazed at how much energy they've wasted by being scattered and disorganized.

Adopting a few new habits to keep track of your commitments will free up time to cultivate your amazing creativity. It is possible to maintain big-picture clarity and attend to details. It's a matter of changing the way you think and behave. Strive to achieve balance between cultivating your creative mind and keeping yourself grounded in the real world. You are a capable and strong human being. Keep reminding yourself with the affirmation "I am the operator of my brain. I love myself just the way I am. I AM good enough. All is well."

In addition to affirmations, there are a number of behavioral changes that will help bring balance to the brains of people with developmental and learning issues. To begin your emotional healing, work to move toward the other side of the brain. For example, detail-oriented, structure-loving left-brain folks need to do everything they can to incorporate more free-flowing emotion and creativity into their lives. This will be very scary, so don't do it on your own. Ask someone you trust to plan a day—or an hour—when you will just go along with whatever they suggest. You won't know what's going to happen, but you will be able to set out on the journey knowing that someone who has your best interest in mind created the structure for you. Easing into this type of spontaneity provides you with a safe structure, even though it may not feel like it. It's also important for you to employ the help of a professional therapist. Try a cognitive behavioral therapist or a dialectical behavioral therapist to help you identify and handle thought patterns that lead to anxiety and fear.

If you are a free-flowing, creative, right-brained person, you'll want to do just the opposite. You need to work on slowly bringing structure into your life. Don't throw yourself in all at once because this will overwhelm you and destroy your efforts. One handy strategy to use is called the Two-Step Technique. If you find yourself unable to focus your mind enough to make a decision or solve a problem, simply take it two steps at a time. To do this, get a pen and paper, and write down two things that you know to be true about the situation. Then come up with two more related facts. And then two more. If you repeat this process, you will find that you eventually zero in on the heart of the problem.

This technique will help you achieve focus, even if your brain feels scattered.

You can also look for someone who can ease you into organization. An educational coach can introduce you to some of the basic tenets involved in living a more structured life. They can also help you find tools that will work for you—be it a scheduling book, index cards, or some other method that helps you put things in order. If you're feeling really daring, you could try to pick up a part-time job or an internship that uses your creative skills but also requires some focus on details.

From the Clinic Files: Learning Disorders Case Study

Tara, now in her 30s, grew up in a home that was run like a military unit—her father was a Marine, and he insisted on discipline, structure, and focus. Some children would respond well to this style of parenting but Tara did not. To make matters worse, the school she attended was on the military base and had a similar strict philosophy, where memorization and other traditional teaching methods were used. Tara was lost. She couldn't concentrate and had trouble finishing her assignments on time. Concerned about her academic performance, her parents took her to a psychiatrist, who diagnosed ADHD and prescribed Ritalin.

Tara's concentration improved a bit, but Ritalin could not fix her primary problem—she just didn't respond to a conventional education. As soon as she became an adult, Tara decided to move to New York City to focus her considerable creativity by attending design school and getting a job in fashion. Almost immediately she had problems fulfilling her academic requirements. Although design came naturally to her, she had problems taking the required exams and finishing projects because of her incapacity to organize and plan her projects. She found herself on academic probation despite the fact that her instructors praised her designs and her brilliant, creative mind. Lack of focus had derailed her in school when she was younger and it was happening again.

Tara started by trying to reprogram her thoughts using an affirmation for ADHD (Life loves me. I love myself just the way I am. I am free to create a joyous life that works for me. All is well in my world). When she came to see us, we recommended that she also use the affirmations for anxiety (I love and approve of myself and I trust the process of life. I am safe) and hyperactivity (I am safe. All pressure dissolves. I AM good enough).

Although she had gone to her physician and was considering Ritalin again, she wanted to learn about all the options available to help her learn. So the first thing we did was teach her how the brain generally functions in people who have the ability to focus and pay attention. Here's what we told her: The right brain focuses primarily on shapes, colors, emotion, and overall themes; the left brain is more drawn to key into details, words, and logic. As humans there are also four ways we can pay attention:

- Focused attention: We can ignore distractions and prioritize what to pay attention to first, next, and last.

- Divided attention: This allows us to spread our focus among an array of things in our environment.

- Sustained attention: This state involves vigilance and mental endurance.

- Emotional and intuitive attention: This style drives our focus to elements in our lives where we or someone near us is in distress, in love, or in some other emotionally charged circumstance.

The way your brain is wired will make you more prone to one type of attention style but this also changes with age. At age three to four, emotional and intuitive attention runs our life, so we focus on what we want, whether it's a candy bar or a nap. As we get older, other members of our attention network usually come on board; we start to develop our capacity for focused, divided, sustained, and emotional attention. For example, by the time most of us get to high school, we have learned to divide our attention between what the teacher is saying and what our "crush" is doing at the same moment. We also may become better at blocking out the distraction of music while we focus on our homework. I say "most of us" because not everyone develops these abilities. But this doesn't mean they can't learn to tap into any one of the attention styles that are within all of us. Each and every one of us has strengths and weakness that can be addressed with instructional, pharmaceutical, and nutritional support.

Tara went for a complete a neuropsychological assessment to pinpoint her brain style for attention, learning, and memory. As one would expect from an artist, Tara had good attention to three-dimensional shapes and other right-brain elements but was easily distracted when it came to left-brain details. She could get completely lost when she received written or verbal directions. In fact, her left-brain developmental language deficit was diagnosed for the first time as dyslexia.

When Tara's neuropsychologist explained her true brain style, she was elated! All of a sudden she realized why it was so difficult for her to finish her reading assignments on time. She wasn't stupid. And the fact that her right brain "visuospatial" IQ scores were superior or "off the charts high" indicated that her brain was born to be an artist's brain. She just needed to adapt her learning style so she could do the required reading and pay attention to details in class to finish her assignments.

Armed with a newfound confidence, Tara looked for a mentor; she found a professor who was known to have dyslexia and ADD but had somehow made it through the maze of training. Under his wing, she learned a variety of compensatory techniques including (1) the use of a color-coded calendar system to keep her on a schedule; (2) the use of a loud timer that was set so that when she started to get stuck on one detail, it would remind her that she needed to move on to complete the assignment; and (3) the tool of diagramming and flowcharting assignments so she could keep her priorities and timing more on task.

Under her doctor's guidance and support, she worked out a system in which she took the stimulant Metadate, a drug similar to Ritalin, at times when she was experiencing the most pressure, and then took the less-powerful stimulant Wellbutrin at times when she wasn't under as much pressure. She even worked with her doctor to spend some vacation months where she was, in fact, drug free. However, we did recommend daily supplements of acetyl-L-carnitine, DHA, and Gingko biloba to help her focus.

On the dietary front, we told Tara to keep her caffeine intake to a minimum because this is also a stimulant, and it might complicate her attention problem. And finally, we told her to carefully assess her mind state after drinking alcohol or smoking marijuana. In the end, Tara decided that she needed to stay away from these substances because they made her mind muddled.

Using these tactics, Tara graduated from fashion school and is making a living as a designer. She's even sold her products to several major department stores.

Eyes and Ears

People who have problems of the eyes and ears often have trouble balancing logic and spiritual contemplation, prayer, and mysticism. Neither extreme—being lost in the spiritual ethers or fully immersed in earthly matters—is good. But when you're in the spiritual ethers much of the time, you can't have your feet on the ground enough to experience earthly matters such as pop culture, politics, or any other topic around which most people connect. As a result you can often become withdrawn and isolated from friends, lovers, or colleagues.

Disorders of the eyes and ears are caused by thought patterns and behaviors that block your capacity to see and hear what you are being shown or told. So it is important to change these thoughts and behaviors. Louise lays out a number of affirmations that will help address the fear and anxiety that are often associated with eye and ear problems. For example, eye problems in general are about not liking what you see in life. To combat this, you can use the affirmation "I see with love and joy." Nearsightedness (myopia) has to do specifically with fear of the future and not trusting what is ahead. If you are constantly worried about what the future will bring, remind yourself to stay in the present with the affirmation "I trust the process of life. I am safe." Conversely, farsightedness (hyperopia) is fear of the present. If you have trouble seeing what is right in front of you, open your eyes with "I am safe in the here and now. I see that clearly." A disease of the eye such as cataracts, a clouding of the lens of the eye, involves not trusting life and seeing the future as dark and dismal. Try the new thought pattern "Life is eternal and filled with joy. I look forward to every moment. I am safe. Life loves me." Glaucoma, a disease of the optic nerve, involves a distorted perception of life caused by a strong, long-standing hurt. Release the past hurt and start the healing process with "I see with love and tenderness." These are some of the major ailments of the eye, but you can also refer to the table on page 183 to find other eye-specific affirmations.

Ears represent our capacity to hear, so a loss or disruption of ear health or ear function is about not being able to hear—or fully open up your mind to—the outside world. Ear problems also are associated with a lack of trust. A good general healing affirmation is "I now learn to trust my higher self. I release all ideas that are unlike the voice of love. I listen with love to my inner voice." Deafness is related to isolation and stubbornness and what you don't want to hear. Open yourself up to new ideas with the affirmation "I listen to the Divine and rejoice at all that I am able to hear. I am one with all." An earache is about not wanting to hear, combined with anger and memories of turmoil such as parents arguing. Release the anger and chaos in your mind with "Harmony surrounds me. I listen with love to the pleasant and the good. I am a center for love." Middle ear issues such as balance problems and dizziness (vertigo) are caused by flighty or scattered thinking. If you often feel distracted or confused, focus your mind with "I am deeply centered and peaceful in life. It is safe for me to be alive and joyous." Tinnitus, or ringing in the ears, occurs in illnesses such as Ménière's disease; it is associated with stubbornness and a refusal to listen to your inner voice. Remind yourself that you have all the answers within you with the affirmation "I trust my Higher Self. I listen with love to my inner voice. I release all that is unlike the action of love."

You're making these changes in your behavior to bring your-self into a balance between an earth-based way of living and a spiritual life, and this will take conscious effort. So delight in the world around you—the food, the nature, the people. Be tough; you can do it. I'm not saying to drop the mystical realm altogether, but do something that will give you an ability to relate to people around you. Watch some TV. Pick up a best-selling novel. Listen to the radio or a podcast. Get a little more familiar with the things that are happening in the world today. How 'bout those Mets!

You must also avoid the urge to seclude yourself. Armed with your new knowledge of the world, try talking to people. Take a minute or two in the kitchen at work to relay your thoughts on the latest episode of *Dancing with the Stars*. Really, try watching some show that everyone is talking about: not to watch the show per se but to be able to join in on the conversation and social festivities the next day. You can even jump-start your interaction skills by making small talk with a cashier at the grocery store—the weather is always a good topic of conversation. How 'bout those Mets!!

Finally, try to do some activities that involve physical sensa-tion. Get a massage, go to the gym, or go dancing. Any physical activity will connect you to your body, grounding you here on Earth, which will eventually connect you back to the divine.

From the Clinic Files: Eyes and Ears Case Study

Wanda, 44 years old, was one of the most sensitive people we'd ever met, and also one of the most spiritual. By the time she came to us, she had been having mystical visions for more than a decade. Wanda had to wear glasses at a very early age. Through her teen years, she struggled with weight problems, anxiety, and irritability, so she withdrew into her books and became more and more solitary. She graduated from high school and became a book-keeper—the perfect job for someone who was hiding from life. But after years of doing the same job, adding columns of numbers, she began having trouble seeing and found herself making errors she had never made before. She also started experiencing a glaring light distortion as she was driving home from work at night. Assuming she needed glasses, she made an appointment with an eye doctor, who quickly diagnosed her with a cataract.

Our first step to healthier vision for Wanda was to help her visualize (pun intended) what a healthy eye looked like. The eyeball is a globe with light-sensitive nerves in the back, called the retina, and a lens in the front. Lining the front of the lens is a very sensitive, fine layer called the cornea.

In a normal eye, the lens is nice and clear. When someone develops cataracts, the lens of the eye becomes cloudy, sometimes to the point of blocking vision. This is what happened to Wanda.

The risk of getting cataracts can be increased by a number of causes, including eye trauma, an autoimmune disease of the eye (uveitis), diabetes, radiation, and steroid use. To reduce her current problem, not to mention preventing a cataract in her other eye, we needed to figure out if Wanda had any of these possible contributing factors. We noted that she was 50 pounds overweight, but because she had been avoiding doctors for years, she was unsure whether or not she had diabetes. At our urging she went to her internist, had her blood sugar checked, and was diagnosed with type 2 diabetes. To help with this part of the problem, Wanda's doctor put her on an aggressive carbohydrate-restricted diet to lose weight. And we helped her find a form of aerobic exercise that she could do for 30 minutes each day. Wanda embraced the exercise plan, inspired by the fact that she was improving her blood sugar, her heart health, and ultimately her vision.

Wanda saw that the surgery might not help her visual problem, but the eye surgeon assured her that 95 percent of patients do see clearly after the procedure. With this bit of information, Wanda elected to have surgery on her cataract.

But she didn't stop there. She wanted to know how to prevent a cataract from forming in her other eye. We recommended that she continue to work on dropping weight, but we also sent her to an acupuncturist and Chinese herbalist and a nutritionist who would try to extinguish the inflammation in her body that was increasing her chances of creating cataracts. The acupuncturist and Chinese herbalist suggested Huang Lian, which contained coptidis, Bupleurean, and scutellariae.

The nutritionist gave Wanda a nutritional supplement specifically aimed at creating eye health. It contained vitamin E, vitamin A, DHA, vitamin C, riboflavin, zinc, selenium, copper, turmeric, grape seed extract, lutein, and glutathione. Wanda also took antioxidants, including alpha lipoic acid, coenzyme Q10, acetyl-L-carnitine, and quercetin. In addition to the supplements, the nutritionist told her that cow's milk may make her cataracts worse, so Wanda began to avoid dairy products.

She also began to change the behaviors and thoughts that could be contributing to her ailment. To become less reclusive, she decided to go to two movies each month to get a taste of pop culture. This was something she could do on her own that would give her something to talk about with other people. She also began making small talk anywhere she could. To help her change the underlying thoughts that were likely affecting her eyesight, Wanda worked with affirmations for general eye health (I see with love and joy); eye problems (I now create a life I love to look at); cataracts (Life is eternal and filled with joy. I look forward to every moment. I am safe. Life loves me); and anxiety (I love and approve of myself and I trust the process of life. I am safe).

These changes helped her gain a greater connection to the world around her, rather than the world above her. Wanda's vision improved. She lost 25 pounds, her blood sugar normalized, and her other eye remained cataract free.

All Is Well in the Sixth Emotional Center

When people develop brain, sight, or hearing problems, they must look, once again, toward balance. Health in the sixth emotional center is all about being able to take in information from both the world around you and the Divine realm. These different perspectives will help you move through life smoothly—giving you a well-rounded base of knowledge from which to approach every situation.

Your brain and your abilities to see and solve problems are unique to you. Don't deny your special talents, but try to create a vast, multifaceted approach to gaining knowledge. Learn to trust and have faith, embrace meditation, prayer, or quiet times but also hold on to the logic, structure, and creativity of the earthly world.

To facilitate a more mindful approach to your life, try Louise's sixth emotional center affirmation "When I balance my creativity, intellect, and spirituality with discipline and flexibility, I always succeed."

Your heart and mind are open. All is well.

Chapter 10

CHANGES

The Seventh Emotional Center: Chronic and Degenerative Disorders and Life-Threatening Illnesses

The seventh emotional center differs slightly from the others because this center is about problems that often begin in other emotional centers but progress to their extremes. For example, breast health is a matter of the fourth emotional center but life-threatening breast cancer falls both into the fourth and the seventh emotional centers. This same pattern can be held for any ailment that becomes chronic or life threatening—everything from weight problems to immune system health.

To move toward health in the seventh emotional center involves overcoming a lifelong emotional pattern of hopelessness and despair. It's about finding life's purpose and a spiritual connection at the same time. If you believe that you are powerless or if you have lost your connection to something bigger than yourself—whether it's God or some other greater force—you may find yourself experiencing the problems of the seventh emotional center. An immediately life-threatening or slowly degenerative disease could be your body letting you know that you need to reevaluate your life purpose, free yourself from the grudges and resentments you carry, and access a higher power. To live healthfully, you must realize that your life is guided by both Divine grace and personal choice.

The negative thoughts and behaviors that are associated with chronic or degenerative diseases as well as cancer involve fear, worry, hopelessness, and feeling that you're not good enough. The process of identifying the thoughts and behaviors that may be making you ill or making your symptoms worse is not about blaming yourself. You did not cause your illness. Every illness is in part due to factors such as diet, the environment, and genetics. But every illness also can be made worse or better by your emotions. So the goal is to transform your thoughts and behaviors into healing ones by incorporating Louise's affirmations and behavioral changes into your daily life. These can help you align your earthbound mind with your higher power so you can be well.

Seventh Emotional Center Affirmation Theory and Science

When it comes to the seventh emotional center, Louise's affirmation theory explores the emotions behind chronic, life-threatening diseases such as cancer, amyotrophic lateral sclerosis (ALS, commonly known as Lou Gehrig's disease), or other degenerative disorders. For Louise, these diseases are a sign of stagnation—whether it's in a job, marriage, or life in general. Seventh emotional center thought patterns associated with cancer and chronic or degenerative disorders often have to do with a denial of success and, ultimately, unwillingness to believe you are good enough or worthy.

What does medical science have to say about the mind-body connection of seventh emotional center life-threatening health problems?

There is a clear historic pattern of emotion that has been established for people with chronic health problems or life-threatening illnesses.[1] For example, studies show that people with degenerative illnesses are often dealing with the depression, hopelessness, and anxiety associated with losing someone or something central to their life, something that gave their life purpose and meaning. While these emotions can increase the risk of chronic illness in general, one study showed that these feelings are directly associated with multiple sclerosis. Losing a relationship because of death or infidelity, experiencing the death of a child, or even learning that you can't have children—all of these situations have been shown to precipitate the onset of multiple sclerosis.[2]

The death of a loved one or other significant loss often leads people to evaluate their purpose in life. However, another study showed that people who were unable to reconstitute their life with a purpose and meaning—to find loving support through creating new relationships, or find an avocation or calling—had a worse prognosis after the diagnosis of multiple sclerosis.[3]

Studies have also shown that the degree of disease progression, or even remission of neurodegenerative illnesses like ALS, can be influenced by how we handle stress and find meaning and purpose in life's adversities.[4] A landmark study on ALS by Evelyn McDonald showed that people who had a strong life purpose, a belief that they could change their lives, and a high level of psychological health lived on the average four years after the diagnosis compared to only one year for those who did not have this positive frame of mind.[5] This study, published in the *Archives of Neurology*, had such an impact on the medical community that it influenced how ALS is diagnosed and categorized. Before the study, a diagnosis of ALS was uniformly considered a grim prognosis. Apparently, it is possible to heal your body and change your life in the face of a fatal, degenerative illness.

People who "come down" with chronic or life-threatening illnesses such as MS, ALS, and cancer often have major depression or are chronically anxious and angry about some past unhealed, unresolved traumatic experience, whether it's a contentious drawn-out divorce, the death of a child, or some other catastrophe.[6] And we see that effectively dealing with these emotions, whether they take the form of anxiety, sadness, or frustration, even in the midst of cancer treatment, can make a great difference in the ability to have an optimal result in the end. In one study of men before and after prostate cancer surgery, there was a marked difference between the control group that used only supportive therapy and the group that used guided imagery and other stress-reduction techniques. The latter group had better immune system parameters and recovered from the surgery more quickly.[7] This shows that if we are able to identify and process the stress; change the negative thought patterns through affirmations, imagery, or other means; and use all the available medical options, it is possible to heal our bodies and live with purpose and passion.

Chronic and Degenerative Disorders

People who are prone to chronic or degenerative diseases such as fibromyalgia, Lyme disease, or ALS try to control their destiny. They often have lists of life goals—a successful career, having a lot of money, being thin, or having the perfect family life—that guide all of their actions. However, it's likely that they haven't accounted for the possibility of some sort of Divine intervention. Unfortunately, if you have been going through life considering only your own plans—with no room for deviation—the universe is apt to throw you a curveball. To overcome the forced sense of simmering helplessness that often accompanies unexpected events, it is important to cultivate a healthy balance between earthbound purpose and heavenly intervention.

If you are one of the millions of people who suffer from a serious progressive illness that has been labeled incurable, you've probably tried everything—from conventional medical treatments to alternative therapies. But does your illness seem to get worse no matter how much money and resources you pour into the problem? Maybe you need to try a new tack. In our experience medicine is helpful but it is not the complete answer. If you can combine medicine, affirmations, and intuition to guide behavioral changes you are much more likely to see shifts in your health and in your life. There's nothing like a health crisis to help you take stock of your past, present, and future—and reevaluate your priorities.

Louise believes that at the heart of the imbalance between the personal and the spiritual is a fundamental refusal to change old ways of thinking; an inability to let go of old hurts, resentments, patterns, and beliefs; and a failure to believe in oneself. Chronic disease in general is about refusing to change because of fear of the future. To foster the ability to change in spite of your fears, use the affirmation "I am willing to change and to grow. I now create a safe, new future." Looking at some of the degenerative diseases, we see a similar pattern of fear. People with ALS are often extremely capable but deep down believe that they are just a sham. They live with the terror that arises from thinking "If only people really knew . . ." They have deep feelings of not being good enough, and the closer they get to success, the harder they are on themselves. Remind yourself that you are powerful and talented with the affirmation "I know I am worthwhile. It is safe for me to succeed. Life loves me." AIDS is associated with similar thought patterns of being defenseless, hopeless, and alone. To combat these feelings, you can use the affirmation "I am part of the Universal design. I am important and I am loved by Life itself. I am powerful and capable. I love and appreciate all of myself." If you are told that your illness is incurable, offer yourself hope by meditating on the affirmation "Miracles happen every day. I go within to dissolve the pattern that created this, and I now accept a Divine healing. And so it is!"

Changing thought patterns is vital to achieving health in the seventh emotional center. As you begin to shift your negative thoughts and behaviors to healthier ones, it is also important to look at your relationship to the mystical world and realize that your life's purpose is not something you decide and carry out on your own. This life-altering condition can help you evaluate what your life's true purpose is, if you are open to it. Search for guidance using more than just your own logic. Accept that there is a higher power there to support you in your efforts and try to tap into the wisdom inherent in this. Your belief in something greater than yourself will help you banish the fear and hopelessness that come when you experience chaos in your life.

One tool that we recommend to people who are trying to create a connection with the Divine is something called a Life Grant Proposal. This is like the grant proposals researchers or nonprofit organizations write to get funding. But this is one that you send to the universe, God, or whatever higher power you believe in, outlining how much longer you want to live and what you intend to do with whatever additional years you're allowed to have.

To do this, take a piece of paper and write your name and date at the top. Then, along the top of the page, write: LIFE GRANT PROPOSAL. Follow that with a time period in parentheses, such as "for the interval 2013–2048," using the current year and whatever year reflects how much longer you want to live. Underneath this heading, break up the proposal into five-year phases. So in the above example, Phase 1 would be 2013–2017, Phase 2 would be 2018–2022, and so on.

Under each phase, write what you think your Divinely guided life purpose would be during that period of time. Then itemize what supplies you'd need to accomplish the plans you're proposing. Don't write down goals that you're already involved in, like volunteering at the soup kitchen or enjoying nature. That's for a grant-renewal form—not a grant proposal. With this exercise, you're preparing a whole new purpose, not renewing the old ones. Also, avoid vague purposes, such as "creating world peace" or "loving my grandchildren." Chances are you already love your grandchildren, and creating world peace isn't specific enough; these phrases weaken your proposal and making it less likely to fly.

A better life purpose would sound something like this:

> I used to work 12 hours a day, 7 days a week. In the first phase of my new life I intend to decrease my workday to 8 hours, 6 days a week. I will spend the rest of my day engaging in loving and leisurely activities with my grandchildren, including but not limited to going camping at least once a year, coaching their soccer team, and teaching them fishing and needlepoint.

Got it? Be detailed, but not so much so that you don't leave room for a higher power to have some input. The process of writing a Life Grant Proposal is truly a profound exercise in reevaluating your life design, enabling you to set your Divine purpose into motion, with humility and intention.

Many aspects of how a disease progresses are well out of your control, but there is much you do control. Try not to let anxiety overwhelm you. Be in touch with your friends and family to form a supportive circle around you. Learn to listen to your instincts and gut reactions, as these are Divinely guided signs leading you toward your true purpose. Choose to believe in yourself but also in something more.

From the Clinic Files: Degenerative Disorders Case Study

Yvette was 62 and in excellent physical shape when she first came to us. Everyone in her family was an athlete. Yvette appreciated the rituals and structure of sports and had become an avid long-distance runner in her teens.

As an adult, Yvette kept up her running, even through her pregnancy, and she was still running when we met. Throughout her life she'd had occasional injuries to her knees and back but her positive attitude and belief that she would get better helped her through these times. For the most part, Yvette was content. She had a large house, a handsome husband, plenty of money, and her health.

Then things started to fall apart. One night Yvette was awakened by strange tremors in her side. They continued for days. She saw her doctor, then a neurologist, and then another neurologist. There was no definitive answer, but the doctors thought it might be ALS. Yvette was devastated.

The first thing we did was to explain that before "cementing" her mind to the label of a diagnosis, she needed to remember what her physician had said: she *might* have ALS, and there was "no definitive answer." We stressed to Yvette that it was good news that her symptoms fell only in the "gray area"—the "prediagnostic" phase. This may not seem very comforting, because people often want a definitive name for what they are suffering. But from our point of view this was key, because without a firm diagnosis, it is easier to reverse your symptoms and put them in remission. ALS is a perfect example of that kind of disease.

ALS causes a progressive degeneration of the nerve cells in the brain and spinal cord that control movement. An individual can experience arm and leg weakness and, at later stages, difficulty talking and swallowing. This disease used to be universally thought of as fatal but this is no longer the case. It has been shown that if a person with ALS is engaged in their life purpose, they will have fewer physical symptoms and live longer.

Although she had resisted her neurologist's earlier suggestions, we recommended that she go back for more in-depth diagnostic testing to find out if another illness was causing her tremors. Everything checked out okay. She didn't have problems with her neck, thyroid, or parathyroid, and she didn't have any other oddball disease that could account for her illness. Her MRI and EMG were both normal. So Yvette focused on finding a way to put her ALS into remission.

Yvette went to see an integrative or holistic neurologist, who would follow her symptoms over time but also suggest a series of nutritional supplements to help stop the degeneration in her nervous system and promote its recovery through a process called plasticity. The first treatment he suggested was a series of hyperbaric oxygen treatments. This method has been shown to have some effect in the neurodegeneration of multiple sclerosis, so physicians are beginning to use it to treat ALS as well. In addition, the physician recommended a series of potent antioxidant treatments, including glutathione and a pharmaceutical-grade multivitamin, along with DHA.

The final physical treatment for Yvette was a combination of tai chi and *qigong,* as these practices have been used for centuries in China to counteract complex neurological disorders that are especially common as people age.

Yvette also started working with affirmations to address the ALS (I know I am worthwhile. It is safe for me to succeed. Life loves me); general brain health (I am the loving operator of my mind); and tics and twitches (I am approved of by all Life. All is well. I am safe).

Empowered by all of her treatments and the affirmations, Yvette began to take a long, hard look at her life and what she wanted to accomplish with it. It took the crisis of a possible illness like ALS to force her to begin to listen to her intuition and live with passion and purpose. And when her physician examined her once a year, her illness had not progressed. From time to time when she was stressed she would get an arm tremor, but there was no escalation.

Life-Threatening Illness

What is it about someone's life that would increase the chances that disease would progress to threaten it? People who are prone to life-threatening illness have often felt helpless about their lives for a long, long time—even before they got sick. They believe that all events in their lives are in the hands of fate. They feel powerless to make their lives better, and they wait, wait, wait, hoping things will somehow get better. But they don't.

The treatment of life-threatening diseases is varied and unique to each case; however, we can see a string of similar behaviors and thought patterns that may contribute to the disease. After working with your medical provider to figure out what treatments are right for your situation, it's important to incorporate intuitive thinking and affirmations into your plan. Since life-threatening illnesses stem from ill health associated with other emotional centers, you must change the thoughts associated with both centers. So, for example, with breast cancer, there is a tendency to mother and nurture others but also a deep hurt and long-standing resentment. To free yourself from these thoughts, you would work with the affirmation for breast problems (I am important. I count. I now care for and nourish myself with love and with joy. I allow others the freedom to be who they are. We are all safe and free) and the affirmation for cancer (I lovingly forgive and release all of the past. I choose to fill my world with joy. I love and approve of myself). This is just one example. You may want to refer to the table on page 183 to find out the connection between the organ of the body your cancer is in and the thoughts associated with that area.

To address the behaviors that may be contributing to rapid progression of your disease, you have to take healthy control of your life. You need to realize that though there is a Divine presence supporting your life, it is not in charge of everything. You also have personal power. You can co-create your world.

With this knowledge you can work with the health issue using the recommendations in the other chapters of this book. If you have leukemia, work with the information in the blood section of Chapter 4 to help you create safety and security in your family and friendships. If you have breast cancer, turn to Chapter 7 and learn how to care about yourself as much as you care about others. If your weight has become life threatening, realize your power and go to Chapter 6 to create balance in the third emotional center.

The most important step to take when addressing health in the seventh emotional center is realizing the balance between the power of the Divine and the power in you. Take action. Free yourself.

From the Clinic Files: Cancer Case Study

Angelina is 50 years old. She has been tested in every way someone can be—financially, physically, and emotionally—but she is still standing. Her life has mostly been defined by ill health: it has been one disaster after another. When she was a child, her appendix burst, causing a serious blood infection that forced her to be hospitalized. She had chronic headaches and back pain from a car accident in her 20s. She had thyroid problems that led to weight gain in her 30s. She had asthma. And in her early 40s, she was diagnosed with breast cancer. She fought and won the battle with breast cancer in her left breast, choosing to have a lumpectomy followed by radiation. Physically Angelina was healthy for probably the first time in her life. But emotionally she was a wreck—always on edge waiting for the next medical disaster. So when she developed a persistent cough and her doctor found a shadow on the mammogram of her right breast, she was sure her breast cancer had returned.

By the time we met Angelina, her health history read like the table of contents of this book. She had had a major problem associated with each and every emotional center: blood infection (first), chronic back pain (second), weight gain (third), asthma (fourth), hypothyroidism (fifth), chronic headaches (sixth), and cancer (seventh). Whereas in the past she had seemingly endless energy and a positive attitude that never wavered, now she was exhausted, and for the first time she felt hopeless.

When we started pulling together a health plan for Angelina she became overwhelmed, so we broke up her plan into two parts: one short term and one long term.

We began with the short-term health goals. These goals all dealt with bringing love and joy into her life. She needed to focus for at least one hour each day on each emotional center, for a total of at least seven hours of daily work. To help her schedule this, Angelina got a daytimer calendar and programmed her phone with reminders to help her follow this new system.

Our goal was to inundate Angelina's life with love and joy. These emotions elevate opiates and natural killer cell activity, and they decrease inflammatory mediators that maintain health problems. Here is a typical day for Angelina under our new plan:

- First emotional center (blood): Spend time with a friend or family member over coffee (maybe decaf); look at old pictures of family and friends during pleasant times.

- Second emotional center (lower back): Make a date, even if it's just with a friend. Dress up and have an evening out on the town. Buy a small gift and give it to someone you love. Watch children playing at a playground.

- Third emotional center (weight): Allow yourself one 100-calorie treat before 3 P.M. Have a friend help you reorganize your closet, and go to a makeup counter for a makeover. Do aerobic exercise on a bicycle or treadmill while listening to upbeat music. Dance like a banshee.

- Fourth emotional center (asthma): Go to a funny movie or watch comedies on TV. Your goal is to laugh. Go to an art store and buy some watercolors, crayons, or colored pencils and paper or coloring books, and start coloring.

- Fifth emotional center (low thyroid): Go driving in the car. Play the radio and sing at the top of your lungs. Play with an animal, even if it belongs to a friend.

- Sixth emotional center (headache): Remember the deeds of loving people in your life and have gratitude. Reflect on how you have improved from last week. Learn a new language. Take dance lessons.

- Seventh emotional center (possible cancer recurrence): Wake up each day with your first thought being "I'm thrilled and grateful to be alive." Try something new, whether it's a new station on the radio, eating a food you have never tried, watching a new TV program, or visiting a different place on the web. Go outside and look into the sky and try to reach your higher power.

During the other hours of her day, we addressed her long-term health goals:

- First emotional center (blood): Go to an acupuncturist and Chinese herbalist who can nourish your blood with herbs, including angelica, gecko, Fructus lycii, Paeoniae, and others. Take a pharmaceutical-grade multivitamin that includes folic acid, pantothenic acid, riboflavin, thiamine, copper, iron, zinc, DHA, and vitamins A, B6, B12, and E.

- Second emotional center (lower back): Take SAMe and Wellbutrin given to her by her internist to relieve back pain and a multivitamin for anemia. In addition, to ease the pain of lower-back arthritis, take grape seed extract and glucosamine sulfate. Also do Yamuna body rolling to improve the flexibility and pain in your spine and joints.

- Third emotional center (weight): Lose weight by eating a big breakfast, a larger lunch, and a tiny dinner. Every meal except dinner must have sensible portions, ⅓ carbohydrates, ⅓ protein, and ⅓ vegetable. Dinner is simply a small piece of protein and some dark, leafy vegetables. Also feel free to eat half of a protein bar with a bottle of water at 10 A.M. and 3 P.M. No carbohydrates after 3 P.M. Check out a macrobiotic healing diet, which may help support the immune system's capacity to keep cancer at bay.

- Fourth emotional center (asthma): Use the Advair inhaler she got from her pulmonologist and visit an acupuncturist and Chinese Herbalist for Crocody Smooth Tea Pills, Andrographis, and respiryn to further decrease shortness of breath. Also take the nutritional supplement coenzyme Q10 for immune system support.

- Fifth emotional center (low thyroid): Visit an integrative physician to find out if it would help to stop taking only Synthroid (T4) and replace it with a thyroid hormone that is partly T4 and partly T3.

- Sixth emotional center (headache): Go back to the neurologist to decide whether you want to take migraine medication such as Imitrex or Topamax. If not, visit an acupuncturist and Chinese herbalist for weekly treatments and the herb Tian Ma Huan.

- Seventh emotional center (possible cancer recurrence): Get a second and third medical opinion to verify results of first mammogram.

With these instructions, Angelina started on her new regimen. The first thing she did, because she was so scared about a recurrence of her earlier breast cancer and thus a "life-threatening" prognosis, was go for a second and third opinion. Fortunately, after a biopsy was performed, both opinions suggested that this was a second primary cancer, meaning that Angelina had a new cancer in the right breast; it wasn't a recurrence of the original breast cancer. She had a lumpectomy and radiation again, but this time, unlike her first occurrence, the cancer had spread to one lymph node. Although he was concerned, her oncologist agreed to continue to work with her after she elected not to do chemotherapy. Since it was only one lymph node, he felt that his knowledge could be of help—even without the typical treatments. But the spread of cancer did something to Angelina: it made her realize that she had to make *major* life-saving changes. She needed to figure out her life's purpose.

Angelina began to work with a vocational coach twice a month, focusing on a long-range map of what she wanted her career to look like at certain intervals—in six months, one year, two years, and five years from that point. She made a list of all the people she had "unfinished business with"—those people against whom she harbored a grudge—and she immediately called them to set up lunch dates and clear the air.

Angelina took a weekend solitary retreat at a friend's cabin in the woods to map out her future. She wrote a Life Grant Proposal to her higher power, outlining what people and financial support she needed to carry out her life goals. She put the grant in a journal and said a prayer over it.

Next, Angelina worked with a life coach to make sure she was able to skillfully work with healing affirmations to optimize her body's capacity to keep cancer at bay. To address the underlying thought patterns that were affecting her health, we had to incorporate many affirmations. In addition to body-part-specific affirmations (for example, breasts and lungs), we also brought in the affirmations for cancer (I lovingly forgive and release all of the past. I choose to fill my world with joy. I love and approve of myself); depression (I now go beyond other people's fears and limitations. I create my life); facing possible death (I joyfully move on to new levels of experience. All is well); and chronic diseases (I am willing to change and to grow. I now create a safe, new future).

By using all of these techniques, and working tirelessly to bring joy and love back into her life, Angelina was able to overcome her cancer and move forward with her life.

All Is Well in the Seventh Emotional Center

In this chapter we have explored seventh emotional center health issues, which are some of the most devastating emotionally and physically. If you have a chronic, degenerative, or life-threatening disease, you will be tested in all sorts of ways you may never have imagined. You may be forced to contemplate your mortality and ask yourself "What is the meaning of my life?" or "How can I find peace with a higher power?" How you handle these difficult concepts may dictate how long you live and how healthy and happy you are while you are alive.

To achieve and maintain health in the seventh emotional center, search for your purpose in life, strengthen your faith, and strive to keep learning and changing. If the negative thought pattern for chronic and degenerative illnesses and cancers is "Why me?" the new thought pattern is "In partnership with the universe, I move through emotional conflicts to find a peaceful resolution. Listening to my own intuition, I simultaneously try to tune in to the wisdom of a higher power."

I have survived and thrived. All is well.

Chapter 11

ALL IS WELL TABLES

PROBLEM	PROBABLE CAUSE	NEW THOUGHT PATTERN
Abdominal Cramps	Fear. Stopping the process.	I trust the process of life. I am safe.
Abscess	Fermenting thoughts over hurts, slights, and revenge.	I allow my thoughts to be free. The past is over. I'm at peace.
Accidents	Inbility to speak up for the self. Rebellion against authority. Belief in violence.	I release the pattern in me that created this. I am at peace. I am worthwhile.
Aches	Longing for love. Longing to be held.	I love and approve of myself. I am loving and lovable.
Acne	Not accepting the self. Dislike of the self.	I am a Divine expression of life. I love and accept myself where I am right now.
Addictions	Running from the self. Fear. Not knowing how to love the self.	I now discover how wonderful I am. I choose to love and enjoy myself.
Addison's Dis-ease *See: Adrenal Problems*	Severe emotional malnutrition. Anger at the self.	I lovingly take care of my body, my mind, and my emotions.

Adenoids	Family friction, arguments. Child feeling unwelcome, in the way.	This child is wanted and welcomed and deeply loved.
Adrenal Problems *See: Addison's Dis-ease, Cushing's Dis-ease*	Defeatism. No longer caring for the self. Anxiety.	I love and approve of myself. It is safe for me to care for myself.
Aging Problems	Social beliefs. Old thinking. Fear of being oneself. Rejection of the now.	I love and accept myself at every age. Each moment in life is perfect.
AIDS	Feeling defenseless and hopelessness. Nobody cares. A strong belief in not being good enough. Denial of the self. Sexual guilt.	I am part of the universal design. I am important and I am loved by life itself. I am powerful and capable. I love and appreciate all of myself.
Alcoholism	"What's the use?" Feeling of futility, guilt, inadequacy. Self-rejection.	I live in the now. Each moment is new. I choose to see my self-worth. I love and approve of myself.
Allergies *See: Hay Fever*	Who are you allergic to? Denying your own power.	The world is safe and friendly. I am safe. I am at peace with life.
Alzheimer's Dis-ease *See: Dementia, Senility*	Refusal to deal with the world as it is. Hopelessness and helplessness. Anger.	There is always a new and better way for me to experience life. I forgive and release the past. I move into joy.
Amenorrhea *See: Female Problems, Menstrual Problems*	Not wanting to be a woman. Dislike of the self.	I rejoice in who I am. I am a beautiful expression of life, flowing perfectly at all times.
Amnesia	Fear. Running from life. Inability to stand up for the self.	Intelligence, courage, and self-worth are always present. It is safe to be alive.
Amyotrophic Lateral Sclerosis (ALS, or Lou Gehrig's Dis-ease)	Unwillingness to accept self-worth. Denial of success.	I know I am worthwhile. It is safe for me to succeed. Life loves me.
Anemia	"Yes-but" attitude. Lack of joy. Fear of life. Not feeling good enough.	It is safe for me to experience joy in every area of my life. I love life.

Ankle(s)	Inflexibility and guilt. Ankles represent the ability to receive pleasure.	I deserve to rejoice in life. I accept all the pleasure life has to offer.
Anorectal Bleeding (Hematochezia)	Anger and frustration.	I trust the process of life. Only right and good action is taking place in my life.
Anorexia *See: Appetite, Loss of*	Denying the self. Extreme fear, self-hatred, and rejection.	It is safe to be me. I am wonderful just as I am. I choose to live. I choose joy and self-acceptance.
Anus *See: Hemorrhoids*	Releasing point. Dumping ground.	I easily and comfortably release that which I no longer need.
—Abscess	Anger in relation to what you don't want to release.	It is safe to let go. Only that which I no longer need leaves my body.
—Bleeding *See: Anorectal Bleeding*		
—Fistula	Incomplete releasing of trash. Holding on to the garbage of the past.	It is with love that I totally release the past. I am free. I am love.
—Itching (Pruritis Ani)	Guilt over the past. Remorse.	I lovingly forgive myself. I am free.
—Pain	Guilt. Desire for punishment. Not feeling good enough.	The past is over. I choose to love and approve of myself in the now.
Anxiety	Not trusting the flow and the process of life.	I love and approve of myself and I trust the process of life. I am safe.
Apathy	Resistance to feeling. Deadening of the self. Fear.	It is safe to feel. I open myself to life. I am willing to experience life.
Appendicitis	Fear. Fear of life. Blocking the flow of good.	I am safe. I relax and let life flow joyously.

Appetite		
—Excessive	Fear. Needing protection. Judging the emotions.	I am safe. It is safe to feel. My feelings are normal and acceptable.
—Loss of *See: Anorexia*	Fear. Protecting the self. Not trusting life.	I love and approve of myself. I am safe. Life is safe and joyous.
Arm(s)	Represents the capacity and ability to hold the experiences of life.	I lovingly hold and embrace my experiences with ease and with joy.
Arteries	Carry the joy of life.	I am filled with joy. It flows through me with every beat of my heart.
Arteriosclerosis	Resistance, tension. Hardened narrow-mindedness. Refusing to see good.	I am completely open to life and to joy. I choose to see with love.
Arthritic Fingers	A desire to punish. Blame. Feeling victimized.	I see with love and understanding. I hold all my experiences up to the light of love.
Arthritis *See: Joints*	Feeling unloved. Criticism, resentment.	I am love. I now choose to love and approve of myself. I see others with love.
Asphyxiating Attacks *See: Breathing Problems, Hyperventilation*	Fear. Not trusting the process of life. Getting stuck in childhood.	It is safe to grow up. The world is safe. I am safe.
Asthma	Smother love. Inability to breathe for one's self. Feeling stifled. Suppressed crying.	It is safe now for me to take charge of my own life. I choose to be free.
—Babies and Children	Fear of life. Not wanting to be here.	This child is safe and loved. This child is welcomed and cherished.
Athlete's Foot	Frustration at not being accepted. Inability to move forward with ease.	I love and approve of myself. I give myself permission to go ahead. It is safe to move.

Attention Deficit Hyperactive Disorder (ADHD)	Inflexibility. Fear of the world.	Life loves me. I love myself just the way I am. I am free to create a joyous life that works for me. All is well in my world.
Back	Represents the support of life.	I know that life always supports me.
Back Problems —Lower	Fear of money. Lack of financial support.	I trust the process of life. All I need is always taken care of. I am safe.
—Middle	Guilt. Stuck in all that stuff back there. "Get off my back."	I release the past. I am free to move forward with love in my heart.
—Upper	Lack of emotional support. Feeling unloved. Holding back love.	I love and approve of myself. Life supports me and loves me.
Bad Breath *See: Halitosis*	Anger and revenge thoughts. Experiences backing up.	I release the past with love. I choose to voice only love.
Balance, Loss of	Scattered thinking. Not centered.	I center myself in safety and accept the perfection of my life. All is well.
Baldness	Fear. Tension. Trying to control everything. Not trusting the process of life.	I am safe. I love and approve of myself. I trust life.
Bedwetting (Enuresis)	Fear of parent, usually the father.	This child is seen with love, with compassion, and with understanding. All is well.
Belching	Fear. Gulping life too quickly.	There is time and space for everything I need to do. I am at peace.
Bell's Palsy *See: Palsy, Paralysis*	Extreme control over anger. Unwillingness to express feelings.	It is safe for me to express my feelings. I forgive myself.
Birth	Represents the entering of this segment of the movie of life.	This baby now begins a joyous and wonderful new life. All is well.
—Defects	Karmic. You selected to come that way. We choose our parents and our children. Unfinished business.	Every experience is perfect for our growth process. I am at peace with where I am.

Bites	Fear. Open to every slight.	I forgive myself and I love myself now and forevermore.
—Animal	Anger turned inward. A need for punishment.	I am free.
—Bug	Guilt over small things	I am free of all irritations. All is well.
Blackheads	Small outbursts of anger.	I calm my thoughts and I am serene.
Bladder Problems (Cystitis)	Anxiety. Holding on to old ideas. Fear of letting go. Being pissed off.	I comfortably and easily release the old and welcome the new in my life. I am safe.
Bleeding	Joy running out. Anger. But where?	I am the joy of Life expressing and receiving perfect rhythm.
Bleeding Gums	Lack of joy in the decision made in life.	I trust that right action is always taking place in my life. I am at peace.
Blisters	Resistance. Lack of emotional protection.	I gently flow with life and each new experience. All is well.
Blood	Represents joy in the body, flowing freely.	I am the joy of Life expressing and receiving.
Blood Pressure		
—High (Hypertension)	Long-standing emotional problem not solved.	I joyously release the past. I am at peace.
—Low	Lack of love as a child. Defeatism. "What's the use? It won't work anyway."	I now choose to live in the ever-joyous NOW. My life is a joy.
Blood Problems *See: Leukemia*	Lack of joy. Lack of circulation of ideas.	Joyous new ideas are circulating freely within me.
—Anemic *See: Anemia*		
—Clotting	Closing down the flow of joy.	I awaken new life within me. I flow.
Body Odor	Fear. Dislike of the self. Fear of others.	I love and approve of myself. I am safe.
Boils (Furuncle) *See: Carbuncle*	Anger. Boiling over. Seething.	I express love and joy and I am at peace.

Bone(s) *See: Skeleton*	Represent the structure of the Universe	I am well structured and balanced.
Bone Marrow	Represents your deepest beliefs about the self. How you support and care for yourself.	Divine Spirit is in the structure of my life. I am safe and loved and totally supported.
Bone Problems —Breaks/Fractures	Rebelling against authority.	In my world, I am my own authority, for I am the only one who thinks in my mind.
—Deformity *See: Osteomyelitis, Osteoporosis*	Mental pressures and tightness. Muscles can't stretch. Loss of mental mobility.	I breathe in life fully. I relax and trust the flow and the process of life.
Bowels	Represent the release of waste.	Letting go is easy.
—Problems	Fear of letting go of the old and no longer needed.	I freely and easily release the old and joyously welcome the new.
Brain	Represents the computer, the switchboard.	I am the loving operator of my mind.
—Tumor	Incorrect computerized beliefs. Stubbornness. Refusing to change old patterns.	It is easy for me to reprogram the computer of my mind. All of life is change, and my mind is ever new.
Breast(s)	Represents mothering and nurturing and nourishment.	I take in and give out nourishment in perfect balance.
Breast Problems —Cysts, Lumps, Soreness (Mastitis)	A refusal to nourish the self. Putting everyone else first. Overmothering. Overprotection. Overbearing attitudes.	I am important. I count. I now care for and nourish myself with love and with joy. I allow others the freedom to be who they are. We are all safe and free.
Breath	Represents the ability to take in life.	I love life. It is safe to live.
Breathing Problems *See: Asphyxiating Attacks, Hyperventilation*	Fear or refusal to take in life fully. Not feeling the right to take up space or even exist.	It is my birthright to live fully and freely. I am worth loving. I now choose to live life fully.

Bright's Dis-ease See: Nephritis	Feeling like a kid who can't do it right and is not good enough. A failure. Loss.	I love and approve of myself. I care for me. I am totally adequate at all times.
Bronchitis See: Respiratory Ailments	Inflamed family environment. Arguments and yelling. Sometimes silent.	I declare peace and harmony within me and around me. All is well.
Bruises (Ecchymoses)	The little bumps in life. Self-punishment.	I love and cherish myself. I am kind and gentle with me. All is well.
Bulimia	Hopeless terror. A frantic stuffing and purging of self-hatred.	I am loved and nourished and supported by Life itself. It is safe for me to be alive.
Bunions	Lack of joy in meeting the experience of life.	I joyously run forward to greet life's wonderful experiences.
Burns	Anger. Burning up. Incensed.	I create only peace and harmony within myself and my environment. I deserve to feel good.
Bursitis	Repressed anger. Wanting to hit someone.	Love relaxes and releases all unlike itself.
Buttocks	Represents power. Loose buttocks, loss of power.	I use my power wisely. I am strong. I am safe. All is well.
Callouses	Hardened concepts and ideas. Fear solidified.	It is safe to see and experience new ideas and new ways. I am open and receptive to good.
Cancer	Deep hurt. Long-standing resentment. Deep secret or grief eating away at the self. Carrying hatreds. "What's the use?"	I lovingly forgive and release all of the past. I choose to fill my world with joy. I love and approve of myself.
Candida (Candidiasis) See: Thrush, Yeast Infections	Feeling very scattered. Lots of frustration and anger. Demanding and untrusting in relationships. Great takers.	I give myself permission to be all that I can be, and I deserve the very best in life. I love and appreciate myself and others.
Canker Sores	Festering words held back by the lips. Blame.	I create only joyful experiences in my loving world.

Carbuncle *See: Boils*	Poisonous anger about personal injustices.	I release the past and allow time to heal every area of my life.
Carpal-Tunnel Syndrome *See: Wrist*	Anger and frustration at life's seeming injustices.	I now choose to create a life that is joyous and abundant. I am at ease.
Car Sickness *See: Motion Sickness*	Fear. Bondage. Feeling of being trapped.	I move with ease through time and space. Only love surrounds me.
Cataracts	Inability to see ahead with joy. Dark future.	Life is eternal and filled with joy. I look forward to every moment.
Cellulite	Stored anger and self-punishment.	I forgive others. I forgive myself. I am free to love and enjoy life.
Cerebral Palsy *See: Palsy*	A need to unite the family in an action of love.	I contribute to a united, loving, and peaceful family life. All is well.
Cerebrovascular Accident *See: Stroke*		
Childhood Dis-ease	Belief in calendars and social concepts and false laws. Childish behavior in the adults around them.	This child is Divinely protected and surrounded by love. We claim mental immunity.
Chills	Mental contraction, pulling away and in. Desire to retreat. "Leave me alone."	I am safe and secure at all times. Love surrounds me and protects me. All is well.
Cholelithiasis *See: Gallstones*		
Cholesterol (Atherosclerosis)	Clogging the channels of joy. Fear of accepting joy.	I choose to love life. My channels of joy are wide open. It is safe to receive.
Chronic Dis-eases	A refusal to change. Fear of the future. Not feeling safe.	I am willing to change and to grow. I now create a safe, new future.
Circulation	Represents the ability to feel and express the emotions in positive ways.	I am free to circulate love and joy in every part of my world. I love life.

Cold Sores (Fever Blisters) See: Herpes Simplex	Festering angry words and fear of repressing them.	I only create peaceful experiences because I love myself. All is well.
Colds (Upper-Respiratory Illness) See: Respiratory Ailments	Too much going on at once. Mental confusion, disorder. Small hurts. "I get three colds every winter" type of belief.	I allow my mind to relax and be at peace. Clarity and harmony are within me and around me. All is well.
Colic	Mental irritation, impatience, annoyance in the surroundings.	This child responds only to love and having loving thoughts. All is peaceful.
Colon	Fear of letting go. Holding on to the past.	I easily release that which I no longer need. The past is over, and I am free.
Colitis See: Colon, Intestines, Mucus Colon, Spastic Colitis	Insecurity. Represents the ease of letting go of that which is over.	I am part of the perfect rhythm and flow of life. All is in Divine right order.
Coma	Fear. Escaping something or someone.	We surround you with safety and love. We create a space for you to heal. You are loved.
Comedones	Small outbursts of anger.	I calm my thoughts and I am serene.
Congestion See: Bronchitis, Colds, Influenza		
Conjunctivitis See: Pink Eye	Anger and frustration at what you are looking at in life.	I see with the eyes of love. There is a harmonious solution, and I accept it now.
Constipation	Refusing to release old ideas. Stuck in the past. Sometimes stinginess.	As I release the past, the new and fresh and vital enter. I allow life to flow through me.
Corns	Hardened areas of thought—stubbornly holding on to the pain of the past.	I move forward, free from the past. I am safe, I am free.

Coronary Thrombosis *See: Heart Attack*	Feeling alone and scared. "I'm not good enough. I don't do enough. I'll never make it."	I am one with all of life. The Universe totally supports me. All is well.
Coughs *See: Respiratory Ailments*	A desire to bark at the world. "See me! Listen to me!"	I am noticed and appreciated in the most positive ways. I am loved.
Cramps	Tension. Fear. Gripping, holding on.	I relax and allow my mind to be peaceful.
Croup *See: Bronchitis*		
Crying	Tears are the river of life, shed in joy as well as in sadness and fear.	I am peaceful with all my emotions. I love and approve of myself.
Cushing's Dis-ease *See: Adrenal Problems*	Mental imbalance. Overproduction of crushing ideas. A feeling of being overpowered.	I lovingly balance my mind and my body. I now choose thoughts that make me feel good.
Cuts *See: Injuries, Wounds*	Punishment for not following your own rules.	I create a life filled with rewards.
Cyst(s)	Running the old painful movie. Nursing hurts. A false growth.	The movies of my mind are beautiful because I choose to make them so. I love me.
Cystic Fibrosis	A thick belief that life won't work for you. "Poor me."	Life loves me, and I love life. I now choose to take in life fully and freely.
Cystitis *See: Bladder Problems*		
Deafness	Rejection, stubbornness, isolation. What don't you want to hear? "Don't bother me."	I listen to the Divine and rejoice at all that I am able to hear. I am one with all.
Death	Represents leaving the movie of life.	I joyfully move on to new levels of experience. All is well.

Defects	Karmic. You selected to come that way. We choose our parents and our children. Unfinished business.	Every experience is perfect for our growth process. I am at peace with where I am.
Degenerative Disk	Lack of support. Fear of life. Inability to trust.	I am willing to learn to love myself. I allow my love to support me. I am learning to trust life and accept its abundance. It is safe for me to trust.
Dementia See: Alzheimer's Dis-ease, Senility	A refusal to deal with the world as it is. Hopelessness and anger.	I am in my perfect place, and I am safe at all times.
Depression	Anger you feel you do not have a right to have. Hopelessness.	I now go beyond other people's fears and limitations. I create my life.
Diabetes (Hyperglycemia, Mellitus)	Longing for what might have been. A great need to control. Deep sorrow. No sweetness left.	This moment is filled with joy. I now choose to experience the sweetness of today.
Diarrhea	Fear. Rejection. Running off.	My intake, assimilation, and elimination are in perfect order. I am at peace with life.
Dizziness (Vertigo)	Flighty, scattered thinking. A refusal to look.	I am deeply centered and peaceful in life. It is safe for me to be alive and joyous.
Dry Eye	Angry eyes. Refusing to see with love. Would rather die than forgive. Being spiteful.	I willingly forgive. I breathe life into my vision and see with compassion and understanding.
Dysentery	Fear and intense anger.	I create peacefulness in my mind, and my body reflects this.
—Amoebic	Believing they are out to get you.	I am the power and authority in my world. I am at peace.
—Bacillary	Oppression and hopelessness.	I am filled with life and energy and the joy of living.
Dysmenorrhea See: Female Problems, Menstrual Problems	Anger at the self. Hatred of the body or of women.	I love my body. I love myself. I love all my cycles. All is well.

Ear	Represents the capacity to hear.	I hear with love.
Ear Problems	Inability to hear or fully open up your mind to the outside world. Lack of trust.	I now learn to trust my higher self. I release all ideas that are unlike the voice of love.
Earache (Otitis: External/Ear Canal Media/ Inner Ear)	Anger. Not wanting to hear. Too much turmoil. Parents arguing.	Harmony surrounds me. I listen with love to the pleasant and the good. I am a center for love.
Ecchymoses *See: Bruises*		
Eczema	Breath-taking antagonism. Mental eruptions.	Harmony and peace, love and joy surround me and indwell me. I am safe and secure.
Edema *See: Holding Fluids, Swelling*	What or who won't you let go of?	I willingly release the past. It is safe for me to let go. I am free now.
Elbow *See: Joints*	Represents changing directions and accepting new experiences.	I easily flow with new experiences, new directions, and new changes.
Emphysema	Fear of taking in life. Not worthy of living.	It is my birthright to live fully and freely. I love life. I love me.
Endometriosis	Insecurity, disappointment, and frustration. Replacing self-love with sugar. Blamers.	I am both powerful and desirable. It is wonderful to be a woman. I love myself, and I am fulfilled.
Enuresis *See: Bedwetting*		
Epilepsy	Sense of persecution. Rejection of life. A feeling of great struggle. Self-violence.	I choose to see life as eternal and joyous. I am eternal and joyous and at peace.
Epstein-Barr Virus	Pushing beyond one's limits. Fear of not being good enough. Draining all inner support. Stress virus.	I relax and recognize my self-worth. I am good enough. Life is easy and joyful.
Exotropia *See: Eye Problems*		

Eye(s)	Represents the capacity to see clearly—past, present, and future.	I see with love and joy.
Eye Problems *See: Sty*	Not liking what you see in your own life.	I now create a life I love to look at.
—Astigmatism	"I" trouble. Fear of really seeing the self.	I am now willing to see my own beauty and magnificence.
—Cataracts	Inability to see ahead with joy. Dark future.	Life is eternal and filled with joy.
—Children	Not wanting to see what is going on in the family.	Harmony and joy and beauty and safety now surround this child.
—Crossed *See: Keratitis*	Not wanting to see what's out there. Crossed purposes.	It is safe for me to see. I am at peace.
—Farsighted (Hyperopia)	Fear of the present.	I am safe in the here and now. I see that clearly.
—Glaucoma	Stony unforgiveness. Pressure from long-standing hurts. Overwhelmed by it all.	I see with love and tenderness.
—Nearsighted *See: Myopia*	Fear of the future.	I accept Divine guidance and am always safe.
—Wall Eyed (Exotropia)	Fear of looking at the present, right here.	I accept Divine guidance and am always safe.
Face	Represents what we show the world.	It is safe to be me. I express who I am.
Fainting (Vasovagal Attack)	Fear. Can't cope. Blacking out.	I have the power and the strength and knowledge to handle everything in my life.
Fat *See: Overweight*	Oversensitivity. Often represents fear and shows a need for protection. Fear may be a cover for hidden anger and a resistance to forgive.	I am protected by Divine Love. I am always safe and secure. I am willing to grow up and take responsibility for my life. I forgive others and I now create my own life the way I want it. I am safe.
—Arms	Anger at being denied love	It is safe for me to create all the love I want.

—Belly	Anger at being denied nourishment.	I nourish myself with spiritual food, and I am satisfied and free.
—Hips	Lumps of stubborn anger at the parents.	I am willing to forgive the past. It is safe for me to go beyond my parents' limitations.
—Thighs	Packed childhood anger. Often rage at the father.	I see my father as a loveless child, and I forgive easily. We are both free.
Fatigue	Resistance, boredom. Lack of love for what one does.	I am enthusiastic about life and filled with energy and enthusiasm.
Feet *See: Foot Problems*	Represents our understanding—of ourselves, of life, of others.	My understanding is clear, and I am willing to change with the times. I am safe.
Female Problems *See: Amenorrhea, Dysmenorrhea, Fibroid Tumors, Leukorrhea, Menstrual Problems, Vaginitis*	Denial of the self. Rejecting femininity. Rejection of the feminine principle.	I rejoice in my femaleness. I love being a woman. I love my body.
Fertility Problems	Fear. Worry about not being good enough. Resistance to the process of life.	I love and cherish my inner child. I love and adore myself. I am the most important person in my life. All is well and I am safe.
Fever	Anger. Burning up.	I am the cool, calm expression of peace and love.
Fever Blisters *See: Cold Sores, Herpes Simplex*		
Fibroid Tumors & Cysts *See: Female Problems*	Nursing a hurt from a partner. A blow to the feminine ego.	I release the pattern in me that attracted this experience. I create only good in my life.
Fingers	Represent the details of life.	I am peaceful with the details of life.
—Thumb	Represents intellect and worry.	My mind is at peace.
—Index Finger	Represents ego and fear.	I am secure.

—Middle Finger	Represents anger and sexuality.	I am comfortable with my sexuality.
—Ring Finger	Represents unions and grief.	I am peacefully loving.
—Little Finger	Represents the family and pretending.	I am myself with the family of Life.
Fistula	Fear. Blockage in the letting-go process.	I am safe. I trust fully in the process of life. Life is for me.
Flatulence *See: Gas Pains*		
Flu *See: Influenza*		
Food Poisoning	Allowing others to take control. Feeling defenseless.	I have the strength, power, and skill to digest whatever comes my way.
Foot problems	Fear of the future and of not stepping forward in life.	I move forward in life with joy and with ease.
Frigidity	Fear. Denial of pleasure. A belief that sex is bad. Insensitive partners. Fear of father.	It is safe for me to enjoy my own body. I rejoice in being a woman.
Fungus	Stagnating beliefs. Refusing to release the past. Letting the past rule today.	I live in the present moment, joyous and free.
Furuncle *See: Boils*		
Gallstones (Cholelithiasis)	Bitterness. Hard thoughts. Condemning. Pride.	There is joyous release of the past. Life is sweet, and so am I.
Gangrene	Mental morbidity. Drowning of joy with poisonous thoughts.	I now choose harmonious thoughts and let the joy flow freely through me.
Gas Pains (Flatulence)	Gripping. Fear. Undigested ideas.	I relax and let life flow through me with ease.
Gastritis *See: Stomach Problems*	Prolonged uncertainty. A feeling of doom.	I love and approve of myself. I am safe.
Genitals	Represents the masculine and feminine principles.	It is safe to be who I am.

—Problems	Worry about not being good enough.	I rejoice in my own expression of life. I am perfect just as I am. I love and approve of myself.
Gland(s)	Represent holding stations. Self-starting activity.	I am a creative power in my world.
Glandular Fever *See: Mononucleosis*		
Glandular Problems	Poor distribution of get-up-and-go ideas. Holding yourself back.	I have all the Divine ideas and activity I need. I move forward right now.
Globus Hystericus *See: Lump in Throat*		
Goiter *See: Thyroid*	Hatred for being inflicted upon. Victim. Feeling thwarted in life. Unfulfilled.	I am the power and authority in my life. I am free to be me.
Gonorrhea *See: Venereal Dis-ease*	A need for punishment for being a bad person.	I love my body. I love my sexuality. I love me.
Gout	The need to dominate. Impatience, anger.	I am safe and secure. I am at peace with myself and with others.
Gray Hair	Stress. A belief in pressure and strain.	I am at peace and comfortable in every area of my life. I am strong and capable.
Growths	Nursing those old hurts. Building resentments.	I easily forgive. I love myself and will reward myself with thoughts of praise.
Gum Problems	Inability to back up decisions. Wishy-washy about life.	I am a decisive person. I follow through and support myself with love.
Halitosis *See: Bad Breath*	Rotten attitudes, vile gossip, foul thinking.	I speak with gentleness and love. I exhale only the good.
Hands	Hold and handle. Clutch and grip. Grasping and letting go. Caressing. Pinching. All ways of dealing with experiences.	I choose to handle all my experiences with love and with joy and with ease.

Hay Fever *See: Allergies*	Emotional congestion. Fear of the calendar. A belief in persecution. Guilt.	I am one with ALL OF LIFE. I am safe at all times.
Headaches *See: Migraine Headaches*	Invalidating the self. Self-criticism. Fear.	I love and approve of myself. I see myself and what I do with eyes of love. I am safe.
Heart *See: Blood*	Represents the center of love and security.	My heart beats to the rhythm of love.
—**Attack (M.I./ Myocardial Infarction)** *See: Coronary Thrombosis*	Squeezing all the joy out of the heart in favor of money or position, etc.	I bring joy back to the center of my heart. I express love to all.
—**Problems**	Long-standing emotional problems. Lack of joy. Hardening of the heart. Belief in strain and stress.	Joy. Joy. Joy. I lovingly allow joy to flow through my mind and body and experience.
Heartburn *See: Peptic Ulcer, Stomach Problems, Ulcers*	Fear. Fear. Fear. Clutching fear.	I breathe freely and fully. I am safe. I trust the process of life.
Hematochezia *See: Anorectal Bleeding*		
Hemorrhoids *See: Anus*	Fear of deadlines. Anger of the past. Afraid to let go. Feeling burdened.	I release all that is unlike love. There is time and space for everything I want to do.
Hepatitis *See: Liver Problems*	Resistance to change. Fear, anger, hatred. Liver is the seat of anger and rage.	My mind is cleansed and free. I leave the past and move forward into the new. All is well.
Hernia	Ruptured relationships. Strain, burdens, incorrect creative expression.	My mind is gentle and harmonious. I love and approve of myself. I am free to be me.
Herpes (Herpes Genitalis) *See: Venereal Dis-ease*	Mass belief in sexual guilt and the need for punishment. Public shame. Belief in a punishing God. Rejection of the genitals.	My concept of God supports me. I am normal and natural. I rejoice in my own sexuality and in my own body. I am wonderful.

Herpes Simplex (Herpes Labialis) *See: Cold Sores*	Burning to bitch. Bitter words left unspoken.	I think and speak only words of love. I am at peace with life.
Hip(s)	Carries the body in perfect balance. Major thrust in moving forward.	Hip Hip Hooray—there is joy in every day. I am balanced and free.
Hip Problems	Fear of going forward in major decisions. Nothing to move forward to.	I am in perfect balance. I move forward in life with ease and with joy at every age.
Hirsutism	Anger that is covered over. The blanket used is usually fear. A desire to blame. There is often an unwillingness to nurture the self.	I am a loving parent to myself. I am covered with love and approval. It is safe for me to show who I am.
Hives (Urticaria) *See: Rash*	Small, hidden tears. Mountains out of molehills.	I bring peace to every corner of my life.
Hodgkin's Dis-ease	Blame and a tremendous fear of not being good enough. A frantic race to prove oneself until the blood has no substance left to support itself. The joy of life is forgotten in the race for acceptance.	I am perfectly happy to be me. I am good enough just as I am. I love and approve of myself. I am joy expressing and receiving.
Holding Fluids *See: Edema, Swelling*	What are you afraid of losing?	I willingly release with joy.
Huntington's Dis-ease	Resentment at not being able to change others. Hopelessness.	I release all control to the Universe. I am at peace with myself and with life.
Hyperactivity	Fear. Feeling pressured and frantic.	I am safe. All pressure dissolves. I AM good enough.
Hyperglycemia *See: Diabetes*		
Hyperopia *See: Eye Problems*		
Hypertension *See: Blood Problems*		

| Hyperthyroidism

See: Thyroid	Rage at being left out.	I am at the center of life, and I approve of myself and all that I see.
Hyperventilation

See: Asphyxiating Attacks, Breathing Problems | Fear. Resisting change. Not trusting the process. | I am safe everywhere in the Universe. I love myself and trust the process of life. |
| Hypoglycemia | Overwhelmed by the burdens in life. "What's the use?" | I now choose to make my life light and easy and joyful. |
| Hypothyroidism

See: Thyroid | Giving up. Feeling hopelessly stifled. | I create a new life with new rules that totally support me. |
Ileitis (Crohn's Dis-ease, Regional Enteritis)	Fear. Worry. Not feeling good enough.	I love and approve of myself. I am doing the best I can. I am wonderful. I am at peace.
Impotence	Sexual pressure, tension, guilt. Social beliefs. Spite against a previous mate. Fear of mother.	I now allow the full power of my sexual principle to operate with ease and with joy.
Incontinence	Emotional overflow. Years of controlling the emotions.	I am willing to feel. It is safe for me to express my emotions. I love myself.
Incurable	Cannot be cured by outer means at this point. We must go within to effect the cure. It came from nowhere and will go back to nowhere.	Miracles happen every day. I go within to dissolve the pattern that created this, and I now accept a Divine healing. And so it is!
Indigestion	Gut-level fear, dread, anxiety. Griping and grunting.	I digest and assimilate all new experiences peacefully and joyously.
Infection

See: Viral Infection | Irritation, anger, annoyance. | I choose to be peaceful and harmonious. |
| Infertility

See: Fertility Problems | | |
| Inflammation

See: "Itis" | Fear. Seeing red. Inflamed thinking. | My thinking is peaceful, calm, and centered. |

Influenza *See: Respiratory Ailments*	Response to mass negativity and beliefs. Fear. Belief in statistics.	I am beyond group beliefs or the calendar. I am free from all congestion and influence.
Ingrown Toenail	Worry and guilt about your right to move forward.	It is my Divine right to take my own direction in life. I am safe. I am free.
Injuries *See: Cuts, Wounds*	Anger at the self. Feeling guilty.	I now release anger in positive ways. I love and appreciate myself.
Insanity (Psychiatric Illness)	Fleeing from the family. Escapism, withdrawal. Violent separation from life.	This mind knows its true identity and its creative point of Divine Self-Expression.
Insomnia	Fear. Not trusting the process of life. Guilt.	I lovingly release the day and slip into peaceful sleep, knowing tomorrow will take care of itself.
Intestines *See: Colon*	Assimilation. Absorption. Elimination with ease.	I easily assimilate and absorb all that I need to know and release the past with joy.
Itching (Pruritis)	Desires that go against the grain. Unsatisfied. Remorse. Itching to get out or get away.	I am at peace just where I am. I accept my good, knowing that all my needs and desires will be fulfilled.
"Itis" *See: Inflammation*	Anger and frustration about conditions you are looking at in your life.	I am willing to change all patterns of criticism. I love and approve of myself.
Jaundice *See: Liver Problems*	Internal and external prejudice. Unbalanced reason.	I feel tolerance and compassion and love for all people, myself included.
Jaw Problems (Temporomandibular Joint [TMJ] Syndrome)	Anger. Resentment. Desire for revenge.	I am willing to change the patterns in me that created this condition. I love and approve of myself. I am safe.
Joints *See: Arthritis, Elbow, Knee, Shoulders*	Represent changes in direction in life and the ease of these movements.	I easily flow with change. My life is Divinely guided, and I am always going in the best direction.
Keratitis *See: Eye Problems*	Extreme anger. A desire to hit those or what you see.	I allow the love from my own heart to heal all that I see. I choose peace. All is well in my world.

Kidney Problems	Criticism, disappointment, failure. Shame. Reacting like a little kid.	Divine right action is always taking place in my life. Only good comes from each experience. It is safe to grow up.
Kidney Stones	Lumps of undissolved anger.	I dissolve all past problems with ease.
Knee *See: Joints*	Represents pride and ego.	I am flexible and flowing.
Knee Problems	Stubborn ego and pride. Inability to bend. Fear. Inflexibility. Won't give in.	Forgiveness. Understanding. Compassion. I bend and flow with ease, and all is well.
Laryngitis	So mad you can't speak. Fear of speaking up. Resentment of authority.	I am free to ask for what I want. It is safe to express myself. I am at peace.
Left Side of Body	Represents receptivity, taking in, feminine energy, women, the mother.	My feminine energy is beautifully balanced.
Leg(s)	Carry us forward in life.	Life is for me.
Leg Problems —Lower	Fear of the future. Not wanting to move.	I move forward with confidence and joy, knowing that all is well in my future.
Leprosy	Inability to handle life at all. A long-held belief in not being good enough or clean enough.	I rise above all limitations. I am Divinely guided and inspired. Love heals all life.
Leukemia *See: Blood Problems*	Brutally killing inspiration. "What's the use?"	I move beyond past limitations into the freedom of the now. It is safe to be me.
Leukorrhea *See: Female Problems, Vaginitis*	A belief that women are powerless over the opposite sex. Anger at a mate.	I create all my experiences. I am the power. I rejoice in my femaleness. I am free.
Liver	Seat of anger and primitive emotions.	Love and peace and joy are what I know.
Liver Problems *See: Hepatitis, Jaundice*	Chronic complaining. Justifying fault-finding to deceive yourself. Feeling bad.	I choose to live through the open space in my heart. I look for love and find it everywhere.

Lockjaw *See: Tetanus*	Anger. A desire to control. A refusal to express feelings.	I trust the process of my life. I easily ask for what I want. Life supports me.
Lou Gehrig's Dis-ease *See: Amyotrophic Lateral Sclerosis*		
Lump in Throat (Globus Hystericus)	Fear. Not trusting the process of life.	I am safe. I trust that Life is here for me. I express myself freely and joyously.
Lung	The ability to take in life.	I take in life in perfect balance.
—Problems *See: Pneumonia*	Depression. Grief. Fear of taking in life. Not feeling worthy of living life fully.	I have the capacity to take in the fullness of life. I lovingly live life to the fullest.
Lupus (Erythematosis)	A giving up. Better to die than stand up for one's self. Anger and punishment.	I speak up for myself freely and easily. I claim my own power. I love and approve of myself. I am free and safe.
Lymph Problems	A warning that the mind needs to be recentered on the essentials of life. Love and joy.	I am now totally centered in the love and joy of being alive. I flow with life. Peace of mind is mine.
Malaria	Out of balance with nature and with life.	I am united and balanced with all of my life. I am safe.
Mastitis *See: Breast Problems*		
Mastoiditis	Anger and frustration. A desire not to hear what is going on. Usually in children. Fear infecting the understanding.	Divine peace and harmony surround and indwell me. I am an oasis of peace and love and joy. All is well in my world.
Mellitus *See: Diabetes*		
Menopause Problems	Fear of no longer being wanted. Fear of aging. Self-rejection. Not feeling good enough.	I am balanced and peaceful in all changes of cycles, and I bless my body with love.

Menstrual Problems *See: Amenorrhea, Dysmenorrhea, Female Problems*	Rejection of one's femininity. Guilt, fear. Belief that the genitals are sinful or dirty.	I accept my full power as a woman and accept all my bodily processes as normal and natural. I love and approve of myself.
Migraine Headaches *See: Headaches*	Dislike of being driven. Resisting the flow of life. Sexual fears. (Can usually be relieved by masturbation.)	I relax into the flow of life and let life provide all that I need easily and comfortably. Life is for me.
Miscarriage (Abortion, Spontaneous)	Fear. Fear of the future. "Not now—later." Inappropriate timing.	Divine right action is always taking place in my life. I love and approve of myself. All is well.
Mono, Mononucleosis (Pfeiffer's Disease, Glandular Fever)	Anger at not receiving love and appreciation. No longer caring about the self.	I love and appreciate and take care of myself. I am enough.
Motion Sickness *See: Car Sickness, Seasickness*	Fear. Fear of not being in control.	I am always in control of my thoughts. I am safe. I love and approve of myself.
Mouth	Represents taking in of new ideas and nourishment.	I nourish myself with love.
—Problems	Set opinions. Closed mind. Incapacity to take in new ideas.	I welcome new ideas and new concepts and prepare them for digestion and assimilation.
Mucus Colon *See: Colitis, Colon, Intestines, Spastic Colitis*	Layered deposits of old, confused thoughts clogging the channel of elimination. Wallowing in the gummed mire of the past.	I release and dissolve the past. I am a clear thinker. I live now in peace and joy.
Multiple Sclerosis	Mental hardness, hard-heartedness, iron will, inflexibility. Fear.	By choosing loving, joyous thoughts, I create a loving, joyous world. I am safe and free.
Muscles	Resistance to new experiences. Muscles represent our ability to move in life.	I experience life as a joyous dance.

Muscular Dystrophy	"It's not worth growing up."	I go beyond my parents' limitations. I am free to be the best me I can.
Myocardial Infarction *See: Heart Attack*		
Myopia *See: Eye Problems*	Fear of the future. Not trusting what is ahead.	I accept Divine guidance and am always safe.
Nail(s)	Represents protection.	I reach out safely.
Nail Biting	Frustration. Eating away at the self. Spite of a parent.	It is safe for me to grow up. I now handle my own life with joy and with ease.
Narcolepsy	Can't cope. Extreme fear. Wanting to get away from it all. Not wanting to be here.	I rely on Divine wisdom and guidance to protect me at all times. I am safe.
Nausea	Fear. Rejecting an idea or experience.	I am safe. I trust the process of life to bring only good to me.
Nearsightedness *See: Eye Problems, Myopia*		
Neck (Cervical Spine)	Represents flexibility. The ability to see what's back there.	I am peaceful with life.
Neck Problems	Refusing to see other sides of a question. Stubbornness, inflexibility.	It is with flexibility and ease that I see all sides of an issue. There are endless ways of doing things and seeing things. I am safe.
Nephritis *See: Bright's Disease*	Overreaction to disappointment and failure.	Only right action is taking place in my life. I release the old and welcome the new. All is well.
Nerves	Represent communication. Receptive reporters.	I communicate with ease and with joy.
Nervous Breakdown	Self-centeredness. Jamming the channels of communication.	I open my heart and create only loving communication. I am safe. I am well.

Nervousness	Fear, anxiety, struggle, rushing. Not trusting the process of life.	I am on an endless journey through eternity, and there is plenty of time. I communicate with my heart. All is well.
Neuralgia	Punishment for guilt. Anguish over communication.	I forgive myself. I love and approve of myself. I communicate with love.
Nodules	Resentment and frustration and hurt ego over career.	I release the pattern of delay within me, and I now allow success to be mine.
Nose	Represents self-recognition.	I recognize my own intuitive ability.
—Bleeds	A need for recognition. Feeling unrecognized and unnoticed. Crying for love.	I love and approve of myself. I recognize my own true worth. I am wonderful.
—Runny	Asking for help. Inner crying.	I love and comfort myself in ways that are pleasing to me.
—Stuffy	Not recognizing the self-worth.	I love and appreciate myself.
Numbness (Parasthesia)	Withholding love and consideration. Going dead mentally.	I share my feelings and my love. I respond to love in everyone.
Osteomyelitis *See: Bone Problems*	Anger and frustration at the very structure of life. Feeling unsupported.	I am peaceful with and trust the process of life. I am safe and secure.
Osteoporosis *See: Bone Problems*	Feeling there is no support left in life.	I stand up for myself, and Life supports me in unexpected, loving ways.
Ovaries	Represent point of creation. Creativity.	I am balanced in my creative flow.
Overweight *See: Fat*	Fear, need for protection. Running away from feelings. Insecurity, self-rejection. Seeking fulfillment.	I am at peace with my own feelings. I am safe where I am. I create my own security. I love and approve of myself.
Paget's Dis-ease	Feeling there is no longer any foundation to build on. "Nobody cares."	I know I am supported by Life in grand and glorious ways. Life loves me and cares for me.

Pain	Guilt. Guilt always seeks punishment.	I lovingly release the past. They are free and I am free. All is well in my heart now.
Palsy *See: Bell's Palsy, Cerebral Palsy, Parkinson's Dis-ease*	Paralyzing thoughts. Getting stuck.	I am a freethinker, and I have wonderful experiences with ease and with joy.
Pancreas	Represents the sweetness of life.	My life is sweet.
Pancreatitis	Rejection. Anger and frustration because life seems to have lost its sweetness.	I love and approve of myself, and I alone create sweetness and joy in my life.
Panic	Fear. Inability to move with the flow of life.	I am capable and strong. I can handle all situations in my life. I know what to do.
Paralysis See: Palsy	Fear. Terror. Escaping a situation or person. Resistance.	I am one with all of life. I am totally adequate for all situations.
Parasites	Giving power to others, letting them take over.	I lovingly take back my power and eliminate all interference.
Parkinson's Dis-ease *See: Palsy*	Fear and an intense desire to control everything and everyone.	I relax knowing I am safe. Life trusts me, and I trust the process of life.
Peptic Ulcer *See: Heartburn, Stomach Problems, Ulcers*	Fear. A belief that you are not good enough. Anxious to please.	I love and approve of myself. I am at peace with myself. I am wonderful.
Periodontitis *See: Pyorrhea*		
Petit Mal *See: Epilepsy*		
Pfeiffer's Dis-ease *See: Mononucleosis*		
Phlebitis	Anger and frustration. Blaming others for the limitations and lack of joy in life.	Joy now flows freely within me, and I am at peace with life.

Piles *See: Hemorrhoids*		
Pimples *See: Blackheads, Whiteheads*	Small outbursts of anger.	I calm my thoughts, and I am serene.
Pink Eye *See: Conjunctivitis*	Anger and frustration. Not wanting to see.	I release the need to be right. I am at peace. I love and approve of myself.
Pituitary Gland	Represents the control center.	My mind and body are in perfect balance. I control my thoughts.
Plantar Wart	Anger at the very basis of your understanding. Spreading frustration about the future.	I move forward with confidence and ease. I trust and flow with the process of life.
Pneumonia *See: Lung Problems*	Desperate. Tired of life. Emotional wounds that are not allowed to heal.	I freely take in Divine ideas that are filled with the breath and intelligence of Life. This is a new moment.
Poison Ivy	Feeling defenseless and open to attack.	I am powerful, safe, and secure. All is well.
Poison Oak *See: Poison Ivy*		
Polio	Paralyzing jealously. A desire to stop someone.	There is enough for everyone. I create my good and my freedom with loving thoughts.
Postnasal Drip	Inner crying. Childish tears. Victim.	I acknowledge and accept that I am the creative power in my world. I now choose to enjoy my life.
Premenstrual Syndrome (PMS)	Allowing confusion to reign. Giving power to outside influences. Rejection of the feminine processes.	I now take charge of my mind and my life. I am a powerful, dynamic woman! Every part of my body functions perfectly. I love me.
Prostate	Represents the masculine principle.	I love and approve of myself. I accept my own power. I am forever young in spirit.

Prostate Problems	Mental fears weaken the masculinity. Giving up. Sexual pressure and guilt. Belief in aging.	I accept and rejoice in my masculinity.
Pruritus *See: Itching*		
Pruritus Ani *See: Anus*		
Psoriasis *See: Skin Problems*	Fear of being hurt. Deadening the senses of the self. Refusing to accept responsibility for your own feelings.	I am alive to the joys of living. I deserve and accept the very best in life. I love and approve of myself.
Psychiatric Illness *See: Insanity*		
Pubic Bone	Represent genital protection.	My sexuality is safe.
Pyelonephritis *See: Urinary Infections*		
Pyorrhea (Periodontitis)	Anger at the inability to make decisions. Wishy-washy people.	I approve of myself, and my decisions are always perfect for me.
Quinsy (Peritonsillar Abscess) *See: Sore Throat, Tonsillitis*	A strong belief that you cannot speak up for yourself and ask for your needs.	It is my birthright to have my needs met. I now ask for what I want with love and with ease.
Rabies	Anger. A belief that violence is the answer.	I am surrounded and indwelled with peace.
Rash *See: Hives*	Irritation over delays. Babyish way to get attention.	I love and approve of myself. I am at peace with the process of life.
Rectum *See: Anus*		

Respiratory Ailments *See: Bronchitis, Colds, Coughs, Influenza*	Fear of taking in life fully.	I am safe. I love my life.
Rheumatism	Feeling victimized. Lack of love. Chronic bitterness. Resentment.	I create my own experiences. As I love and approve of myself and others, my experiences get better and better.
Rheumatoid Arthritis	Deep criticism of authority. Feeling very put-upon.	I am my own authority. I love and approve of myself. Life is good.
Rickets	Emotional malnutrition. Lack of love and security.	I am secure and am nourished by the love of the Universe itself.
Right Side of Body	Giving out, letting go, masculine energy, men, the father.	I balance my masculine energy easily and effortlessly.
Ringworm	Allowing others to get under your skin. Not feeling good enough or clean enough.	I love and approve of myself. No person, place, or thing has any power over me. I am free.
Root Canal *See: Teeth*	Can't bite into anything anymore. Root beliefs being destroyed.	I create firm foundations for myself and for my life. I choose my beliefs to support me joyously.
Round Shoulders *See: Shoulders, Spinal Curvature*	Carrying the burdens of life. Helpless and hopeless.	I stand tall and free. I love and approve of me. My life gets better every day.
Sagging Lines	Sagging lines on the face come from sagging thoughts in the mind. Resentment of life.	I express the joy of living and allow myself to enjoy every moment of every day totally. I become young again.
Scabies	Infected thinking. Allowing others to get under your skin.	I am the living, loving, joyous expression of life. I am my own person.
Sciatica	Being hypocritical. Fear of money and of the future.	I move into my greater good. My good is everywhere, and I am secure and safe.

Scleroderma	Protecting the self from life. Not trusting yourself to be there and to take care of yourself.	I relax completely, for I now know I am safe. I trust life and I trust myself.
Scoliosis *See: Round Shoulders, Spinal Curvature*		
Scratches	Feeling life tears at you, life is a ripoff, and that you are being ripped off.	I am grateful for life's generosity to me. I am blessed.
Seasickness *See: Motion Sickness*	Fear. Fear of death. Lack of control.	I am totally safe in the Universe. I am at peace everywhere. I trust Life.
Seizures	Running away from the family, from the self, or from life.	I am at home in the Universe. I am safe and secure and understood.
Senility *See: Alzheimer's Dis-ease*	Returning to the so-called safety of childhood. Demanding care and attention. A form of control of those around you. Escapism.	Divine protection. Safety. Peace. The intelligence of the Universe operates on every level of life.
Shin(s)	Breaking down ideals. Shins represent the standards of life.	I live up to my highest standards with love and with joy.
Shingles (Varicella)	Waiting for the other shoe to drop. Fear and tension. Too sensitive.	I am relaxed and peaceful because I trust in the process of life. All is well in my world.
Shoulders *See: Joints, Round Shoulders*	Represent our ability to carry out experiences in life joyously. We make life a burden by our attitude.	I choose to allow all my experiences to be joyous and loving.
Sickle-Cell Anemia	A belief that one is not good enough, which destroys the very joy of life.	This child lives and breathes in the joy of life and is nourished by love. God works miracles every day.
Sinus Problems (Sinusitis)	Irritation to one person, someone close.	I declare peace and harmony indwell me and surround me at all times. All is well.

Skeleton *See: Bones*	Crumbling of structure. Bones represent the structure of your life.	I am strong and sound. I am well structured.
Skin	Protects our individuality. A sense organ.	I feel safe to be me.
Skin problems *See: Hives, Psoriasis, Rash*	Anxiety, fear. Old, buried guck. I am being threatened.	I lovingly protect myself with thoughts of joy and peace. The past is forgiven and forgotten. I am free in this moment.
Slipped Disc	Feeling totally unsupported by life. Indecisive.	Life supports all of my thoughts; therefore, I love and approve of myself and all is well.
Snoring	Stubborn refusal to let go of old patterns.	I release all that is unlike love and joy in my mind. I move from the past into the new and fresh and vital.
Solar Plexus	Gut reactions. Center of our intuitive power.	I trust my inner voice. I am strong, wise, and powerful.
Sores	Unexpressed anger that settles in.	I express my emotions in joyous, positive ways.
Sore Throat *See: Quinsy, Throat, Tonsillitis*	Holding in angry words. Feeling unable to express the self.	I release all restrictions, and I am free to be me.
Spasms	Tightening our thoughts through fear.	I release, I relax, and I let go. I am safe in life.
Spastic Colitis *See: Colitis, Colon, Intestines, Mucus Colon*	Fear of letting go. Insecurity.	It is safe for me to live. Life will always provide for me. All is well.
Spinal Curvature (Scoliosis Kyphosis) *See: Round Shoulders*	The inability to flow with the support of Life. Fear and trying to hold on to old ideas. Not trusting life. Lack of integrity. No courage of conviction.	I release all fears. I now trust the process of life. I know that life is for me. I stand straight and tall with love.
Spinal Meningitis	Inflamed thinking and rage at life.	I release all blame and accept the peacefulness and joy of life.
Spine	Flexible support of life.	I am supported by Life.

Spleen	Obsessions. Being obsessed about things.	I love and approve of myself. I trust the process of life to be there for me. I am safe. All is well.
Sprains	Anger and resistance. Not wanting to move in a certain direction in life.	I trust the process of life to take me to only my highest good. I am at peace.
Sterility	Fearful and resistance to the process of life, OR not needing to go through the parenting experience.	I trust in the process of life. I am always in the right place, doing the right thing, at the right time. I love and approve of myself.
Stiff Neck *See: Neck Problems*	Unbending bullheadedness.	It is safe to see other viewpoints.
Stiffness	Rigid, stiff thinking.	I am safe enough to be flexible in my mind.
Stomach	Holds nourishment. Digests ideas.	I digest life with ease.
Stomach Problems *See: Gastritis, Heartburn, Peptic Ulcer, Ulcers*	Dread. Fear of the new. Inability to assimilate the new.	Life agrees with me. I assimilate the new every moment of every day. All is well.
Stroke (Cerebrovascular Accident/CVA)	Giving up. Resistance. "Rather die than change." Rejection of life.	Life is change, and I adapt easily to the new. I accept life—past, present, and future.
Stuttering	Insecurity. Lack of self-expression. Not being allowed to cry.	I am free to speak up for myself. I am now secure in my own expression. I communicate only with love.
Sty *See: Eye Problems*	Looking at life through angry eyes. Angry at someone.	I choose to see everyone and everything with joy and love.
Suicide	See life only in black and white. Refusal to see another way out.	I live in the totality of possibilities. There is always another way. I am safe.
Swelling *See: Edema, Holding Fluids*	Being stuck in thinking. Clogged, painful ideas.	My thoughts flow freely and easily. I move through ideas with ease.

Syphilis *See: Venereal Disease*	Giving away your power and effectiveness.	I decide to be me. I approve of myself as I am.
Tapeworm	Strong belief in being a victim or unclean. Helpless to the seeming attitudes of others.	Others only reflect the good feelings I have about myself. I love and approve of all that I am.
Teeth	Represent decisions.	
—Decay	Inability to make decisions. Tendency to give up easily.	I fill my decisions with love and compassion. My new decisions support me and strengthen me. I have new ideas and put them into action. I am safe in my new decisions.
—Problems	Long-standing indecisiveness. Inability to break down ideas for analysis and decisions.	I make decisions based on the principles of truth, and I rest securely knowing that only right action is taking place in my life.
Temporomandibular Joint *See: Jaw Problems*		
Testicles	Masculine principles. Masculinity.	It is safe to be a man.
Tetanus *See: Lockjaw*	A need to release angry, festering thoughts.	I allow the love from my own heart to wash through me and cleanse and heal every part of my body and my emotions.
Throat	Avenue of expression. Channel of creativity.	I open my heart and sing the joys of love.
—Problems *See: Sore Throat*	The inability to speak up for one's self. Swallowed anger. Stifled creativity. Refusal to change.	It is okay to make noise. I express myself freely and joyously. I speak up for myself with ease. I express my creativity. I am willing to change.

Thrush *See: Candida, Mouth, Yeast Infections*	Anger over making the wrong decisions.	I lovingly accept my decisions, knowing I am free to change. I am safe.
Thymus	Master gland of the immune system. Feeling attacked by Life. They are out to get me.	My loving thoughts keep my immune system strong. I am safe inside and out. I hear myself with love.
Thyroid *See: Goiter, Hyperthyroidism, Hypothyroidism*	Humiliation. "I never get to do what I want to do. When is it going to be my turn?"	I move beyond old limitations and now allow myself to express freely and creatively.
Tics, Twitches	Fear. A feeling of being watched by others.	I am approved of by all Life. All is well. I am safe.
Tinnitus	Refusal to listen. Not hearing the inner voice. Stubbornness.	I trust my Higher Self. I listen with love to my inner voice. I release all that is unlike the action of love.
Toes	Represent the minor details of the future.	All details take care of themselves.
Tongue	Represents the ability to taste the pleasures of life with joy.	I rejoice in all of my life's bountiful givingness.
Tonsillitis *See: Quinsy, Sore Throat*	Fear. Repressed emotions. Stifled creativity.	My good now flows freely. Divine ideas express through me. I am at peace.
Tooth Problems *See: Root Canal*	Long-standing indecisiveness. Inability to break down ideas for analysis and decisions.	I make my decisions based on the principles of truth, and I rest securely, knowing that only right action is taking place in my life.
Tuberculosis	Wasting away from selfishness. Possessiveness. Cruel thoughts. Revenge.	As I love and approve of myself, I create a joyful, peaceful world to live in.
Tumors	Nursing old hurts and shocks. Building remorse.	I lovingly release the past and turn my attention to this new day. All is well.

Ulcers *See: Heartburn, Peptic Ulcer, Stomach Problems*	Fear. A strong belief that you are not good enough. What is eating away at you?	I love and approve of myself. I am at peace. I am calm. All is well.
Urethritis	Angry, emotions. Being pissed off. Blame.	I only create joyful experiences in my life.
Urinary infections (Cystitis, Pyelonephritis)	Pissed off. Usually at the opposite sex or a lover. Blaming others.	I release the pattern in my consciousness that created this condition. I am willing to change. I love and approve of myself.
Urticaria *See: Hives*		
Uterus	Represents the home of creativity.	I am at home in my body.
Vaginitis *See: Female Problems, Leukorrhea*	Anger at a mate. Sexual guilt. Punishing the self.	Others mirror the love and self-approval I have for myself. I rejoice in my sexuality.
Varicella *See: Shingles*		
Varicose Veins	Standing in a situation you hate. Discouragement. Feeling overworked and overburdened.	I stand in truth and live and move in joy. I love Life, and circulate freely.
Vasovagal Attack *See: Fainting*		
Venereal Dis-ease *See: AIDS, Gonorrhea, Herpes, Syphilis*	Sexual guilt. Need for punishment. Believe that the genitals are sinful or dirty. Abusing another.	I lovingly and joyously accept my sexuality and its expression. I accept only thoughts that support me and make me feel good.
Vertigo *See: Dizziness*		
Viral Infections *See: Infection*	Lack of joy flowing through life. Bitterness.	I lovingly allow joy to flow freely in my life. I love me.

Vitiligo	Feeling completely outside of things. Not belonging. Not one of the group.	I am at the very center of Life, and I am totally connected in Love.
Vomiting	Violent rejection of ideas. Fear of the new.	I digest life safely and joyously. Only good comes to me and through me.
Vulva	Represents vulnerability.	It is safe to be vulnerable.
Warts	Little expressions of hate. Belief in ugliness.	I am the love and the beauty of Life in full expression.
Weakness	A need for mental rest.	I give my mind a joyous vacation.
Whiteheads *See: Pimples*	Hiding ugliness.	I accept myself as beautiful and loved.
Wisdom Tooth, Impacted	Not giving yourself mental space to create a firm foundation.	I open my consciousness to the expansion of life. There is plenty of space for me to grow and to change.
Wounds *See: Cuts, Injuries*	Anger and guilt at the self.	I forgive myself, and I choose to love myself.
Wrist	Represents movement and ease.	I handle all my experiences with wisdom, with love, and with ease.
Yeast Infections *See: Candida, Thrush*	Denying your own needs. Not supporting yourself.	I now choose to support myself in loving, joyous ways.

A Final Note from Louise

Thank you, dear readers, for coming on this journey with me. Creating this book with Mona Lisa has provided ample opportunity for me to learn even more about my own work. I now have a much deeper understanding of what I have been teaching for years. I see the depth of patterns—both in wellness and in disease—and how these affect our lives. And I see even more vividly just how connected our thoughts, emotions, and health are.

I know you will use the information in this book to create a healthy and happy life. Here's to a new wave of personal healing!

Endnotes

First Emotional Center

1. M.L. Laudenslager et al., "Suppression of Specific Antibody Production by Inescapable Shock," *Brain, Behavior, and Immunity* 2, no. 2 (June 1988): 92–101; M.L. Laudenslager et al., "Suppressed Immune Response in Infant Monkeys Associated with Maternal Separation," *Behavioral Neural Biology* 36, no. 1 (September 1982): 40–48; S. Cohen and T. Wills, "Stress, Social Support, and the Buffering Hypothesis," *Psychological Bulletin* 98, no. 2 (September 1985): 310–357; J. Kiecolt-Glaser et al., "Psychosocial Modifiers of Immunocompetence in Medical Students," *Psychosomatic Medicine* 46, no. 1 (January 1984): 7–14; M. Seligman et al., "Coping Behavior," *Behaviour Research and Therapy* 18, no. 5 (1980): 459–512.

2. M. Mussolino, "Depression and Hip Fractures Risk," *Public Health Reports* 120, no. 1 (January–February 2005): 71–75; J. Serovich et al., "The Role of Family and Friend Social Support in Reducing Emotional Distress Among HIV-positive Women," *AIDS Care* 13, no. 3 (June 2001): 335–341; P. Solomon et al., eds., *Sensory Deprivation* (Cambridge, Mass.: Harvard University Press, 1961); E. Lindemann, "The Symptomatology and Management of Acute Grief," *American Journal of Psychiatry* 101 (1944): 141–148.

3. G. Luce, *Biological Rhythms in Psychiatry and Medicine, Public Health Service Publication No. 288* (Washington, D.C.: National Institutes of Mental Health, 1970); J. Vernikos-Danellis and C.M. Wingest, "The Importance of Social Cues in the Regulation of Plasma Cortisol in Man," in A. Reinberg and F. Halbers, eds., *Chronopharmacology* (New York: Pergamon, 1979).

4. M. Moore-Ede et al., *The Clocks That Time Us* (Cambridge, Mass.: Harvard University Press, 1961).

5. J. Chiang et al., "Negative and Competitive Social Interactions are Related to Heightened Proinflammatory Cytokine Activity," *Proceedings of National Academy of Sciences of the USA* 109, no. 6 (February 7, 2012): 1878–1882; S. Hayley, "Toward an Anti-inflammatory Strategy for Depression," *Frontiers in Behavioral Neuroscience* 5 (April 2011): 19; F. Eskandari et al., "Low Bone Mass in Premenopausal Women With Depression," *Archives of Internal Medicine* 167, no. 21 (November 26, 2007): 2329–2336.

6. L. LeShan, "An Emotional Life-History Pattern Associated with Neoplastic Disease," *Annals of the New York Academy of Sciences* 125, no. 3 (January 21, 1966): 780–793.

7. R. Schuster et al., "The Influence of Depression on the Progression of HIV: Direct and Indirect Effects," *Behavior Modification* 36, no. 2 (March 2012): 123–145; J.R. Walker et al., "Psychiatric Disorders in Patients with Immune-Mediated Inflammatory Diseases: Prevalence, Association with Disease Activity, and Overall Patient Well-Being," *Journal of Rheumatology Supplement* 88 (November 2011): 31–35; D. Umberson and J.K. Montez, "Social Relationships and Health: A Flashpoint for Health Policy," *Journal of Health and Social Behavior* 51 (2010): S54–S66; M. Hofer, "Relationships as Regulators," *Psychosomatic Medicine* 46, no. 3 (May 1984): 183–197; C.B. Thomas et al., "Family Attitudes Reported in Youth as Potential Predictors of Cancer," *Psychosomatic Medicine* 41 (June 1979): 287–302; C.B. Thomas and K.R. Duszynski, "Closeness to Parents and the Family Constellation in a Prospective Study of Five Disease States: Suicide, Mental Illness, Malignant Tumor, Hypertension and Coronary Heart Disease," *Johns Hopkins Medical Journal* 134, no. 5 (May 1974): 251–70; C.B. Thomas and R.L. Greenstreet, "Psychobiological Characteristics in Youth as Predictors of Five Disease States: Suicide, Mental Illness, Hypertension, Coronary Heart Disease and Tumor," *Johns Hopkins Medical Journal* 132, no. 1 (January 1973): 16–43; L.D. Egbert et al., "Reduction of Post-operative Pain by Encouragement and Instruction of Patients," *New England Journal of Medicine* 270 (April 16, 1964): 825–827.

8. F. Poot et al., "A Case-control Study on Family Dysfunction in Patients with Alopecia Areata, Psoriasis and Atopic Dermatitis," *Acta Dermato-Venereologica* 91, no. 4 (June 2011): 415–421.

9. S. Cohen et al., "Social Ties and Susceptibility to the Common Cold," *Journal of the American Medical Association* 277, no. 24 (June 25, 1997): 1940–1944; J. House et al., "Social Relationships and Health," *Science* 241, no. 4865 (July 29, 1988): 540–545; L.D. Egbert et al., "Reduction of Postoperative Pain by Encouragement and Instruction of Patients. A Study of Doctor-Patient Rapport," *New England Journal of Medicine* 16 (April 1964): 825–827.

10. R.P. Greenberg and P.J. Dattore, "The Relationship Between Dependency and the Development of Cancer," *Psychosomatic Medicine* 43, no. 1 (February 1981): 35–43.

11. T.M. Vogt et al., "Social Networks as Predictors of Ischemic Heart Disease, Cancer, Stroke, and Hypertension: Incidence, Survival and Mortality," *Journal of Clinical Epidemiology* 45, no. 6 (June 1992): 659–666; L.F. Berkman and

S.L. Syme, "Social Networks, Host Resistance, and Mortality: A Nine-Year Follow-up Study of Alameda County Residents," *American Journal of Epidemiology* 109, no. 2 (February 1979): 186–204; S.B. Friedman et al., "Differential Susceptibility to a Viral Agent in Mice Housed Alone or in Groups," *Psychosomatic Medicine* 32, no. 3 (May–June 1970): 285–299.

12. U. Schweiger et al., "Low Lumbar Bone Mineral Density in Patients with Major Depression: Evidence of Increased Bone Loss at Follow-Up," *American Journal of Psychiatry* 157, no. 1 (January 2000): 118–120; U. Schweiger et al., "Low Lumbar Bone Mineral Density in Patients with Major Depression," *American Journal of Psychiatry* 151, no. 11 (November 1994): 1691–1693.

Second Emotional Center

1. A. Ambresin et al., "Body Dissatisfaction on Top of Depressive Mood Among Adolescents with Severe Dysmenorrhea," *Journal of Pediatric and Adolescent Gynecology* 25, no. 1 (February 2012): 19–22;

2. P. Nepomnaschy et al., "Stress and Female Reproductive Function," *American Journal of Human Biology* 16, no. 5 (September–October 2004): 523–532; B. Meaning, "The Emotional Needs of Infertile Couples," *Fertility and Sterility* 34, no. 4 (October 1980): 313–319; B. Sandler, "Emotional Stress and Infertility," *Journal of Psychosomatic Research* 12, no. 1 (June 1968): 51–59; B. Eisner, "Some Psychological Differences between Fertile and Infertile Women," *Journal of Clinical Psychology* 19, no. 4 (October 1963): 391–395; J. Greenhill, "Emotional Factors in Female Infertility," *Obstetrics & Gynecology* 7, no. 6 (June 1956): 602–607.

3. F. Judd et al., "Psychiatric Morbidity in Gynecological Outpatients," *Journal of Obstetrics and Gynaecology Research* 38, no. 6 (June 2012): 905–911; D. Hellhammer et al., "Male Infertility," *Psychosomatic Medicine* 47, no. 1 (January–February 1985): 58–66; R.L. Urry, "Stress and Infertility," in: A.T.K. Cockett and R.L. Urry, eds., *Male Infertility* (New York: Grune & Stratton, 1977), 145–162.

4. Niravi Payne, *The Language of Fertility* (New York: Harmony Books, 1997); Christiane Northrup, *Women's Bodies, Women's Wisdom* (New York: Bantam, 1994), 353; A. Domar et al., "The Prevalence and Predictability of Depression in Infertile Women," *Fertility & Sterility* 58, no. 6 (December 1992): 1158–1163; P. Kemeter, "Studies on Psychosomatic Implications of Infertility on Effects of Emotional Stress on Fertilization and Implantation in In Vitro Fertilization," *Human Reproduction* 3, no. 3 (1988): 341–352; S. Segal et al., "Serotonin and 5-hydroxyindoleacetic Acid in Fertile and Subfertile Men," *Fertility & Sterility* 26, no. 4 (April 1975): 314–316; R. Vanden Burgh et al., "Emotional Illness in Habitual Aborters Following Suturing of Incompetent Os," *Psychosomatic Medicine* 28, no. 3 (1966): 257–263; B. Sandler, "Conception after Adoption," *Fertility & Sterility* 16 (May–June 1965): 313–333; T. Benedek et al., "Some Emotional Factors in Fertility," *Psychosomatic Medicine* 15, no. 5 (1953): 485–498.

5.   H.B. Goldstein et al., "Depression, Abuse and Its Relationship to Internal
     Cystitis," *International Urogynecology Journal and Pelvic Floor Dysfunction* 19,
     no. 12 (December 2008): 1683–1686; R. Fry, "Adult Physical Illness and
     Childhood Sexual Abuse," *Journal of Psychosomatic Research* 37, no. 2 (1993):
     89–103; R. Reiter et al., "Correlation between Sexual Abuse and Somatization
     in Women with Somatic and Nonsomatic Pelvic Pain," *American Journal
     of Obstetrics and Gynecology* 165, no. 1 (July 1991): 104–109; G. Bachmann
     et al., "Childhood Sexual Abuse and the Consequences in Adult Women,"
     Obstetrics and Gynecology 71, no. 4 (April 1988): 631–642.

6.   S. Ehrström et al., "Perceived Stress in Women with Recurrent Vulvovaginal
     Candidiasis," *Journal of Psychosomatic Obstetrics and Gynaecology* 28, no. 3
     (September 2007): 169–176; C. Wira and C. Kauschic, "Mucosal Immunity
     in the Female Reproductive Tract," in H. Kiyono et al., eds., *Mucosal
     Vaccines* (New York: Academic Press, 1996); J.L. Herman, *Father-Daughter
     Incest* (Cambridge, Mass.: Harvard University Press, 1981); R.J. Gross et
     al., "Borderline Syndrome and Incest in Chronic Pelvic Pain Patients,"
     International Journal of Psychiatry in Medicine 10, no. 1 (1980–1981): 79–96;
     A. Pereya, "The Relationship of Sexual Activity to Cervical Cancer," *Obstetrics
     & Gynecology* 17, no. 2 (February 1961): 154–159; M. Tarlan and I. Smalheiser,
     "Personality Patterns in Patients with Malignant Tumors of the Breast and
     Cervix," *Psychosomatic Medicine* 13, no. 2 (March–April 1951): 117–121.

7.   K. Goodkin et al., "Stress and Hopelessness in the Promotion of Cervical
     Intraepithelial Neoplasia to Invasive Squamous Cell Carcinoma of the
     Cervix," *Journal of Psychosomatic Research* 30, no. 1 (1986): 67–76; A. Schmale
     and H. Iker, "Hopelessness as a Predictor of Cervical Cancer," *Social Science
     & Medicine* 5, no. 2 (April 1971): 95–100; M. Antoni and K. Goodkin, "Host
     Moderator Variables in the Promotion of Cervical Neoplasia-I," *Journal of
     Psychosomatic Research* 32, no. 3 (1988): 327–338; A. Schmale and H. Iker,
     "The Psychological Setting of Uterine and Cervical Cancer," *Annals of the
     New York Academy of Sciences* 125 (1966): 807–813; J. Wheeler and
     B. Caldwell, "Psychological Evaluation of Women with Cancer of the Breast
     and Cervix," *Psychosomatic Medicine* 17, no. 4 (1955): 256–268; J. Stephenson
     and W. Grace, "Life Stress and Cancer of the Cervix," *Psychosomatic Medicine*
     16, no. 4 (1954): 287–294.

8.   S. Currie and J. Wang, "Chronic Back Pain and Major Depression in the
     General Canadian Population," *Pain* 107, nos. 1 and 2 (January 2004):
     54–60; B.B. Wolman, *Psychosomatic Disorders* (New York: Plenum Medical
     Books, 1988); S. Kasl et al., "The Experience of Losing a Job," *Psychosomatic
     Medicine* 37, no. 2 (March 1975): 106–122; S. Cobb, "Physiological Changes
     in Men Whose Jobs Were Abolished," *Journal of Psychosomatic Research* 18,
     no. 4 (August 1974): 245–258; T.H. Holmes and H.G. Wolff, "Life Situations,
     Emotions, and Backache," *Psychosomatic Medicine* 14, no. 1 (January–
     February 1952): 18–32.

9.   S.J. Linton and L.E. Warg, "Attributions (Beliefs) and Job Dissatisfaction
     Associated with Back Pain in an Industrial Setting," *Perceptual and Motor Skills*
     76, no. 1 (February 1993): 51–62.

10. K. Matsudaira et al., "Potential Risk Factors for New Onset of Back Pain Disability in Japanese Workers: Findings from the Japan Epidemiological Research of Occupation-Related Back Pain Study," *Spine* 37, no. 15 (July 1, 2012): 1324–1333; M.T. Driessen et al., "The Effectiveness of Physical and Organisational Ergonomic Interventions on Low Back Pain and Neck Pain: A Systematic Review," *Occupational and Environmental Medicine* 67, no. 4 (April 2010): 277–285; N. Magnavita, "Perceived Job Strain, Anxiety, Depression and Musculo-Skeletal Disorders in Social Care Workers," *Giornale Italiano di Medicina del Lavoro ed Ergonomia* 31, no. 1, suppl. A (January–March 2009): A24–A29.

11. S. Saarijarvi et al., "Couple Therapy Improves Mental Well-being in Chronic Lower Back Pain Patients," *Journal of Psychosomatic Research* 36, no. 7 (October 1992): 651–656.

Third Emotional Center

1. D. O'Malley et al., "Do Interactions Between Stress and Immune Responses Lead to Symptom Exacerbations in Irritable Bowel Syndrome?" *Brain, Behavior, and Immunity* 25, no. 7 (October 2011): 1333–1341; C. Jansson et al., "Stressful Psychosocial Factors and Symptoms of Gastroesophageal Reflux Disease: a Population-based Study in Norway," *Scandinavian Journal of Gastroenterology* 45, no. 1 (2010): 21–29; J. Sareen et al., "Disability and Poor Quality of Life Associated With Comorbid Anxiety Disorders and Physical Conditions," *Archives of Internal Medicine* 166, no. 19 (October 2006): 2109–2116; R.D. Goodwin and M.B. Stein, "Generalized Anxiety Disorder and Peptic Ulcer Disease Among Adults in the United States," *Psychosomatic Medicine Journal of Behavioral Medicine* 64, no. 6 (November–December 2002): 862–866; P.G. Henke, "Stomach Pathology and the Amygdala," in J.P. Aggleton, ed., *The Amygdala: Neurobiological Aspects of Emotion, Memory, and Mental Dysfunction* (New York: Wiley-Liss, 1992): 323–338.

2. L.K. Trejdosiewicz et al., "Gamma Delta T Cell Receptor-positive Cells of the Human Gastrointestinal Mucosa: Occurrence and V Region Expression in Heliobacter Pylori-Associated Gastritis, Celiac Disease, and Inflammatory Bowel Disease," *Clinical and Experimental Immunology* 84, no. 3 (June 1991): 440–444.

3. T.G. Digan and J.F. Cryan, "Regulation of the Stress Response by the Gut Microbiota: Implications for Psychoneuroendocrinology," *Psychoneuroendocrinology* 37, no. 9 (September 2012): 1369–1378; G.B. Glavin, "Restraint Ulcer: History, Current Research and Future Implications," *Brain Research Bulletin* Supplement, no. 5 (1980): 51–58.

4. J.M. Lackner et al., "Self Administered Cognitive Behavior Therapy for Moderate to Severe IBS: Clinical Efficacy, Tolerability, Feasibility," *Clinical Gastroenterology and Hepatology* 6, no. 8 (August 2008): 899–906; F. Alexander, "Treatment of a Case of Peptic Ulcer and Personality Disorder," *Psychosomatic Medicine* 9, no. 5 (September 1947): 320–330; F. Alexander, "The Influence of Psychologic Factors upon Gastro-Intestinal Disturbances: A Symposium—I.

General Principles, Objectives, and Preliminary Results," *Psychoanalytic Quarterly* 3 (1934): 501–539.

5. S.J. Melhorn et al., "Meal Patterns and Hypothalamic NPY Expression During Chronic Social Stress and Recovery," *American Journal of Physiology Regulatory, Integrative and Comparative Physiology* 299, no. 3 (July 2010): R813–R822; I.K. Barker et al., "Observations on Spontaneous Stress-Related Mortality Among Males of the Dasyurid Marsupial Antechinus Stuartii Macleay," *Australian Journal of Zoology* 26, no. 3 (1978): 435–447; J.L. Barnett, "A Stress Response in Som Antechinus Stuartii (Macleay)," *Australian Journal of Zoology* 21, no. 4 (1973): 501–513; R. Ader, "Effects of Early Experience and Differential Housing on Susceptibility to Gastric Erosions in Lesion-Susceptible Rats," *Psychosomatic Medicine Journal of Behavioral Medicine* 32, no. 6 (November 1970): 569–580.

6. G.L. Flett et al., "Perfectionism, Psychosocial Impact and Coping with Irritable Bowel Disease: A study of Patients with Crohn's Disease and Ulcerative colitis," *Journal of Health Psychology* 16, no. 4 (May 2011): 561–571; P. Castelnuovo-Tedesco, "Emotional Antecedents of Perforation of Ulcers of the Stomach and Duodenum," *Psychosomatic Medicine* 24, no. 4 (July 1962): 398–416.

7. R.K. Gundry et al., "Patterns of Gastric Acid Secretion in Patients with Duodenal Ulcer: Correlations with Clinical and Personality Features," *Gastroenterology* 52, no. 2 (February 1967): 176–184; A. Stenback, "Gastric Neurosis, Pre-ulcers Conflict, and Personality in Duodenal Ulcer," *Journal of Psychosomatic Research* 4 (July 1960): 282–296; W.B. Cannon, "The Influence of Emotional States on the Functions of the Alimentary Canal," *The American Journal of the Medical Sciences* 137, no. 4 (April 1909): 480–486.

8. E. Fuller-Thomson et al., "Is Childhood Physical Abuse Associated with Peptic Ulcer Disease? Findings From a Population-based Study," *Journal of Interpersonal Violence* 26, no. 16 (November 2011): 3225–3247; E.J. Pinter et al., "The Influence of Emotional Stress on Fat Mobilization: The Role of Endogenous Catecholamines and the Beta Adrenergic Receptors," *The American Journal of the Medical Sciences* 254, no. 5 (November 1967): 634–651.

9. S. Minuchin et al., "Psychosomatic Families: Anorexia Nervosa in Context," (Harvard University Press, 1978): 23–29; G.L. Engel, "Studies of Ulcerative Colitis: V. Psychological Aspects and Their Implications for Treatment," *The American Journal of Digestive Diseases and Nutrition* 3, no. 4 (April 1958): 315–337; J.J. Groen and J.M. Van der Valk, "Psychosomatic Aspects of Ulcerative Colitis," *Gastroenterologia* 86, no. 5 (1956): 591–608; G.L. Engel, "Studies of Ulcerative Colitis. III. The Nature of the Psychologic Process," *The American Journal of Medicine* 19, no. 2 (August 1955): 231–256.

10. S.J. Melhorn et al., "Meal Patterns and Hypothalamic NPY Expression During Chronic Social Stress and Recovery," *American Journal of Physiology-Regulatory, Integrative and Comparative Physiology* 299, no. 3 (September 2010): R813–R822; P.V. Cardon, Jr., and P.S. Mueller, "A Possible Mechanism: Psychogenic Fat Mobilization," *Annals of the New York Academy of Sciences* 125 (January 1966): 924–927; P.V. Cardon, Jr., and R.S. Gordon, "Rapid

Increase of Plasma Unesterified Fatty Acids in Man during Fear," *Journal of Psychosomatic Research* 4 (August 1959): 5–9; M.D. Bogdonoff et al., "Acute Effect of Psychologic Stimuli upon Plasma Non-esterified Fatty Acid Level," *Experimental Biology and Medicine* 100, no. 3 (March 1959): 503–504.

11. R.N. Melmed et al., "The Influence of Emotional State on the Mobilization of Marginal Pool Leukocytes after Insulin-Induced Hypoglycemia. A Possible Role for Eicosanoids as Major Mediators of Psychosomatic Processes," *Annals of the New York Academy of Sciences* 496 (May 1987): 467–476; H. Rosen and T. Lidz, "Emotional Factors in the Precipitation of Recurrent Diabetic Acidosis," *Psychosomatic Medicine Journal of Behavioral Medicine* 11, no. 4 (July 1949): 211–215; A. Meyer et al., "Correlation between Emotions and Carbohydrate Metabolism in Two Cases of Diabetes Mellitus," *Psychosomatic Medicine Journal of Behavioral Medicine* 7, no. 6 (November 1945): 335–341.

12. S.O. Fetissov and P. Déchelotte, "The New Link between Gut-Brain Axis and Neuropsychiatric Disorders," *Current Opinion in Clinical Nutrition and Metabolic Care* 14, no. 5 (September 2011): 477–482; D. Giugliano et al., "The Effects of Diet on Inflammation: Emphasis on the Metabolic Syndrome," *Journal of the American College of Cardiology* 48, no. 4 (August 2006): 677–685; G. Seematter et al., "Stress and Metabolism," *Metabolic Syndrome and Related Disorders* 3, no. 1 (2005): 8–3; A.M. Jacobson and J.B. Leibovitch, "Psychological Issues in Diabetes Mellitus," *Psychosomatics: Journal of Consultation Liaison Psychiatry* 25, no. 1 (January 1984): 7–15; S.L. Werkman and E.S. Greenberg, "Personality and Interest Patterns in Obese Adolescent Girls," *Psychosomatic Medicine Journal of Biobehavirial Medicine* 29, no. 1 (January 1967): 72–80.

13. J.H. Fallon et al., "Hostility Differentiates the Brain Metabolic Effects of Nicotine," *Cognitive Brain Research* 18, no. 2 (January 2004): 142–148; R.N. Melmed et al., "The Influence of Emotional Stress on the Mobilization of Marginal Pool Leukocytes after Insulin-Induced Hypoglycemia. A Possible Role for Eicosanoids as Major Mediators of Psychosomatic Processes," *Annals of the New York Academy of Sciences* 496 (May 1987): 467–476; P.V. Cardon Jr. and P.S. Mueller, "A Possible Mechanism: Psychogenic Fat Mobilization," *Annals of the New York Academy of Sciences* 125 (January 1966): 924–927; M.D. Bogdonoff et al., "Acute Effect of Psychologic Stimuli upon Plasma Non-Esterified Fatty Acid Level," *Experimental Biology and Medicine* 100, no. 3 (March 1959): 503–504; P.V. Cardon, Jr., and R.S. Gordon, "Rapid Increase of Plasma Unesterified Fatty Acids in Man during Fear," *Journal of Psychosomatic Research* 4 (August 1959): 5–9; A. Meyer et al., "Correlation between Emotions and Carbohydrate Metabolism in Two Cases of Diabetes Mellitus," *Psychosomatic Medicine Journal of Behavioral Medicine* 7, no. 6 (November 1945): 335–341.

Fourth Emotional Center

1. H.P. Kapfhammer, "The Relationship between Depression, Anxiety and Heart Disease—a Psychosomatic Challenge," *Psychiatr Danubina* 23, no. 4 (December 2011): 412–424; B.H. Brummett et al., "Characteristics of Socially

Isolated Patients With Coronary Artery Disease Who Are at Elevated Risk for Mortality," *Psychosomatic Medicine Journal of Biobehavioral Medicine* 63, no. 2 (March 2001): 267–272; W.B. Cannon, *Bodily Changes in Pain, Hunger, Fear and Rage* (New York: D. Appleton & Co., 1929).

2. K.S. Whittaker et al., "Combining Psychosocial Data to Improve Prediction of Cardiovascular Disease Risk Factors and Events: The National Heart, Lung, and Blood Institute–Sponsored Women's Ischemia Syndrome Evaluation Study," *Psychosomatic Medicine Journal of Biobehavioral Medicine* 74, no. 3 (April 2012): 263–270; A. Prasad et al., "Apical Ballooning Syndrome (Tako-Tsubo or Stress Cardiomyopathy): A mimic of Acute Myocardial Infarction," *American Heart Journal* 155, no. 3 (March 2008): 408–417; Wittstein, I.S. et al. "Neurohumoral Features of Myocardial Stunning Due to Sudden Emotional Stress," *The New England Journal of Medicine* 352, no. 6 (February 2005): 539–548; M.A. Mittleman et al., "Triggering of Acute Myocardial Infarction Onset of Episodes of Anger," *Circulation* 92 (1995): 1720–1725; G. Ironson et al., "Effects of Anger on Left Ventricular Ejection Fraction in Coronary Artery Disease," *American Journal of Cardiology* 70, no. 3 (August 1992): 281–285; R.D. Lane and G.E. Schwartz, "Induction of Lateralized Sympathetic Input to the Heart by the CNS During Emotional Arousal: A Possible Neurophysiologic Trigger of Sudden Cardiac Death," *Psychosomatic Medicine* 49, no. 3 (May–June 1987): 274–284; S.G. Haynes et al., "The Relationship of Psychosocial Factors to Coronary Heart Disease in the Framingham Study. III. Eight-Year Incidence of Coronary Heart Disease," *American Journal of Epidemiology* 111, no. 1 (January 1980): 37–58.

3. T.W. Smith et al., "Hostility, Anger, Aggressiveness, and Coronary Heart Disease: An Interpersonal Perspective on Personality, Emotion, and Health." *Journal of Personality* 72, no. 6 (December 2004): 1217–1270; T.M. Dembroski et al., "Components of Hostility as Predictors of Sudden Death and Myocardial Infarction in the Multiple Risk Factor Intervention Trial," *Psychosomatic Medicine* 51, no. 5 (September–October 1989): 514–522; K.A. Matthews et al., "Competitive Drive, Pattern A, and Coronary Heart Disease," *Journal of Chronic Diseases* 30, no. 8 (August 1977): 489–498; I. Pilowsky et al., "Hypertension and Personality," *Psychosomatic Medicine* 35, no. 1 (January–February 1973): 50–56.

4. M.D. Boltwood et al., "Anger Reports Predict Coronary Artery Vasomotor Response to Mental Stress in Atherosclerotic Segments," *American Journal of Cardiology* 72, no. 18 (December 15, 1993): 1361–1365; P.P. Vitaliano et al., "Plasma Lipids and Their Relationships with Psychosocial Factors in Older Adults," *Journal of Gerontology, Series B, Psychological Sciences and Social Sciences* 50, no. 1 (January 1995): 18–24.

5. H.S. Versey and G.A. Kaplan, "Mediation and Moderation of the Association Between Cynical Hostility and Systolic Blood Pressure in Low-Income Women," *Health Education & Behavior* 39, no. 2 (April 2012): 219–228.

6. P.J. Mills and J.E. Dimsdale, "Anger Suppression: Its Relationship to Beta-Adrenergic Receptor Sensitivity and Stress-Induced Changes in Blood Pressure," *Psychological Medicine* 23, no. 3 (August 1993): 673–678.

7.   M.Y. Gulec et al., "Cloninger's Temperament and Character Dimension of Personality in Patients with Asthma," *International Journal of Psychiatry in Medicine* 40, no. 3 (2010): 273–287; P.M. Eng et al., "Anger Expression and Risk of Stroke and Coronary Heart Disease Among Male Health Professionals," *Psychosomatic Medicine* 65, no. 1 (January–February 2003): 100–110; L. Musante et al., "Potential for Hostility and Dimensions of Anger," *Health Psychology* 8, no. 3 (1989): 343–354; M.A. Mittleman et al., "Triggering of Acute Myocardial Infarction Onset of Episodes of Anger," *Circulation* 92 (1995): 1720–1725; M. Koskenvuo et al., "Hostility as a Risk Factor for Mortality and Ischemic Heart Disease in Men," *Psychosomatic Medicine* 50, no. 4 (July–August 1988): 330–340; J.E. Williams et al, "The Association Between Trait Anger and Incident Stroke Risk: The Atherosclerosis Risk in Communities (ARIC) Study," *Stroke* 33, no. 1 (January 2002): 13–19; N. Lundberg et al., "Type A Behavior in Healthy Males and Females as Related to Physiological Reactivity and Blood Lipids," *Psychosomatic Medicine* 51, no. 2 (March–April 1989): 113–122; G. Weidner et al., "The Role of Type A Behavior and Hostility in an Elevation of Plasma Lipids in Adult Women and Men," *Psychosomatic Medicine* 49, no. 2 (March–April 1987): 136–145.

8.   L.H. Powell et al., "Can the Type A Behavior Pattern Be Altered after Myocardial Infarction? A Second-Year Report for the Recurrent Coronary Prevention Project," *Psychosomatic Medicine* 46, no. 4 (July–August 1984): 293–313.

9.   D. Giugliano et al., "The Effects of Diet on Inflammation: Emphasis on the Metabolic Syndrome," *Journal of the American College of Cardiology* 48, no. 4 (August 15, 2006): 677–685; C.M. Licht et al., "Depression Is Associated With Decreased Blood Pressure, but Antidepressant Use Increases the Risk for Hypertension," *Hypertension* 53, no. 4 (April 2009): 631–638; G. Seematter et al., "Stress and Metabolism," *Metabolic Syndrome and Related Disorders* 3, no. 1 (2005): 8–13; I. Pilowsky et al., "Hypertension and Personality," *Psychosomatic Medicine* 35, no. 1 (January–February 1973): 50–56; J.P. Henry and J.C. Cassel, "Psychosocial Factors in Essential Hypertension. Recent Epidemiologic and Animal Experimental Evidence," *American Journal of Epidemiology* 90, no. 3 (September 1969): 171–200.

10.   P.J. Clayton, "Mortality and Morbidity in the First Year of Widowhood," *Archives of General Psychiatry* 30, no. 6 (June 1974): 747–750; C.M. Parkes and R.J. Brown, "Health After Bereavement: A Controlled Study of Young Boston Widows and Widowers," *Psychosomatic Medicine* 34, no. 5 (September–October 1972): 449–461; M. Young et al., "The Mortality of Widowers," *The Lancet* 282, no. 7305 (August 1963): 454–457.

11.   W.T. Talman, "Cardiovascular Regulation and Lesions of the Central Nervous System," *Annals of Neurology* 18, no. 1 (July 1985): 1–13; P.D. Wall and G.D. Davis, "Three Cerebral Cortical Systems Affecting Autonomic Function," *Journal of Neurophysiology* 14, no. 6 (November 1951): 507–517; G.R. Elliot and C. Eisdorfer, *Stress and Human Health: Analysis and Implications of Research* (New York: Springer, 1982).

12. R.J. Tynan et al., "A Comparative Examination of the Anti-inflammatory Effects of SSRI and SNRI Antidepressants on LPS Stimulated Microglia," *Brain, Behavior, and Immunity* 26, no. 3 (March 2012): 469–479; L. Mehl-Madrona, "Augmentation of Conventional Medical Management of Moderately Severe or Severe Asthma with Acupuncture and Guided Imagery/Meditation," *The Permanente Journal* 12, no. 4 (Fall 2008): 9–14.

13. A.C. Ropoteanu, "The Level of Emotional Intelligence for Patients with Bronchial Asthma and a Group Psychotherapy Plan in 7 Steps," *Romanian Journal of Internal Medicine* 49, no. 1 (2011): 85–91.

14. C. Jasmin et al., "Evidence for a Link Between Certain Psychological Factors and the Risk of Breast Cancer in a Case-Control Study. Psycho-Oncologic Group (P.O.G.)," *Annals of Oncology* 1, no. 1 (1990): 22–29; M. Tarlau and I. Smalheiser, "Personality Patterns in Patients with Malignant Tumors of the Breast and Cervix," *Psychosomatic Medicine* 13, no. 2 (March 1951): 117–121; L. LeShan, "Psychological States as Factors in the Development of Malignant Disease: A Critical Review," *Journal of the National Cancer Institute* 22, no. 1 (January 1959): 1–18; H. Becker, "Psychodynamic Aspects of Breast Cancer. Differences in Younger and Older Patients," *Psychotherapy and Psychosomatics* 32, nos. 1–4 (1979): 287–296; H. Snow, *The Proclivity of Women to Cancerous Diseases and to Certain Benign Tumors* (London: J. & A. Churchill, 1891); H. Snow, *Clinical Notes on Cancer* (London: J. & A. Churchill, 1883).

15. D. Razavi et al., "Psychosocial Correlates of Oestrogen and Progesterone Receptors in Breast Cancer," *The Lancet* 335, no. 3695 (April 21, 1990): 931–933; S.M. Levy et al., "Perceived Social Support and Tumor Estrogen/ Progesterone Receptor Status as Predictors of Natural Killer Cell Activity in Breast Cancer Patients," *Psychosomatic Medicine* 52, no. 1 (January–February 1990): 73–85; S. Levy et al., "Correlation of Stress Factors with Sustained Depression of Natural Killer Cell Activity and Predicted Prognosis in Patients with Breast Cancer," *Journal of Clinical Oncology* 5, no. 3 (March 1987): 348–353; A. Brémond et al., "Psychosomatic Factors in Breast Cancer Patients: Results of a Case Control Study," *Journal of Psychosomatic Obstetrics & Gynecology* 5, no. 2 (January 1986): 127–136; K.W. Pettingale et al., "Mental Attitudes to Cancer: An Additional Prognostic Factor," *The Lancet* 1, no. 8431 (March 1985): 750; M. Wirsching et al., "Psychological Identification of Breast Cancer Patients before Biopsy," *Journal of Psychosomatic Research* 26, no. 1 (1982): 1–10; K.W. Pettingale et al., "Serum IgA and Emotional Expression in Breast Cancer Patients," *Journal of Psychosomatic Research* 21, no. 5 (1977): 395–399.

16. M. Eskelinen and P. Ollonen, "Assessment of 'Cancer-prone Personality' Characteristics in Healthy Study Subjects and in Patients with Breast Disease and Breast Cancer Using the Commitment Questionnaire: A Prospective Case–Control Study in Finland," *Anticancer Research* 31, no. 11 (November 2011): 4013–4017.

17. J. Giese-Davis et al., "Emotional Expression and Diurnal Cortisol Slope in Women with Metastatic Breast Cancer in Supportive-Expressive Group Therapy: A Preliminary Study," *Biological Psychology* 73, no. 2 (August 2006): 190–198; D. Spiegel et al., "Effect of Psychosocial Treatment on Survival of

Patients with Metastatic Breast Cancer," *The Lancet* 2, no. 8668 (October 14, 1989): 888–891; S.M. Levy et al., "Prognostic Risk Assessment in Primary Breast Cancer by Behavioral and Immunological Parameters," *Health Psychology* 4, no. 2 (1985): 99–113; S. Greer et al., "Psychological Response to Breast Cancer: Effect of Outcome," *The Lancet* 314, no. 8146 (October 13, 1979): 785–787.

Fifth Emotional Center

1. A.W. Bennett and C.G. Cambor, "Clinical Study of Hyperthyroidism: Comparison of Male and Female Characteristics," *Archives of General Psychiatry* 4, no. 2 (February 1961): 160–165.

2. American Association of University Women, *Shortchanging Girls, Shortchanging America* (Washington, D.C.: American Association of University Women, 1991); G. Johansson et al., "Examination Stress Affects Plasma Levels of TSH and Thyroid Hormones Differently in Females and Males," *Psychosomatic Medicine* 49, no. 4 (July–August 1987): 390–396; J.A. Sherman, *Sex-Related Cognitive Differences: An Essay on Theory and Evidence,* (Springfield, Ill.: Charles C. Thomas, 1978).

3. K. Yoshiuchi et al., "Stressful Life Events and Smoking Were Associated With Graves' Disease in Women, but Not in Men," *Psychosomatic Medicine* 60, no. 2 (March–April 1998): 182–185; J.L. Griffith and M.E. Griffith, *The Body Speaks: Therapeutic Dialogues for Mind-Body Problems* (New York: Basic Books, 1994); D. Kimura, "Sex Differences in Cerebral Organization for Speech and Praxic Functions," *Canadian Journal of Psychology* 37, no. 1 (March 1983): 19–35.

4. G. Johansson et al., "Examination Stress Affects Plasma Levels of TSH and Thyroid Hormones Differently in Females and Males," *Psychosomatic Medicine* 49, no. 4 (July–August 1987): 390–396.

5. S.K. Gupta et al., "Thyroid Gland Responses to Intermale Aggression in an Inherently Aggressive Wild Rat," *Endokrinologie* 80, no. 3 (November 1982): 350–352.

6. American Association of University Women, *Shortchanging Girls, Shortchanging America* (Washington, D.C.: American Association of University Women, 1991).

7. American Association of University Women, *Shortchanging Girls, Shortchanging America* (Washington, D.C.: American Association of University Women, 1991).

8. H. Glaesmer et al., "The Association of Traumatic Experiences and Posttraumatic Stress Disorder with Physical Morbidity in Old Age: A German Population-Based Study," *Psychosomatic Medicine* 73, no. 5 (June 2011): 401–406; T. Mizokami et al., "Stress and Thyroid Autoimmunity," *Thyroid* 14, no. 12 (December 2004): 1047–1055; V.R. Radosavljevi et al., "Stressful

Life Events in the Pathogenesis of Graves' Disease," *European Journal of Endocrinology* 134, no. 6 (June 1996): 699–701; N. Sonino et al., "Life Events in the Pathogenesis of Graves' Disease: A Controlled Study," *Acta Endocrinologica* 128, no. 4 (April 1993): 293–296; T. Harris et al., "Stressful Life Events and Graves' Disease," *The British Journal of Psychiatry* 161 (October 1992): 535–541; B. Winsa et al., "Stressful Life Events and Graves' Disease," *The Lancet* 338, no. 8781 (December 14, 1991): 1475–1479; S.A. Weisman, "Incidence of Thyrotoxicosis among Refugees from Nazi Prison Camps," *Annals of Internal Medicine* 48, no. 4 (April 1958): 747–752.

9. I.J. Cook et al., "Upper Esophageal Sphincter Tone and Reactivity to Stress in Patients with a History of Globus Sensation," *Digestive Diseases and Sciences* 34, no. 5 (May 1989): 672–676; J.P. Glaser and G.L. Engel, "Psychodynamics, Psychophysiology and Gastrointestinal Symptomatology," *Clinics in Gastroenterology* 6, no. 3 (September 1977): 507–531.

10. B. Rai et al., "Salivary Stress Markers, Stress, and Periodontitis: A Pilot Study," *Journal of Periodontology* 82, no. 2 (February 2011): 287–292; A.T. Merchant et al., "A Prospective Study of Social Support, Anger Expression and Risk of Periodontitis in Men" *Journal of the American Dental Association* 134, no. 12 (December 2003): 1591–1596; R.J. Genco et al., "Relationship of Stress, Distress and Inadequate Coping Behaviors to Periodontal Disease," *Journal of Periodontology* 70, no. 7 (July 1999): 711–723.

Sixth Emotional Center

1. I. Pilowsky et al., "Hypertension and Personality," *Psychosomatic Medicine* 35, no. 1 (January–February 1973): 50–56; H.O. Barber, "Psychosomatic Disorders of Ear, Nose and Throat," *Postgraduate Medicine* 47, no. 5 (May 1970): 156–159.

2. K. Czubulski et al., "Psychological Stress and Personality in Ménière's Disease," *Journal of Psychosomatic Research* 20, no. 3 (1976): 187–191.

3. A. Brook and P. Fenton, "Psychological Aspects of Disorders of the Eye: A Pilot Research Project," *The Psychiatrist* 18 (1994): 135–137; J. Wiener, "Looking Out and Looking In: Some Reflections on 'Body Talk' in the Consulting Room," *The Journal of Analytic Psychology* 39, no. 3 (July 1994): 331–350; L. Yardley, "Prediction of Handicap and Emotional Distress in Patients with Recurrent Vertigo Symptoms, Coping Strategies, Control Beliefs and Reciprocal Causation," *Social Science and Medicine* 39, no. 4 (1994): 573–581; C. Martin et al., "Ménière's Disease: A Psychosomatic Disease?" *Revue de Laryngologie, Otologie, Rhinologie* 112, no. 2 (1991): 109–111; C. Martin et al., "Psychologic Factor in Ménière's Disease," *Annales d'Oto-laryngologie et de Chirurgie Cervico Faciale* 107, no. 8 (1990): 526–531; M. Rigatelli et al., "Psychosomatic Study of 60 Patients with Vertigo," *Psychotherapy and Psychosomatics* 41, no. 2 (1984): 91–99; F.E. Lucente, "Psychiatric Problems in Otolaryngology," *Annals of Otology, Rhinology, and Laryngology* 82, no. 3 (May–June 1973): 340–346.

4.   V. Raso et al., "Immunological Parameters in Elderly Women: Correlations
      with Aerobic Power, Muscle Strength and Mood State," *Brain, Behavior, and
      Immunity* 26, no. 4 (May 2012): 597–606; O.M. Wolkowitz et al., "Of Sound
      Mind and Body: Depression, Disease, and Accelerated Aging," *Dialogues in
      Clinical Neuroscience* 13, no. 1 (2011): 25–39; M.F. Damholdt et al., "The
      Parkinsonian Personality and Concomitant Depression," *The Journal of
      Neuropsychiatry and Clinical Neurosciences* 23, no. 1 (Fall 2011): 48–55;
      V. Kaasinen et al., "Personality Traits and Brain Dopaminergic Function in
      Parkinson's Disease," *Proceedings of the National Academy of Sciences* 98, no. 23
      (November 6, 2001): 13272–13277; M.A. Menza and M.H. Mark, "Parkinson's
      Disease and Depression: The Relationship to Disability and Personality," *The
      Journal of Neuropsychiatry and Clinical Neurosciences* 6, no. 2 (Spring 1994):
      165–169; G.W. Paulson and N. Dadmehr, "Is There a Premorbid Personality
      Typical for Parkinson's Disease?" *Neurology* 41, no. 5, sup. 2 (May 1991):
      73–76; P. Mouren et al., "Personality of the Parkinsonian: Clinical and
      Psychometric Approach," *Annales Medico-Psychologiques (Paris)* 141, no. 2
      (February 1983): 153–167; R.C. Duvoisin et al., "Twin Study of Parkinson
      Disease," *Neurology* 31, no. 1 (January 1981): 77–80; C.R. Cloninger, "A
      Systematic Method for Clinical Description and Classification of Personality
      Variants," *Archives of General Psychiatry* 44, no. 6 (June 1987): 573–588.

Seventh Emotional Center

1.   A.M. De Vries et al., "Alexithymia in Cancer Patients: Review of the
      Literature," *Psychotherapy and Psychosomatics* 81, no. 2 (2012): 79–86;
      S. Warren et al., "Emotional Stress and Coping in Multiple Sclerosis
      (MS) Exacerbations," *Journal of Psychosomatic Research* 35, no. 1 (1991):
      37–47; V. Mei-Tal et al., "The Role of Psychological Process in a Somatic
      Disorder: Multiple Sclerosis. 1. The Emotional Setting of Illness Onset and
      Exacerbation," *Psychosomatic Medicine* 32, no. 1 (January–February 1970):
      67–86; S. Warren et al., "Emotional Stress and the Development of Multiple
      Sclerosis: Case-Control Evidence of a Relationship," *Journal of Chronic
      Diseases* 35, no. 11 (1982): 821–831.

2.   A. Stathopoulou et al., "Personality Characteristics and Disorders in Multiple
      Sclerosis Patients: Assessment and Treatment," *International Review of
      Psychiatry* 22, no. 1 (2010): 43–54; G.S. Philippopoulos et al., "The Etiologic
      Significance of Emotional Factors in Onset and Exacerbations of Multiple
      Sclerosis; a Preliminary Report," *Psychosomatic Medicine* 20, no. 6 (November–
      December 1958): 458–474; O.R. Langworthy et al., "Disturbances of Behavior
      in Patients with Disseminated Sclerosis," *American Journal of Psychiatry* 98,
      no. 2 (September 1941): 243–249.

3.   X.J. Liu et al., "Relationship Between Psychosocial Factors and Onset of
      Multiple Sclerosis," *European Neurology* 62, no. 3 (2009): 130–136;
      O.R. Langworthy, "Relationship of Personality Problems to Onset and
      Progress of Multiple Sclerosis," *Archives of Neurology Psychiatry* 59, no. 1
      (January 1948): 13–28.

4. C.M. Conti et al., "Relationship Between Cancer and Psychology: An Updated History," *Journal of Biological Regulators and Homeostatic Agents* 25, no. 3 (July–September 2011): 331–339; J.A. Fidler et al., "Disease Progression in a Mouse Model of Amyotrophic Lateral Sclerosis: The Influence of Chronic Stress and Corticosterone," *FASEB Journal* 25, no. 12 (December 2011): 4369–4377.

5. E.R. McDonald et al., "Survival in Amyotrophic Lateral Sclerosis. The Role of Psychological Factors," *Archives of Neurology* 51, no. 1 (January 1994): 17–23.

6. H. Glaesmer et al., "The Association of Traumatic Experiences and Posttraumatic Stress Disorder with Physical Morbidity in Old Age: A German Population-Based Study," *Psychosomatic Medicine* 73, no. 5 (June 2011): 401–406.

7. L. Cohen et al., "Presurgical Stress Management Improves Postoperative Immune Function in Men with Prostate Cancer Undergoing Radical Prostatectomy," *Psychosomatic Medicine* 73, no. 3 (April 2011): 218–225.

Bibliography

First Emotional Center

Bennette, G., "Psychic and Cellular Aspects of Isolation and Identity Impairment in Cancer: A Dialectic Alienation," *Annals of the New York Academy of Sciences* 164 (October 1969): 352–363.

Brown, G.W., et al., "Social Class and Psychiatric Disturbance Among Women in an Urban Population," *Sociology* 9, no. 2 (May 1975): 225–254.

Cobb, S., "Social Support as Moderator of Life Stress," *Psychosomatic Medicine* 38, no. 5 (September–October 1976): 300–314.

Cohen, S., "Social Supports and Physical Health," in E.M. Cummings et al., eds., Life-Span Developmental Psychology: Perspectives on Stress and Coping (Hillsdale, N.J.: Erlbaum, 1991): 213–234.

Goodkin, K., et al., "Active Coping Style is Associated with Natural Killer Cell Cytotoxicity in Asymptomatic HIV-1 Seropositive Homosexual Men," *Journal of Psychosomatic Research* 36, no. 7 (1992): 635–650.

Goodkin, K., et al., "Life Stresses and Coping Style are Associated with Immune Measures in HIV Infection—A Preliminary Report," *International Journal of Psychiatry in Medicine* 22, no. 2 (1992): 155–172.

Jackson, J.K., "The Problem of Alcoholic Tuberculous Patients," in P.J. Sparer, *Personality Stress and Tuberculosis* (New York: International Universities Press, 1956).

Laudenslager, M.L., et al., "Coping and Immunosuppression: Inescapable but not Escapable Shock Suppresses Lymphocyte Proliferation," *Science* 221, no. 4610 (August 1983): 568–570.

Sarason, I.G., et al., "Life Events, Social Support, and Illness," *Psychosomatic Medicine* 47, no. 2 (March–April 1985): 156–163.

Schmale, A.H., "Giving up as a Final Common Pathway to Changes in Health," *Advances in Psychosomatic Medicine* 8 (1972): 20-40.

Spilken, A.Z., and M.A. Jacobs, "Prediction of Illness Behavior from Measures of Life Crisis, Manifest Distress and Maladaptive Coping," *Psychosomatic Medicine* 33, no. 3 (May 1, 1971): 251–264.

Temoshok, L., et al., "The Relationship of Psychosocial Factors to Prognostic Indicators in Cutaneous Malignant Melanoma," *Journal of Psychosomatic Research* 29, no. 2 (1985): 139–153.

Thomas, C.B., and K.R. Duszynski, "Closeness to Parents and Family Constellation in a Prospective Study of Five Disease States," *The Johns Hopkins Medical Journal* 134 (1974): 251–270.

Weiss, J.M., et al., "Effects of Chronic Exposure to Stressors on Avoidance-Escape Behavior and on Brain Norepinephrine," *Psychosomatic Medicine* 37, no. 6 (November–December 1975): 522–534.

Second Emotional Center

Hafez, E., "Sperm Transport," in S.J. Behrman and R.W. Kistner, eds., *Progress in Infertility,* 2d ed. (Boston: Little, Brown, 1975).

Havelock, E., *Studies in the Psychology of Sex* (Philadelphia: Davis, 1928).

Jeker, L., et al., "Wish for a Child and Infertility: Study on 116 Couples," *International Journal of Fertility* 33, no. 6 (November–December 1988): 411–420.

Knight, R.P., "Some Problems in Selecting and Rearing Adopted Children," *Bulletin of the Menninger Clinic* 5 (May 1941): 65–74.

Levy, D.M., "Maternal Overprotection," *Psychiatry* 2 (1939): 99–128.

Mason, J.M., "Psychological Stress and Endocrine Function," in E.J. Sachar, ed., *Topics in Psychoendocrinology* (New York: Grune & Stratton, 1975): 1–18.

Rapkin, A.J., "Adhesions and Pelvic Pain: A Retrospective Study," *Obstetrics and Gynecology* 68, no. 1 (July 1986): 13–15.

Reiter, R.C., "Occult Somatic Pathology in Women with Chronic Pelvic Pain," *Clinical Obstetrics and Gynecology* 33, no. 1 (March 1990): 154–160.

Reiter, R.C., and J.C. Gambore, "Demographic and Historic Variables in Women with Idiopathic Chronic Pelvic Pain," *Obstetrics and Gynecology* 75, no. 3 (March 1990): 428–432.

Slade, P., "Sexual Attitudes and Social Role Orientations in Infertile Women," *Journal of Psychosomatic Research* 25, no. 3 (1981): 183–186.

Van de Velde, T.H., *Fertility and Sterility in Marriage* (New York: Covici Friede, 1931).

Van Keep, P.A., and H. Schmidt-Elmendorff, "Partnerschaft in der Sterilen Ehe," *Medizinische Monatsschrift* 28, no. 12 (1974): 523–527.

Weil, R.J., and C. Tupper, "Personality, Life Situation, and Communication: A Study of Habitual Abortion," *Psychosomatic Medicine* 22, no. 6 (November 1960): 448–455.

Third Emotional Center

Alvarez, W.C., *Nervousness, Indigestion, and Pain* (New York: Hoeber, 1943).

Bradley, A.J., et al., "Stress and Mortality in a Small Marsupial (*Antechinus stuartii*, Macleay)," *General and Comparative Endocrinology* 40, no. 2 (February 1980): 188–200.

Draper, G., and G.A. Touraine, "The Man-Environment Unit and Peptic Ulcers," *Archives of Internal Medicine* 49, no. 4 (April 1932): 616–662.

Dunbar, F., *Emotions and Bodily Changes*, 3d ed. (New York: Columbia University Press, 1947).

Henke, P.G., "The Amygdala and Restraint Ulcers in Rats," *Journal of Comparative Physiology and Psychology* 94, no. 2 (April 1980): 313–323.

Mahl, G.F., "Anxiety, HCI Secretion, and Peptic Ulcer Etiology," *Psychosomatic Medicine* 12, no. 3 (May–June 1950): 158–169.

Sen, R.N., and B.K. Anand, "Effect of Electrical Stimulation of the Hypothalamus on Gastric Secretory Activity and Ulceration," *Indian Journal of Medical Research* 45, no. 4 (October 1957): 507–513.

Shealy, C.N., and T.L. Peele, "Studies on Amygdaloid Nucleus of Cat," *Journal of Neurophysiology* 20 (March 1957): 125–139.

Weiner, H., et al., "I. Relation of Specific Psychological Characteristics to Rate of Gastric Secretion (Serum Pepsinogen)," *Psychosomatic Medicine* 19, no. 1 (January 1957): 1–10.

Zawoiski, E.J., "Gastric Secretory Response of the Unrestrained Cat Following Electrical Stimulation of the Hypothalamus, Amygdala, and Basal Ganglia," *Experimental Neurology* 17, no. 2 (February 1967): 128–139.

Fourth Emotional Center

Alexander, F., *Psychosomatic Medicine* (London: George Allen & Unwin, Ltd., 1952).

Bacon, C.L., et al., "A Psychosomatic Survey of Cancer of the Breast," *Psychosomatic Medicine* 14, no. 6 (November 1952): 453–460.

Dembroski, T.M., ed., *Proceedings of the Forum on Coronary-Prone Behavior* (Washington, D.C.: U.S. Government Printing Office, 1978).

Derogatis, L.R., et al., "Psychological Coping Mechanisms and Survival Time in Metastatic Breast Cancer," *Journal of the American Medical Association* 242, no. 14 (October 1979): 1504–1508.

Friedman, M., and R.H. Rosenman, "Association of Specific Overt Behavior Pattern with Blood and Cardiovascular Findings," *Journal of the American Medical Association* 169, no. 12 (March 1959): 1286–1296.

Helmers, K.F., et al., "Hostility and Myocardial Ischemia in Coronary Artery Disease Patients," *Psychosomatic Medicine* 55, no. 1 (January 1993): 29–36.

Henry, J.P., et al., "Force Breeding, Social Disorder and Mammary Tumor Formation in CBA/USC Mouse Colonies: A Pilot Study," *Psychosomatic Medicine* 37, no. 3 (May 1975): 277–283.

Jansen, M.A., and L.R. Muenz, "A Retrospective Study of Personality Variables Associated with Fibrocystic Disease and Breast Cancer," *Journal of Psychosomatic Research* 28, no. 1 (1984): 35–42.

Kalis, B.L., et al., "Personality and Life History Factors in Persons Who Are Potentially Hypertensive," *The Journal of Nervous and Mental Disease* 132 (June 1961): 457–468.

Kawachi, I., et al., "A Prospective Study of Anger and Coronary Heart Disease," *Circulation* 94 (1996): 2090–2095.

Krantz, D.S., and D.C. Glass, "Personality, Behavior Patterns, and Physical Illness," in W.D. Gentry, ed., *Handbook of Behavioral Medicine* (New York: Guilford, 1984).

Lawler, K.A., et al., "Gender and Cardiovascular Responses: What Is the Role of Hostility?" *Journal of Psychosomatic Research* 37, no. 6 (September 1993): 603–613.

Levy, S.M., et al., "Survival Hazards Analysis in First Recurrent Breast Cancer Patients: Seven-Year Follow-up," *Psychosomatic Medicine* 50, no. 5 (September–October 1988): 520–528.

Lorenz, K., *On Aggression* (London: Methuen & Co., 1966).

Manuck, S.B., et al., "An Animal Model of Coronary-Prone Behavior," in M.A. Chesney and R.H. Rosenman, eds., *Anger and Hostility in Cardiovascular and Behavioral Disorders* (Washington, D.C.: Hemisphere Publishing Corp., 1985).

Marchant, J., "The Effects of Different Social Conditions on Breast Cancer Induction in Three Genetic Types of Mice by Dibenz[a,h]anthracene and a Comparison with Breast Carcinogenesis by 3-methylcholanthrene," *British Journal of Cancer* 21, no. 3 (September 1967): 576–585.

Muhlbock, O., "The Hormonal Genesis of Mammary Cancer," *Advances in Cancer Research* 4 (1956): 371–392.

Parkes, C.M., et al., "Broken Heart: A Statistical Study of Increased Mortality among Widowers," *British Medical Journal* 1, no. 5646 (March 1969): 740–743.

Rees, W.D., and S.G. Lutkins, "Mortality of Bereavement," *British Medical Journal* 4 (October 1967): 13–16.

Reznikoff, M., "Psychological Factors in Breast Cancer: A Preliminary Study of Some Personality Trends in Patients with Cancer of the Breast," *Psychosomatic Medicine* 17, no. 2 (March–April 1955): 96–108.

Seiler, C., et al., "Cardiac Arrhythmias in Infant Pigtail Monkeys Following Maternal Separation," *Psychophysiology* 16, no. 2 (March 1979): 130–135.

Shaywitz, B.A., et al., "Sex Differences in the Functional Organization of the Brain for Language," *Nature* 373, no. 6515 (February 16, 1995): 607–609.

Shekelle, R.B., et al., "Hostility, Risk of Coronary Heart Disease, and Mortality," *Psychosomatic Medicine* 45, no. 2 (1983): 109–114.

Smith, W.K., "The Functional Significance of the Rostral Cingular Cortex as Revealed by Its Responses to Electrical Excitation," *Journal of Neurophysiology* 8, no. 4 (July 1945): 241–255.

Tiger, L., and R. Fox, *The Imperial Animal* (New York: Holt, Rinehart & Winston, 1971).

Van Egeron, L.F., "Social Interactions, Communications, and the Coronary-Prone Behavior Pattern: A Psychophysiological Study," *Psychosomatic Medicine* 41, no. 1 (February 1979): 2–18.

Fifth Emotional Center

Adams, F., *Genuine Works of Hippocrates* (London: Sydenham Society, 1849).

Brown, W.T., and E.F. Gildea, "Hyperthyroidism and Personality," *American Journal of Psychiatry* 94, no.1 (July 1937): 59–76.

Morillo, E., and L.I. Gardner, "Activation of Latent Graves' Disease in Children: Review of Possible Psychosomatic Mechanisms," *Clinical Pediatrics* 19, no. 3 (March 1980): 160–163.

————, "Bereavement as an Antecedent Factor in Thyrotoxicosis of Childhood: Four Case Studies with Survey of Possible Metabolic Pathways," *Psychosomatic Medicine* 41, no. 7 (1979): 545–555.

Voth, H.M., et al., "Thyroid 'Hot Spots': Their Relationship to Life Stress," *Psychosomatic Medicine* 32, no. 6 (November 1970): 561–568.

Wallerstein, R.S., et al., "Thyroid 'Hot Spots': A Psychophysiological Study," *Psychosomatic Medicine* 27, no. 6 (November 1965): 508–523.

Sixth Emotional Center

Booth, G., "Psychodynamics in Parkinsonism," *Psychosomatic Medicine* 10, no. 1 (January 1948): 1–14.

Camp, C.D., "Paralysis Agitans and Multiple Sclerosis and Their Treatment," in W.A. White and S. E. Jelliffe, eds., *Modern Treatment of Nervous and Mental Diseases*, Vol. II (Philadelphia: Lea & Febiger, 1913): 651–671.

Cloninger, C.R., "Brain Networks Underlying Personality Development," in B.J. Carroll and J.E. Barrett, eds., *Psychopathology and the Brain* (New York: Raven Press, 1991), 183–208.

Coker, N.J., et al., "Psychological Profile of Patients with Ménière's Disease," *Archives of Otolaryngology-Head & Neck Surgery* 115, no. 11 (November 1989): 1355–1357.

Crary, W.G., and M. Wexler, "Ménière's Disease: A Psychosomatic Disorder?" *Psychological Reports* 41, no. 2 (October 1977): 603–645.

Eatough, V.M., et al., "Premorbid Personality and Idiopathic Parkinson's Disease," *Advances in Neurology* 53 (1990): 335–337.

Erlandsson, S.I., et al., "Psychological and Audiological Correlates of Perceived Tinnitus Severity," *Audiology* 31, no. 3 (1992): 168–179.

————, "Ménière's Disease: Trauma, Disease, and Adaptation Studied through Focus Interview Analyses," *Scandinavian Audiology*, Supplementum 43 (1996): 45–56.

Groen, J.J., "Psychosomatic Aspects of Ménière's Disease," *Acta Oto-laryngologica* 95, no. 5–6 (May–June 1983): 407–416.

Hinchcliffe, R., "Emotion as a Precipitating Factor in Ménière's Disease," *The Journal of Laryngology & Otology* 81, no. 5 (May 1967): 471–475.

Jellife, S.E., "The Parkinsonian Body Posture: Some Considerations on Unconscious Hostility," *Psychoanalytic Review* 27 (1940): 467–479.

Martin, M.J., "Functional Disorders in Otorhinolaryngology," *Archives of Otolaryngology-Head & Neck Surgery* 91, no. 5 (May 1970): 457–459.

Menza, M.A., et al., "Dopamine-Related Personality Traits in Parkinson's Disease," *Neurology* 43, no. 3, part 1 (March 1993): 505–508.

Minnigerode, B., and M. Harbrecht, "Otorhinolaryngologic Manifestations of Masked Mono- or Oligosymptomatic Depressions," *HNO* 36, no. 9 (September 1988): 383–385.

Mitscherlich, M., "The Psychic State of Patients Suffering from Parkinsonism," *Advances in Psychosomatic Medicine* 1 (1960): 317–324.

Poewe, W., et al., "Premorbid Personality of Parkinson Patients" *Journal of Neural Transmission, Supplementum* 19 (1983): 215–224.

————, "The Premorbid Personality of Patients with Parkinson's Disease: A Comparative Study with Healthy Controls and Patients with Essential Tremor," *Advances in Neurology* 53 (1990): 339–342.

Robins, A.H., "Depression in Patients with Parkinsonism," *British Journal of Psychiatry*, 128 (February 1976): 141–145.

Sands, I., "The Type of Personality Susceptible to Parkinson's Disease," *Journal of the Mount Sinai Hospital,* 9 (1942): 792–94.

Siirala, U., and K. Gelhar, "Further Studies on the Relationship between Ménière, Psychosomatic Constitution and Stress," *Acta Oto-laryngologica* 70, no. 2 (August 1970): 142–147.

Stephens, S.D., "Personality Tests in Ménière's Disorder," *The Journal of Laryngology and Otology* 89, no. 5 (May 1975): 479–490.

Seventh Emotional Center

Adams, D.K., et al., "Early Clinical Manifestations of Disseminated Sclerosis," *British Medical Journal* 2, no. 4676 (August 19, 1950): 431–436.

Allbutt, T. C., and H. D. Rolleston, eds., *A System of Medicine* (London: Macmillan and Co, 1911).

Charcot, J.M., *Lectures on the Diseases of the Nervous System,* George Sigerson (trans.), (London: The New Sydenham Society, 1881).

Firth, D., "The Case of Augustus d'Este (1794–1848): The First Account of Disseminated Sclerosis" *Proceedings of the Royal Society of Medicine* 34, no. 7 (May 1941): 381–384.

McAlpine, D., and N.D. Compston, "Some Aspects of the Natural History of Disseminated Sclerosis," *The Quarterly Journal of Medicine* 21, no. 82 (April 1952): 135–167.

Moxon, W., "Eight Cases of Insular Sclerosis of the Brain and Spinal Cord," *Guy's Hospital Reports* 20 (1875): 437–478.

———, "Case of Insular Sclerosis of Brain and Spinal Cord," *The Lancet* 1, no. 2581 (February 1873): 236.

Acknowledgments

Completing a book is a matter of, in the words of Barbra Streisand, "Putting It Together." And there are many people and companies who have been instrumental in this process and in making it possible for me to teach its material on the road. Some may be obvious and some may surprise you but all have been an enormous help.

I spent a lot of time and work on this with, of course, the wonderful Louise Hay, the great legend in mind-body medicine. The times I spent with Louise on Skype going over case studies have been some of the most monumental of my life. I spent 35 years educating myself in classrooms, hospitals, libraries, and laboratories trying to put together, bit by bit, the connection between emotion, intuition, the brain, the body, and health. She sat in a room listening to clients' stories and came up with the same information. Go figure. I am honored to work with this giant of woman.

To the people who I go to for advice, Hay House CEO Reid Tracy and COO Margarete Nielsen, thank you for giving this kid a chance. And I would never, never, never forget my wonderful editors who help me with my paretic left hemisphere. Patty Gift, true to her name, is a gift—and on her way to becoming a legend in this industry. We go way, way back. And Laura Gray, I have submitted your name to the Vatican for sainthood for what you have done with this book, especially the endnotes. You are brilliant, patient, and calm, and you somehow maintain this stance without a positive tox screen. How do you do it without valium? People want to know. To rockstar Donna Abate, all the people in publicity and production, plus Nancy Levin and all the conference crew—you make Hay House a legend in the publishing industry, so says *The New York Times*.

To my southern family, Miss Naomi, Mr. Larry, and everyone else around Peaceful Valley. You have prayed for me throughout life and back to life. We have laughed, cried, and learned a lot together. Through floods, national and natural disasters, and all the good times, you are always there with that drawl saying, "Well, Honey, we lo'ove you!" I lo'ove you, too, and thank you. And while we're talking southern, thanks also to Helen Snow for those wonderful pseudo-obscene "Cheep Cheerios" chicken graphics. They make my day.

Caroline Myss, my conjoined twin, separated-at-birth and put up for adoption. Who also has the gene for Montblanc pens and animated art, among other biological "conditions"—you make me feel so loved. How about a hand of Portuguese poker? Deuces and one-eyed jacks are wild. Your mom, Delores, the card-shark, can deal.

What would I do without my Sephardic-sister Laura Day? Weekends in the "city" with mad-cap adventures. I love you to pieces. To my Portuguese cousin Barbara Carrellas, an authentic genius in her field. You are always there for me when I need you. And to my Australian aunt, Georgia, who created scandal in the hospital during my recent surgery by bringing genitalia-shaped chocolates to my room. The line of people who wanted a sample wound down the hospital corridor. What an original with a big heart and brain to match.

Helping me hold to my vision, Avis Smith is a rare Hebrew teacher and Torah scholar. I am proud to call her my chavrusa. And thank you to Artscroll for not filing a restraining order because of all those books I ordered.

To my past mentors. Every moment with these people made a contribution to this book in not a small way: Dr. Margaret Naeser,

Deepak Pandya, M.D., Edith Kaplan, Ph.D., Norman Geschwind, M.D., Chris Northup, M.D., and Joan Borysenko, Ph.D.

I wouldn't be able to get to work without my pit crew. Electrical System Tune-up: neurologist Dr. David Perlmutter. Chassis Rebuild: Dr. Kumar Kakarla. Headlight Maintenance: breast surgeon Dr. Rosemary Duda. Meridian Management to keep the motor running: Dr. Fern Tsao, Dr. Dean Deng, and Colleen Tetzloff, R.N., N.P.

To Drs. Janie and Gerald LeMole for being there in Phoenix, Arizona, when I, as they say, almost bought the farm. You saved my life and helped me walk again. Thank you.

Advancing art is easy; financing it is not. Thank you to my money team George Howard, Paul Chabot, and Peter the Accountant. And then there are the web people who keep things going along the ethers. Thank you to Mr. Jeffrey and Wanda Bowring. I do not know how you do what you do, but keep doing it. Ditto for my transcriptionist, Karen Kinne. How would I live without you? You can type the voice in my head. And Marshall Bellovin, thank you for expert, balanced legal advice. You are my Perry Mason.

If it weren't for the skilled people at Hay House Radio, my radio show wouldn't happen. Thank you to the lovely Diane Ray and all the people who work the board. You people keep a cool head even when those strange electrical accidents tend to happen around me. Thank you.

I am blessed to have the loyalty of so many people. Thank you to Omega and Susie "Debbie" Arnett, who's amazing, as is Martha at Kripalu. Thank you also to Marlene and my TV people at Kundali Productions.

And now to thank the people in the orchestra pit—the people who make my day-to-day life go smoothly so I can work on things like this book. Working the bigger instruments on the outside is the wonderful Mike Brewer. He keeps up the lawns, gardens, and my outdoor inflatables all year long and manages to keep the reindeer system lit up year after year. Then Holly Doughty handles the smaller instruments inside. My house has never been so clean. I no longer need an inhaler for asthma; my internist thanks you too. Thanks to Custom Coach who pick me up at God-knows-what hours and do many things outside the call of duty.

Thanks to my appearance team: Joseph Saucier at Boston's Escada who prevents me from looking cheap from a clothing point of view. Darryl who does my hair at Acari salon. You understand my Hair-neurosis. Thank you. And I must acknowledge the makers of Spanx. Thank you for helping women who have abdomens feel normal and not look pregnant. Someone needed to say that. And while we are at it, thanks to Cecilia Romanucci at Chicago's O'Hare Airport Montblanc store who keeps me outfitted with all these fountain pens.

Moving right along . . . the Harraseeket Inn helped keep me stay alive with organic food with spunk, ambience, and just the right amount of attitude. Thanks to owners Rodney "Chip" Gray and Nancy Gray, barkeeper Ronda Real, chef Mary Ann McAllister, manager Marsha, and all the waitstaff. If any of you readers are lucky enough to go there, get the apple and blueberry pie and say I sent you, but don't take my seat at the bar.

Harmonizing every negotiation, Julie Tavares, my CEO, is my voice of reason—a calming presence who delivers a good swift kick when necessary. Thank you. What a peach. Then there's Lizette Paiva, my COO, a Portuguese Hot Tamale, 4'11" and tough as nails. An intuitive genius in her own right.

And to add to the perfect orchestration of my life, my cat kingdom: Miss Dolly, Loretta-Lynn, Conway Twitty, Jethro Bodine (yes, that's a nod to the southern influence), Sigmund "Siggy" Feline, and Horatio.

And finally, I am so grateful to you, the reader, for having been drawn to this work. Thank you for being here.

About the Authors

Louise Hay, the author of the international bestseller *You Can Heal Your Life*, is a metaphysical lecturer and teacher with more than 40 million books sold worldwide.

For more than 30 years, Louise has helped people throughout the world discover and implement the full potential of their own creative powers for personal growth and self-healing. Louise is the founder and chairman of Hay House, Inc., which disseminates books, CDs, DVDs, and other products that contribute to the healing of the planet. Visit www.LouiseHay.com.

Mona Lisa Schulz, M.D., Ph.D., is one of those rare people who can cross the borders of science, medicine, and mysticism. She is a practicing neuropsychiatrist and an associate professor of psychiatry at the University of Vermont College of Medicine. She has been a medical intuitive for 25 years. Dr. Mona Lisa has published three books, *The Intuitive Advisor, The New Feminine Brain,* and *Awakening Intuition.* She lives between Yarmouth, Maine, and Franklin, Tennessee, with her four cats and assorted wildlife. Website: www.DrMonaLisa.com.

Hay House Titles of Related Interest

YOU CAN HEAL YOUR LIFE, the movie,
starring Louise Hay & Friends
(available as a 1-DVD program and an expanded 2-DVD set)
Watch the trailer at: **www.LouiseHayMovie.com**

THE SHIFT, the movie,
starring Dr. Wayne W. Dyer
(available as a 1-DVD program and an expanded 2-DVD set)
Watch the trailer at: **www.DyerMovie.com**

DEFY GRAVITY: Healing Beyond the Bounds of Reason, by Caroliine Myss

HOW YOUR MIND CAN HEAL YOUR BODY, by David R. Hamilton, Ph.D.

THE POWER OF SELF-HEALING: Unlock Your Natural Healing Potential in 21 Days!, by Dr. Fabrizio Mancini

POWER UP YOUR BRAIN: The Neuroscience of Enlightenment, by David Perlmutter, M.D. and Alberto Villoldo, Ph.D.

TRUTH HEALS: What You Hide Can Hurt You, by Deborah King

All of the above are available at your local bookstore,
or may be ordered by contacting Hay House (see next page).

We hope you enjoyed this Hay House book. If you'd like to receive our online catalog featuring additional information on Hay House books and products, or if you'd like to find out more about the Hay Foundation, please contact:

Hay House, Inc., P.O. Box 5100, Carlsbad, CA 92018-5100
(760) 431-7695 or (800) 654-5126
(760) 431-6948 (fax) or (800) 650-5115 (fax)
www.hayhouse.com® • **www.hayfoundation.org**

❁ ❁ ❁

Published and distributed in Australia by:
Hay House Australia Pty. Ltd., 18/36 Ralph St., Alexandria NSW 2015
Phone: 612-9669-4299 • *Fax:* 612-9669-4144 • www.hayhouse.com.au

Published and distributed in the United Kingdom by:
Hay House UK, Ltd., Astley House, 33 Notting Hill Gate, London W11 3JQ •
Phone: 44-20-3675-2450 • *Fax:* 44-20-3675-2451 • www.hayhouse.co.uk

Published and distributed in the Republic of South Africa by:
Hay House SA (Pty), Ltd., P.O. Box 990, Witkoppen 2068
Phone/Fax: 27-11-467-8904 • www.hayhouse.co.za

Published in India by: Hay House Publishers India,
Muskaan Complex, Plot No. 3, B-2, Vasant Kunj,
New Delhi 110 070 • *Phone:* 91-11-4176-1620
Fax: 91-11-4176-1630 • www.hayhouse.co.in

Distributed in Canada by: Raincoast Books,
2440 Viking Way, Richmond, B.C. V6V 1N2
Phone: 1-800-663-5714 • *Fax:* 1-800-565-3770 • www.raincoast.com

❁ ❁ ❁

Take Your Soul on a Vacation

Visit **www.HealYourLife.com®** to regroup,
recharge, and reconnect with your own magnificence.
Featuring blogs, mind-body-spirit news, and
life-changing wisdom from Louise Hay and friends.

Visit **www.HealYourLife.com** today!

Free e~newsletters from Hay House, the Ultimate Resource for Inspiration

Be the first to know about Hay House's dollar deals, free downloads, special offers, affirmation cards, giveaways, contests, and more!

 Get exclusive excerpts from our latest releases and videos from *Hay House Present Moments*.

 Enjoy uplifting personal stories, how-to articles, and healing advice, along with videos and empowering quotes, within *Heal Your Life*.

 Have an inspirational story to tell and a passion for writing? Sharpen your writing skills with insider tips from *Your Writing Life*.

Sign Up Now!

Get inspired, educate yourself, get a complimentary gift, and share the wisdom!

http://www.hayhouse.com/newsletters.php

Visit www.hayhouse.com to sign up today!

 HAY HOUSE

 HAYHOUSE RADIO
radio for your soul

HealYourLife.com